Armies in Europe

Armies in Europe

John Gooch

Department of History
University of Lancaster

Routledge & Kegan Paul
London, Boston and Henley

First published in 1980
by Routledge & Kegan Paul Ltd
39 Store Street, London WC1E 7DD,
Broadway House, Newtown Road,
Henley-on-Thames, Oxon RG9 1EN and
9 Park Street, Boston, Mass. 02108, USA
Set in 11pt IBM Baskerville by Columns
and printed in Great Britain by
Morrison & Gibb Ltd.

British Library Cataloguing in Publication Data

Gooch, John
Armies in Europe.
1. Armies — Europe — History
I. Title
355'.0094   *UA646.*   *79-41297*

ISBN 0 7100 0462 1

For my family

Contents

Preface

Much of the best history that has been written over the past two decades has dealt not with politics, economics or any of the more traditional areas of historical enquiry, but with the development of armies, with their roles in peace-time society, and with the many wars that have marked the course of modern history. Other types of history have their syntheses; this book attempts to put that work together in order to look at what is as self-contained a period as any from a less than traditional angle. The fact that comparative surveys of military affairs have, until now, largely been the realm of sociologists and political scientists was one of the reasons I attempted one, but having completed the task I can now well understand why other historians have, for the most part, avoided it. However, if the result serves to encourage readers to go to the many historians upon whose work I have drawn so heavily, then perhaps it will have performed a useful task. I owe a debt of great professional gratitude to all those whose works I have cited in my notes and in the bibliography at the end of this book; and to those who will detect traces of their work without the compensation of direct acknowledgment my debt, though inadequately publicized, is no less great.

That I have written this book at all is the result of the stimulation I derived from the teaching of Michael Howard. For that experience, and for his long-suffering readiness with

PREFACE

help and advice ever since, I am deeply grateful.

Phillip Bell did all and more that a friend should ever be asked to do and read the entire manuscript in draft at a time when he was deeply involved in a demanding research project of his own. Without his gentle criticism and wise advice this book would be more heavily laden with errors and infelicities than it is. My colleagues Professor J.H. Shennan and Dr M.H. Merriman helped me wrestle the earlier chapters into a more satisfactory shape; and Ralph Gibson, who suffered from being only a few steps down the corridor, gave me valuable references to French material that I should otherwise have missed. To them all, my thanks.

I have benefited also from reading the doctoral theses of Dr I.F.W. Beckett, Dr E.R. Holmes and Dr M.S. Smith — all of which works ought to be in print — and from unpublished manuscripts by Professor John Erickson and Mr I. Worthington. To the authors, and to all the many undergraduates who have taken History 308 and have taught me much more than I can have taught them, I am much indebted.

To Ann, and to Alexander and Julia, I offer the book by way of thanks.

John Gooch
Forton,
Lancaster

A note on the title
This book is about armies, and not navies. There are many good reasons for this, of which the most compelling is that Europe's navies deserve a book to themselves. Perhaps simple annoyance, if nothing else, will stimulate someone to write it.

1

Towards revolution

In the age of combative nationalism which stretched from 1789 to 1945, and which yoked Napoleon to Hitler, the making of military preparations and the act of fighting were two of the most important activities in the life of any state. War was held to be not only a legitimate but also an effective means of furthering the interests of the state, resort to which could resolve those disputes which could not be controlled by the machinery of diplomacy. Conscription provided a means whereby the state both made provision to field large numbers of trained soldiers if war came and demonstrated the extent to which it was prepared to commit its resources to such a war if the need arose. The citizen's obligation to perform military service when required to do so was one of the distinctive characteristics of the nation states as they developed in the nineteenth century, providing a counterweight to the right to vote. In all respects the French Revolution seemed to draw a line which separated two distinct sets of attitudes towards war and military organization. The so-called 'Cabinet Wars' of the eighteenth century are frequently portrayed as taking place outside the general confines of society; as gladiatorial combats held between bands of doughty — or dubious — professional soldiers and watched by 'crowds seated in safety round a bloodstained arena'.[1] War before it was revolutionized by the French

1

conscripts of 1793 thus appears as an activity which was somehow less bloody and less burdensome for the bulk of society, which was called upon to pay its taxes but not to give its personal services.

In reality, the divisions which apparently separated eighteenth-century Europe from what followed the upheaval of July 1789 are as artificial in the sphere of war and military organization as in any other sphere. Casualties in battle were already mounting long before the day of Napoleon: at Blenheim in 1704 the Allies lost 12,000 men and the combined Franco-Bavarian forces 38,000. Nor was war in some sense less barbaric during the Age of Enlightenment: horrific scenes took place after the capture of Ochakov in 1788, when Russian soldiers amused themselves by tossing small children off the ramparts and on to the bayonets of their comrades below. Even the extraordinary punctiliousness of the Brigade of Guards at the battle of Fontenoy (1745) in offering the first volley to their opponents had more to do with cool calculation than with an exaggerated sense of fair play; the poor performance of the musket and the jangling nerves of one's opponent provided some basis for the belief that receiving the first volley was likely to be much less damaging than receiving the second. Once the fighting had begun, war in the eighteenth century was exactly like war in any other age: bloody and unpleasant. Boswell's celebrated remark, 'wars were going out in these days, because of their mildness', is better taken as a measure of the insularity of the British middle classes than as an accurate observation upon the state of the military art.

The essential basis upon which any efficient military organization was built was an efficient bureaucracy, and by the start of the eighteenth century the basic structures through which the state administered its military arm had already been refined to the point at which they were both effective agents of control and efficient organs of management. That this should be the most advanced area of military organization by such a date is scarcely surprising, since the development of national armies and the appearance of the nation state itself were inextricably bound together by virtue of the fact that it was as a 'concentration of fighting power' that the nation state first made its appearance in history.[2] The emergence of state bureaucracies had been accelerated during the sixteenth century, when the princely state had begun to exert its monopolistic right to raise armies, and when princes had begun to refine the argument that the pursuit of their own dynastic rivalries represented a concentration upon interests which were as much those of the whole realm as they were of the monarch. In the military competition which resulted, the need for effective instruments of state control became readily apparent. The first officials to be entrusted with the functions of improving the efficiency of the armies of the day were the *Veedor* of the Spanish army and the Piedmontese *Contador generale*, both of whom made their appearance by the end of the century, whilst Spain's task of maintaining an army in the Netherlands between 1567 and 1659 resulted in the development of a sophisticated administrative machine. More direct royal control over the physical forces of the crown was exercised by the review or muster, in origin a princely device designed to check on the size and quality of the military forces which were being made available. In the course of time the muster roll evolved into the regimental register, a more effective means of watching the constitution of the army, which appeared in Sweden in 1640 and in France in 1670 and which was both the symbol and the instrument of the state's determination to oversee and control military organization.

The forms of state bureaucracy which developed during the seventeenth century, and upon which much of the development of Europe's pre-revolutionary armies was to hinge, represented the emergence of more specialized offices within the general administrative machinery of the state. Now, for the first time, the specialist secretary of war appeared, charged with overseeing military affairs on behalf of the crown. Servien, appointed by Louis XIII of France in 1635, was the first of this new band of civil servants, and this example was soon followed elsewhere: in January 1661 Charles II appointed Sir William Clarke 'Secretary at War to all the forces raised or to be raised in England and Wales' at a salary of £91 9s. per annum. By a natural progression, with which all modern states are familiar, the secretary was soon followed into being by the secretariat, introduced into France by Louvois, into Austria in the twin forms of the *Generalkriegskommissariat* (1650) and the *Hofkriegsrat* (1675), and into Piedmont in 1717. The system in Austria whereby the senior body took over responsibility for the maintenance of the army whilst the junior one exercised command foreshadowed a later development of considerable political significance, shared alike by Austria, Russia and Prussia, in which military administration remained in the charge of the civilians whilst the sovereign exercised operational control over his armies through a military cabinet. By this route the monarchs of all three countries were able to escape all but the financial aspects of parliamentary control until the First World War, and through it they maintained a much closer and more intimate link between the exercise of state power and the work of military command than was to be the case elsewhere in Europe.

The most noteworthy examples of military bureaucracy to be established during the seventeenth century were to be found in France and Prussia, states which were to provide contrasting patterns of civil-military development in the century which followed. In France a modern system of military administration was established by Le Tellier and his son Louvois, who between them held the post of secretary of state for war from 1643 to 1691. Theirs was a system which served two congruent purposes, for it provided the framework for centralized and efficient control of the state's military forces and at the same time helped to accustom the nobility to acquiescence in monarchical control over war and military organization. The medium through which the new system functioned was the *intendant*, an office originally devised in order to supervise and manipulate the tax machine, and thus to produce the money without which military security was not to be had. His functions were soon extended as the interests of military efficiency demanded that regimental recruiting should cease to be an aspect of free enterprise, and in 1644-5 *Intendants* of the Army appeared to take over this responsibility from the regimental commanders. Le Tellier also introduced a system of state-controlled victualling and supply, which both strengthened the bureaucratic machine and added to the attractiveness of military service, and by 1659 conditions in the army had improved to such a degree that arbitrary and compulsory levies were no longer necessary in order to fill up the ranks; instead volunteer recruiting became the order of the day.

This was one example of the benefits which could flow from an efficient military machine. Another was the success of Michel Le Tellier in the task he set himself of reducing aristocratic influence in the army. During the French civil wars a large proportion of the French nobility had avoided royal service and instead had raised their own troops and vigorously pursued their own ends. Le Tellier set himself to reduce this aristocratic independence, which both diminished the crown's sovereign power and reduced the effectiveness of its military forces, with such success that by 1666 the king could nominate and promote all his officers at will. The new system of administration established in the latter part of the seventeenth century enabled France to support a much larger military establishment than she had hitherto been able to afford, and, as a result of the efforts of Le Tellier and Louvois, Louis XIV was able to maintain over 250,000 men under arms at one time. The relationship between military efficiency and bureaucratic machinery lay clearly displayed.

The experience undergone by Prussia at the same period underscored this truth. In 1640 Friedrich Wilhelm I had inherited three widely scattered areas of territory: the Electorate of Brandenburg, the duchy of East Prussia, and Cleves Mark. There was an urgent need for the king to exert his authority and control over these areas, for some parts were overrun and in others local dignitaries controlled the finances and would raise money only for local purposes. In 1641 the king recruited a new army which he managed to keep in being for ten years; then his personal resources ran out and the force had to be disbanded. The king could save from it only a nucleus of 4,000 men with which to garrison key fortresses. In 1654 the imminence of a Polish-Swedish war drove Friedrich Wilhelm to ask the Brandenburg Estates for money. When they refused to give him any, he took the revolutionary step of raising his own land tax without first obtaining their consent, justifying his action with the remark

Not kennt kein Gebot ('Necessity knows no law'). In the out-
burst of amazed annoyance which followed this act, the
nobility made their chief ground for complaint the fact that
they paid a heavier financial contribution than the towns and
thereby exposed themselves to the possibility that they
would forfeit their independent right to grant taxes at all.

By the time the Northern War (1655-60) had ended,
Friedrich Wilhelm had fully realized the possibilities offered
by this *ad hoc* arrangement and was firmly persuaded of the
need to maintain a standing royal force: 'I have become
convinced that I owe the preservation of my position and my
territory to God, and next to God, to my army'.[3] Accordingly
the Great Elector did not fall in with customary practice and
disperse his forces once the Northern War was over. Instead
his military absolutism grew with the years, and in 1667 he
passed on to his son the secret of his own monarchical success: 'Alliances are good to be sure, but a force of one's own,
on which one can more securely rely, is better.' The object
of Friedrich Wilhelm's policy was to make Prussia a great
power of which its monarch was complete master, and to
gain both these ends he saw a standing army as essential.
However, he was also well aware of the need to reconcile his
people to the demands necessary if such a force were to be
kept in being, and he achieved this by skilful use of his army
in peace-time: it helped to dig the Frederick William canal,
linking the Oder to the Elbe, and in 1663 it transformed the
Tiergarten in Berlin into a park and suburb for the benefit of
the populace.

The army had created a united Prussia and it was to be the
institution which first embodied the notion of a unitary and
efficient Prussian state. That this was so was partly the result
of its historic role, but partly also of the fact that the whole
bureaucratic structure of the state was shaped in order to give
support to the military forces of the crown. Nowhere was
this more clearly to be seen than in the fiscal structure, which
was designed specifically to sustain the army. In place of the
old land-tax, the state could now avail itself of a whole series
of imposts designed to maximize revenue: *Aksize* (excise
duty) on meat, grain and beer; *Kopfsteuer*, a form of
graduated income tax; *Stempelsteuer* (stamp tax); and

Chargensteuer, whereby every state official, on receiving a new office, paid half of his first year's salary to the state. By dint of such efforts Prussia, although a poor state, was able to support a standing army of 45,000 men between 1672 and 1679.

In Prussia, as in France and elsewhere in Europe, the eighteenth century thus opened with a formal bureaucratic structure already in existence which was designed to support and maintain an efficient standing army. The difference between the two countries lay in the fact that whereas France had created an efficient military organization, in Prussia an efficient military organization had created the state. Both procedures were, however, different ways of recognizing the same fact; that an efficient state machine which could support and control a strong army was an essential prerequisite for any state which wished to maintain its independence and its territorial integrity. Permanent standing armies of any size certainly needed effective bureaucratic machinery to buttress them, but they also required recognition that the obligation to do military service should fall upon a wide spectrum of the population and not merely upon those accustomed to war or those whom society could well do without. Here the eighteenth century was to provide an important bridge between the limited general obligations of an earlier age and the simple individual obligation of every citizen to serve which was the outcome of the French Revolution.

The progression of society towards acceptance of the obligation of all adult male citizens to enter the ranks had to overcome the notion of a specialized military community which went back at least as far as the end of the twelfth century, when clerics had divided society into three orders: those who prayed, those who worked and those who fought. These were loose and fluctuating divisions, whose boundaries were often crossed in all directions; as late as 1636 a Capuchin priest served with the artillery during the siege of Dôle, whilst Carmelites and Dominicans worked on the town's defences. They did, however, represent an undeniable tendency towards specialization in the military arts, which gathered pace as first the pike and then the hand-gun appeared on the battlefields of Europe. The notion that the best soldiers were those paid to do the fighting for a state rather than its own members became firmly established after 1322, when the city of Siena chartered its 'Great Company' and the first organized band of mercenaries made its appearance.

The social problem that the mercenary presented was one of reliability, and he has gone down in history — not least as a result of Machiavelli's writings — as fickle and untrustworthy, always prepared to fight for whoever offered the most money and reluctant to end campaigns, since in doing so he ended his own employment. Yet the mercenary was in the worst of all possible positions: hired by the state for a fixed period, he lacked the security of a salaried employee or the wealth of a landowner to fall back on when the fighting was over. Moreover, if a *condottiere* lost a battle he risked imprisonment and the need to find a heavy ransom, the loss of his reputation and possibly also of his contract, and the cost of replacing his horse and arms. Micheletto Attendolo showed an acute awareness of the insecurity of the mercenary during his negotiations with the Florentine republic in 1430: 'We know very well how you behave when you no longer have need of us', he remarked, and demanded as security a guarantee of employment in peace-time.[4] Few states were prepared to fall in with such advanced ideas, with the result that, when not actively engaged in war, the bands of semi-professional soldiers which dotted Europe could prove harassingly disruptive of social and political order. The problem of controlling these unemployed *routiers* in mid-fourteenth-century France stimulated the growth of a system of taxes to pay local defence forces, and a second outbreak of the same problem led Charles VII to establish the first salaried army in Europe — the *compagnies d'ordonnance* — in 1445.

The national army, as distinguished from the mercenary forces at the disposal of the state, perhaps first appeared in 1534 when Francis I of France established seven provincial legions, each comprising 6,000 men, recruited on a strictly regional basis. At this time France's military forces were found by a mixture of collective social obligation and straightforward impressment, and reflected the fact that the king had not yet gained a monopoly in the matter of raising armies. Half a century later, Henry III consolidated the monarch's legal supremacy in the matter of military organization, declaring by ordinance in 1583 that the French army was hereafter the king's army. Even in England, a country always distanced from many of the continental pressures which helped create military systems, a statute of 1558 laid down the obligations of every citizen below the rank of baron and between the ages of sixteen and sixty, and would remain in force in the same terms until 1603. Moreover, during the years 1585 to 1603 England enjoyed an experience similar to the continental powers in feeling the need to furnish men for overseas service at a steady rate of 5,000 a year. The equivalent for England of Francis I's raising of the legions, therefore, came in 1588 when Elizabeth I signed the first comprehensive Netherlands contract which provided for the regular provision of an English force in the Low Countries. Spain too created a national militia in 1590, conforming with a common European pattern which was gradually extending the notion of the military community.

The path to the national army was, however, neither smooth nor easy, as was clear from the example of France. That there was considerable political pressure on the French kings to create a national army controlled by the crown is undeniable; the fact that Paris was more or less constantly under threat between 1544 and 1642, and was actually besieged five times during that period, demonstrates this. However, although the process of creating a national army had begun in 1534, it was not until more than one and a half centuries later, in 1694, that France could complete her military organization with the creation of a national militia of her own. The resistance which could be put up by great magnates and by local communities alike to subordination to a powerful central executive authority, whose demands were expressed in terms of military subservience as well as taxation and the acceptance of uniform legal codes, was a force which it took the advanced states of Europe no little time to overcome. While conformity was being enforced and the notion of the national military community beginning to emerge, states were often forced to depend for their soldiery upon the least reliable members of the civilian population. Thus Barnaby Rich observed of military service in Tudor England: 'In London, when they set forth soldiers, either they scour their prisons of thieves, or their streets of rogues and vagabonds, for he that is bound to find a man will seek such a one as is better lost than found.'[5]

Nevertheless the life of the community was far from being divorced from military influence and experience, for over much of Europe the obligation to provide for the army's subsistence fell heavily on the civilian population, both by payment of taxes for the upkeep of the military establishment and by the use of *l'ustensile*, a system under which the householder had to provide heating, lighting, cooking utensils and salt for the soldiers who were billeted upon him. The physical presence of soldiers in the community thus came to be an accepted part of everyday life and civilians grew accustomed to the routine of the soldier's day: 'The street and the town square took on the appearance of a military quarter and the life of the inhabitants was given a rythm by military bugle calls or distraction in the shape of exercises and revues'.[6] Nor were the troops always unpopular guests by any means. As Turgot, the *Intendant* of Metz, pointed out in 1698, in a poor area the presence of soldiery could mean an injection of money into a community and hold out the prospect of wealth for its civilian inhabitants. On the eve of the eighteenth century many of Europe's inhabitants were familiar with military activity, even if they were not directly involved in it.

The determination of many European sovereigns to call more directly and in heavier measure upon their subjects for military service, thereby increasing the size of their armies and also — it was presumed — their efficiency, was powerfully evident in the century before the French Revolution. From 1720 the Russian army recruited by fixed proportions from the provinces, and in 1733 Prussia introduced the *Kanton* system whereby youths were enrolled in the army at the age of ten, spent two years actively learning the military arts from the age of twenty, and subsequently had to serve in the army for several months each year for as long as they remained physically capable of doing so. Although this system was not applied to the western provinces of Prussia, whose social structure was less rigidly hierarchical, it was a distinctive forerunner of nineteenth-century patterns of conscription. In 1781 the Prussian example was followed by Joseph II, who introduced conscription into Austria. This growth of the monarchs' recognition of the need to conscript, and their increasing willingness to do so, was an admission of the importance of military power to the modern state, to which the post-revolutionary age was to be the heir.

Support for the growing practice of extending military service over a wider area of the national community was provided by the maréchal de Saxe, who in 1732 published his *Rêvéries*. 'War', de Saxe informed his readers at the dawn of the age of rationalism, 'is a science covered with shadows.' It was de Saxe's intention to disperse these shadows by means of clearheaded observation and analysis and thereby to increase the efficiency of armies, and in the process he firmly recommended the adoption of conscription for a five-year period, basing his advocacy of this type of military organization chiefly upon a soldier's estimation of the raw material which would result from it: 'an inexhaustable reservoir of fine recruits who would not be subject to desertion'.

This last observation touched upon one of the critical problems inherent in the expansion of obligations to undergo military training, and one to which the Age of Enlightenment could offer no real solution. Almost without exception the armies of eighteenth-century Europe were plagued by desertions, which reached epidemic proportions. The Saxon army, which numbered some 20,000 men, virtually disintegrated between 1717 and 1728 when a total of 8,500 soldiers deserted. The French army, too, suffered its share of the malady: during the War of the Spanish Succession one in four French soldiers left the army without first obtaining their formal release. The problem of desertion was acute everywhere and the penalties were harsh. In France, for most of the eighteenth century, every third deserter who was recaptured was shot, the choice being made by drawing lots; by this and other means wastage had been reduced by 1789 to 4,000 men a year. In Prussia Friedrich Wilhelm I (1713-40) celebrated the first year of his reign with a decree determining that everyone who left the country in order to escape doing military service would be treated as though he had deserted from the ranks. Two years earlier, in 1711, Friedrich I had ordered that deserters were to have their nose and one ear cut off and then serve hard labour for life. Despite even these harsh penalties the rigid discipline of the Prussian army — generally but erroneously associated with the age of Frederick the Great — resulted in 32,216 desertions during Friedrich Wilhelm I's reign. Military service may well have been becoming more widespread in the years before 1789, but it was far from popular.

One of the most powerful brakes which operated to prevent the eighteenth-century rulers from calling a larger proportion of their people into the ranks of their armies was the mercantilist economic system of the day, which sought to produce an amalgam of military efficiency and domestic productivity. For the system to function to its best effect, it was held that the middle classes should not be hindered by military obligations from producing wealth and paying taxes. It was a recognition of the state as a community of economic interests which helped lead William Pitt, on the eve of the Seven Years' War (1756-63), to propound the seductive notion that Britain's way in warfare should be maritime and colonial rather than military and continental:[7]

> We have suffered ourselves to be deceived by names and sounds, the balance of power, the liberty of Europe, a common cause and many more such expressions, without any other meaning than to exhaust our wealth, consume the profits of our trade, and load our prosperity with intolerable burdens.

As a proposition this was eminently palatable to the City of London, since it was buttressed with the argument that an English ship cost the same amount of money as a French one, whereas an English soldier on the continent cost twice as much as a French one. However, in the peace negotiations which followed the end of that war France recovered much of her overseas territory in return for withdrawal in Europe, leaving Pitt to remark ruefully, 'we retain nothing, although we have conquered everything.' That she was a European power and that Europe was not to be controlled by navies were lessons that it would take Britain a long time indeed to absorb; meanwhile, making minimal military demands on the English people conformed with mercantilist ideas and was also safer than following Europe's example and expanding the army. As Blackstone remarked in his celebrated *Commentaries*, the navy was England's greatest defence since it was 'an army from which however strong and powerful, no damage can ever be apprehended to liberty'.[8] Though perhaps less compellingly motivated than England, the European states were also, on occasion, prepared to recognize that disruption was one inevitable and undesirable consequence of military activity; the *Intendant* of Caen remarked that more damage would probably ensue in the course of putting the region into a state of defensibility than would result from several small English landings. In this respect it was to be the changed concept of the national community, resulting from the events of 1789, which was to allow budding ideas of national conscription to reach full flower in Europe.

The feature of the military organizations of eighteenth-century Europe which most obviously passed into the age of mass armies after 1789 was the close and exclusive relationship between aristocrat and officer. Like the development of variants of conscription, this too was a product of the period immediately preceding the Revolution. It would be easy to assume that the nobility had a 'natural' place in the upper levels of military organization which it had enjoyed since feudal times. However, the development of this symbiosis was far from direct and uninterrupted. As early as the fifteenth and sixteenth centuries armies had shown a marked tendency to become more plebeian at the top during wartime and then to experience a noble 'reaction' in the periods of peace which followed: such a pattern had occurred in France in 1447 and again in 1558. In England, in Spain and in the Italian states the link between aristocrat and officer was far from all-encompassing, since on the one hand the small size of the army in each of these states severely limited the prospect of employment, whilst on the other a wider choice of pursuits was open to the nobility in civilian life. The nobility themselves did not always prove eager to stock up the ranks of the kings' officer corps; in Prussia at the start of the seventeenth century noble service in the army was seen not as an attractive social privilege but as a *corvée*, an irksome tax on one's person. And the crown could prove equally reluctant to utilize its rights to demand service from its nobility: the *arrière-ban*, or call-up of all nobles who had not already voluntarily entered into the king's service, fell into disuse in France after 1695, and in Prussia was commuted to a money payment in 1717.

In essence there were two main routes by which Europe's aristocracy came to dominate the officer corps of Europe's armies. One was in response to pressure from the emerging bourgeoisie for admission to the upper reaches of the army as an avenue of social advancement, in the face of which the aristocracy closed ranks and proclaimed their inherent military superiority. This was clearly to be discerned in the process by which Louis XIV created the French officer corps. Until 1684 the nobility did dominate the army, but theirs was far from being a simple or total monopoly, since Louis was using the officer corps as a means of advancing those members of the wealthy bourgeoisie who were content to join the nobility rather than compete against it. Ambitious families could enter their sons for the army with some hopes of achieving the Second Estate: one quarter of Louis XIV's 164 generals did in fact come from families achieving noble status in that or the previous century. The crown also began to pursue a policy of attracting the poorer nobles by suppressing venal offices and making advancement possible to a *gentilhomme sans fortune*.

The nobility were fully capable of putting up a spirited resistance to the direction royal authority was apparently imposing upon the officer corps; in 1672 three marshals of France refused to serve under Turenne, the ablest soldier of the day, because of his humble social origins. Their position became more secure as the king's reign wore on, however, for he became increasingly sparing of ennoblement as a reward and began instead to devise a system of alternatives: pensions in the order of St Lazare, entry into the Hôtel des Invalides (founded in 1670) where appropriate or, for those not quite fitted for social advancement, the cross of St Louis

14

(instituted in 1693). By the end of Louis XIV's reign the domination by the higher nobility — and especially by the 'ancient' nobility whose titles went back before 1300 — was again complete. However, at Louis' death in 1715, two years after the end of the War of the Spanish Succession, the officer corps was faced with the twin problems that it was once again under siege from the bourgeoisie and that there were in any case more noble officers left over as a result of expansion of the army during wartime than there were posts for them to fill.

In order to try to protect their position from external assault the nobility attempted to place social restrictions on entry into the officer corps, and edicts of 1718 and 1727 required all officer candidates to present certification of nobility. By 1728 this defensive social action was over and the bourgeoisie were being admitted in ever growing numbers, with the result that by the middle of the eighteenth century one-third of the French officer corps was of non-noble origin. Making military rank the subject of speculative purchase had helped bring this about, and at the same time had deepened the antagonism between the poorer nobility, who could not afford to buy commissions, and the wealthy middle classes, who had the necessary funds. Attempts to maintain some semblance of employment for an overweight officer corps led to the somewhat bizarre spectacle of commands exercised *de jour* — for the day only — and to many officers rarely making an appearance with the troops at all. Rotational command was the only feasible way to respond to this situation and ensure that all officers had at least some sense of participation in everyday military activities, but it also provided ammunition for those who charged that an aristocratic monopoly in the army was not in the best interests of France. Indifference and neglect on the part of Fleury and Louis XV, and shortage of money, contributed to the deterioration of Louis XIV's army as the post of secretary of state for war slipped into disuse and the nascent army council disappeared.

The second route by which the aristocracy came to dominate the officer corps was typified in the development of the Prussian army during the first half of the eighteenth century.

15

The difference between the economic situation of the Prussian and French nobility was not great, although the growth of the bourgeoisie in Prussia and its consequent pressure for social advance was not as great as in France; what distinguished Prussia from France was the attitude taken by the crown to the opportunities presented to it as much as any greater vulnerability of the Prussian aristocracy to royal manipulation. Long before the middle of the century economic necessity had indeed driven the nobility into the receptive arms of the crown and hence into the army. Prussia had failed to develop credit institutions through which the nobles could raise loans, which left them with no alternative when in debt but to sell off their lands. Allegiance to the crown offered them one compelling attraction: a secure source of revenue. To the kings of Prussia the financial vulnerability of the nobility offered an opportunity from which royal authority might happily benefit. Accordingly, during the reign of Friedrich Wilhelm I, the process by which the nobility entered the officer corps was regularized; it was made illegal for any Prussian noble to enter foreign service and the monarch personally selected the younger sons of the noble houses for entry into the *Kadettenhaus* in Berlin, where they were educated for admission to the officer corps.

The Prussian system welded together the nobility, the army and the monarchy in a way unlike that which operated elsewhere in Europe at the time. It was a successful reciprocal relationship, from which both partners gained. In return for their unswerving loyalty and military energy the nobles received the benefits of an excellent educational system, a marked rise in their political authority as a group and the primary social position in the state. They did, however, pay for their privileges with their independence. Cutting off the last avenue of escape from complete financial dependence on the crown, the king entailed their fiefs, which meant that they no longer even had the freedom to sell their lands to raise money and were thus forced more securely into the ranks of the Prussian officer corps. The much vaunted 'Prussian militarism' was being carefully fostered by a shrewd state policy.

Friedrich Wilhelm built up an army which he had little or

no intention of using in support of diplomacy. It was an expensive capital investment which would be difficult to replace and, in the form of his regiment of giant Potsdam Grenadiers, a costly toy. Moreover, its use outside the boundaries of the kingdom was more than likely, he thought, to undercut the financial stability of the state: 'Let your army march abroad and your taxes will not bring in a third as much as when it is at home' was the king's assessment of the likely effect of foreign entanglements.[9] Frederick the Great differed from him, and from every other European monarch, in being ready to use his troops prodigally. In 1740, the year of his accession to the throne of Brandenburg-Prussia, he threw his army into Silesia in an attempt to expand and solidify the Prussian state. For him, armies existed to fight and decisive results came only from battle, an opinion which few of his contemporaries shared. In his *Instructions*, published in 1747, he offered a brief and all-embracing justification for his novel attitude to his army: 'War is decided only by battles, and it is not finished except by them.'

The prodigality of Frederick's wars made demands upon the Prussian nobility in the course of replenishing the ranks of the officer corps which it was simply not large enough to meet. In order to make good the losses Frederick had to break with tradition during the Seven Years War and admit members of the bourgeoisie to fill up the gaps. This extraordinary measure was, however, in no sense to be regarded as a precedent; as soon as the war ended, middle-class officers were retired or transferred to duty in the less attractive garrisons. Even so the demand for acceptable officers could still exceed supply, and when stocks of noble candidates ran low, Frederick took his conviction that only the nobility were fitted to be officers to its logical extreme by importing aristocrats from outside Prussia sooner than resort to his own middle class. His belief, which came to be widely shared, was that the middle classes, having been exempt from military service, had not acquired the habit of command or the sentiment of honour which were characteristics of the members of the nobility and essential qualifications for any officer. What had begun as a rationalization to justify the exclusion of one social class from power was, in time, to become an article of faith in Germany.

The advantages inherent in the Prussian system of equating nobility and officer corps were also perceived by a number of other central European monarchs. By 1756 the Bavarian army had adopted a similar attitude to the question of nobility and officer status and had established a Cadet Corps modelled on that of Prussia. In Russia the Preobrazhinsky and Semenovsky regiments performed a similar educative function for the aristocracy. In the Habsburg empire Maria Theresa sought to bind the nobility to Vienna after the manner in which the Prussian nobility had been bound to Berlin, issuing an address to the Hungarian aristocracy in 1740 which encouraged them to join the army. The opportunity to gain social prestige was combined with an expansion of the imperial power to exercise a controlling authority on military organization in the attempt to press the nobles into military service: in 1749 Haugwitz created the War Commissariat, which at once set about reducing the military autonomy of different parts of the empire, whilst the empress declared officers to be *Hoffähig* and as a consequence made welcome at court in uniform, a sign of rising social prestige. In the Italian states, in England and in Spain armies were small in the middle years of the eighteenth century and the nobility had other outlets for its energies. Over most of the rest of Europe the noble was coming to military predominance, and with it social pre-eminence: beguiled into service in Austria-Hungary, pressured into the army in Prussia, after having laid hands on the state in Sweden. The striking exception to this pattern was France, where by the middle years of the century the bourgeoisie had gained a substantial foothold from which the aristocracy was about to try to dislodge them.

Just as the Prussian army developed during the first half of the eighteenth century, so the French army declined. It lost the battles of Blenheim, Rossbach and Dettingen and won only at Fontenoy in 1745. Moreover, the wars in which France was engaged during the years after 1739 brought into the army a further influx of bourgeois officers, who showed on the whole that they could fight quite well enough, whilst the nobility revealed on occasions that it was far from possessing a monopoly of the military virtues. One of the most distinguished members of the French aristocracy, prince Louis of Bourbon-Condé, fleeing from the field of Rossbach (1757), enquired of a spectator whether he had seen any fugitives. 'No, monsieur' came the caustic reply, 'you are the first.'[10] It was becoming increasingly difficult to maintain the claim of the noble officer that he demonstrated himself to be a better soldier than his middle-class counterpart by virtue of his innate cultural and moral superiority.

It was against this backcloth that the appearance in 1756 of two important books kindled a debate about the social causes of France's military decline, and more particularly about whether in future the nobility could do the state more service if engaged in commerce or in following the profession of arms. Abbé Coyer's *La Noblesse commerçante* advocated the former course and the Chevalier d'Arc's *La Noblesse militaire* urged the latter. After the defeat at Rossbach the issue of how far the nobility was responsible for that defeat by virtue of its detachment from military service became a predominant one, and in the process a large number of middle-class officers were branded as scapegoats for defeat not as individuals but as members of the bourgeoisie. The nobility put themselves at the head of a new movement for military reform and became loud advocates of the need for greater professionalization in the officer corps and for the suppression of venality in the army. In this they were not without class interests, for by lessening the role of money in the acquisition of a commission they could hope to exclude the wealthy middle classes and gain a more secure monopoly of army ranks. Such a campaign, if successful, would have the added advantage of generating a distinction between the military nobility and other varieties of aristocracy. Under the pressure stimulated by such conditions, the king took over control of all regiments and companies in his army in 1762 and fourteen years later the venality of offices was finally ended.

The first sign of France's aristocratic military renaissance came in 1758 when Belle-Isle became the first soldier ever to occupy the position of secretary of state for war. Thereafter three decades of military reform followed. In 1759 the duc de Broglie became commander-in-chief of the French army and for the first time organized it into permanent divisions for use on the battlefield, an example of the new and more professional approach to questions of military organization. Other innovations quickly followed. In the hands of the duc de Choiseul (1761-71) the Ministry of War, partly driven by force of circumstance to overcome the problem of absentee officers which still existed, built up a corps of exceptionally efficient non-commissioned officers. A successor, the comte de St Germain (1775-7), founded in 1776 twelve provincial military preparatory schools to which the sons of the poorer nobility and the offspring of the bourgeoisie flocked in equal numbers and from which the best pupils passed, until its suppression in 1788, into the *Ecole militaire de Paris*. Such was the power of this example, and the recognition that the nobility had to justify a predominance in Europe's officer corps by bringing with them a greater degree of professional skill, that similar military colleges were set up between 1752 and 1799 at Wiener-Neustadt, St Petersburg, Munich, Naples and Sandhurst. Europe's gentlemen were no longer relying upon the mystic attributes of their class to justify a monopoly in the officer corps, but in France they were fighting determinedly to maintain the military pre-eminence of the second estate, and they gained a notable victory by the terms of a decree of 22 May 1781 which required four quarterings of nobility (i.e. that all four grandparents be of noble birth) in order to become an officer.

Reform in France found practical expression in Gribeauval's reorganization of the artillery, lightening and standardizing guns and increasing their mobility. On the eve of the Revolution the last royal minister, the duc de Brienne (1787-9) created a territorial system designed to unite soldiers and civilians more closely by associating each of the seventeen divisions in the army with a particular geographical region. In the same brief period military manuals were rewritten, pay and conditions of service improved and a top-heavy officer establishment reduced from 35,000 to 9,578. The most striking symbol of the soldiers' control over military affairs came when a *Conseil de guerre* was set up in

1788 to oversee the affairs of the army. Military defeat and social pressure had resulted in massive and wide-ranging military reforms of which the beneficiary was not to be the *ancien régime* which produced them but the Revolution which was its successor.

While it would be tempting to associate this remarkable wave of reform with the influence of the philosophical ideas of the Enlightenment, most of the evidence seems to point in the opposite direction. Montesquieu, Rousseau and Voltaire all shared the belief that standing armies were instruments of tyranny which enabled a monarch to do as he wished. The alternative they offered — a national militia — had well-established antecedents but was quite unsuited to the requirements made of an army of the age in terms of military capacity. Voltaire, in any case, thought that war was unscientific and likely to remain so; coupling it with medicine, he labelled it 'murderous and conjectural'. For the Physiocrats in general the most noteworthy characteristic of an army was that it was unproductive and sterile. While the general effects of the Age of Enlightenment were undoubtedly to encourage enquiry and rational analysis, only one military thinker of primary significance emerged during it — the comte de Guibert, who in 1772 published his *Essai générale de tactique*. This was a work plangent with the tones of romanticism. War, said Guibert — transposing Rousseau — must be 'natural'. Translated into practical terms, 'natural' warfare meant a rejection of Prussian formalism in favour of individualism in officers and non commissioned officers. Guibert also believed that men were perfectable and that the qualities of good citizenship could be encouraged and nurtured. This moral undertone caught more than an echo of the *Arte della guerra* for, like Machiavelli, Guibert wanted a citizen army rather than an old-fashioned militia. The crux of his argument was that the state could only be as strong as the individuals who composed it, and that this was nowhere more true than in the field of military organization.

Guibert saw the practical results of his philosophy as being a greater emphasis on movement, and the use of divisional columns to retain flexibility and initiative. The armies of the future were not to be riveted to chains of magazines but would live off the land — such an alarming and novel method of eroding discipline that Prussian soldiers would be executed in 1806 for following it. The message that fortresses were simply useless appendages was, for the nation which had produced in Vauban the greatest military architect of centuries, a difficult one to accept. In at least one respect, Guibert's practical ideas were to be vindicated; in 1778 the duc de Broglie demonstrated the manoeuvrability of the division column at Vaussieux.

On the eve of the Revolution all the ingredients for a new form of warfare were thus present in France. New techniques, new structures and new ideas about the value of citizen as soldier and the soldier as citizen were in the air. What was missing was a political philosophy to replace absolute monarchy, with its disregard of its humbler subjects, and to provide a stimulus to weld all together. This task would be performed by the nationalism born of the French Revolution.

The contrast between the military affairs of France and Prussia, the two great military powers of the age, under the aegis of an aristocratic military hierarchy, was a striking one for the Prussian system was now in the process of ossifying, largely thanks to Friedrich II himself. The wartime expedient of recruitment by canton was watered down after 1763 as increasing numbers of exemptions from military service were granted, with the result that only 3 per cent of the Prussian populace was inducted into the army and increasing use was made of foreigners and mercenaries. Some areas of Prussia, especially parts of Silesia, were granted total exemption from the military levies. As a result of policies such as these, by 1804 half the army was composed of mercenaries and its reliability was at best problematical. Further military retrenchments which damaged its professional capabilities included reducing the annual periods of manoeuvre and training.

Friedrich continued to follow his rigid beliefs about the innate military superiority of the nobility, with the result that foreign nobles were imported in growing numbers to fill the gaps left by those members of the native Prussian aristocracy who had been killed during the Seven Years' War; the great Scharnhorst himself entered the Prussian army by this route. The Prussian high command progressed only in age, and by 1806 sixty-two generals were over sixty. They tended, quite naturally, to venerate Frederick the Great, but, lacking his military genius, they took refuge in inflexible dogma. The ideas current about war in such circles were best exemplified in the writings of Massenbach, who saw war as a matter of careful manoeuvre and mathematical calculation.

The state of the Prussian army in these years was made worse by acute administrative inflexibility. By the end of the eighteenth century five independent and autonomous agencies operated within the army, chief amongst them the *Militärdepartement*, which was losing its influence, and the *Generaladjutantur*, which was gaining in importance. From the latter was to come the powerful Military Cabinet of the nineteenth century, its predominance resting upon its posses- sion of the right of *vortrag* which meant that it alone com- municated the sovereign's orders to the rest of the army.

On the eve of the French Revolution certain clear patterns had begun to emerge in the way that the major European states ordered their societies for war. Everywhere the tradi- tional personal service which, in one form or another, went back to feudal or early modern times had been overlaid by an obligation to perform some sort of conscript service, though this was as yet far from a universal obligation. Noble pre- dominance was an even more marked feature of military organization and one which was demonstrated in all Europe's officer corps, although it did not extend in an unbroken line back to the *chevaliers* of the Middle Ages; in Austria and in Prussia it had deliberately been sought by the monarch, in France it had been newly won by the nobles themselves, riding the crest of a reformist wave. Hand-in-hand with noble supremacy went a new concern for technical and specialist military education for aspiring officers, one ground for arguing that professionalism did exist in military organiza- tion before the onset of the nineteenth century brought an abundance of technological innovation which had to be mastered.

Neither war nor organization for war could as yet, how- ever, be said in any sense to unify society. Obligations were irregular and uneven and privilege went hand-in-hand with rank: in 1776 Kléber enlisted in an Austrian regiment and seven years later he returned to France still a lieutenant, believing that his lack of noble blood made further promotion impossible. Nor did the causes for which monarchs fought serve to cement together their armies and their peoples. *Raison d'état* could provide a powerful prop to a king in search of legitimate authority for his actions, but it did little to arouse emotion or commitment amongst his people. It was the ideology of revolutionary nationalism which was to add an entirely new dimension to war, to military organization and to government. Arousing popular enthusiasm, it mobilized hitherto unimaginable reserves of manpower for the service of the state. Officers need no longer forbid loose-order manoeuvres through broken or wooded country in the certain knowledge that when they emerged their troops would be fewer in number than when they entered. Military organization had to evolve in order to cope with this new phenomenon, and adaptations had to be made in the field of tactics in order to make good use of the new, enthusiastic but untrained forces. The age of modern warfare, like the age of modern politics, was to be marked out from what had gone before by the addition of one new factor: mass.

2
'Aux armes, citoyens'

━━━◄◄◄◄◄◄◄◄◆►►►►►►►►━━━

The introduction by France of the mass conscript army confronted Europe with a new style of military organization and changed its concepts of the potential size of the military community as the nation-in-arms proved capable of mobilizing its resources and applying them on the battlefield with marked success. The notion of general involvement in military activity did not, however, take hold everywhere on the continent; rather it was to be two states which laid down patterns that were to be the subject of deep scrutiny in the half-century following the defeat of Napoleon. France was the innovator, but her experience demonstrated that certain social tenets which pre-dated the Revolution, especially about the relationship between noble and officer, were not susceptible to revolutionary ideals to the point of being totally undermined. Prussia was the imitator, impelled by a desire to revenge her defeat at the hands of Napoleon in 1806, and driven as a consequence to copy certain aspects of her rival's organization; but she too showed conservatism in several respects and particularly in the matter of her officer corps. Differing markedly in both their political and their social structure, these two countries developed their own patterns of conscription and demonstrated that the new type of military organization might fit the needs of both a society from which it emerged naturally and one on which it

25

was imposed artificially.

Elsewhere in Europe the revolutionary model was not copied, and the armies of Austria and Russia which fought Napoleon were structurally essentially eighteenth-century armies. Later on, during the nineteenth century, they would all succumb to the new military system and introduce variants of the conscript army, with the exception of Britain. She proved that her own blend of organization was both successful and satisfactory, and was subsequently able to use the success of Wellington's armies as a powerful argument against change. Britain's experience during the Napoleonic period was thus of particular importance in explaining her subsequent military development.

Mass armies also changed the shape of war itself. The presence on the battlefield of large, imperfectly trained bodies of men who lacked the discipline of the old, long-service, professional armies meant that the generals who commanded them had more men at their disposal than previously, but also that the troops had to be used in ways which took account of their inability to perform complex tactical manoeuvres during battle. The result was to be a form of combat which drew upon Guibert's notion of 'natural' warfare and upon the experience of war in North America during the last quarter of the eighteenth century to produce much greater flexibility and an emphasis upon the shock which the impact of massed attacks could produce upon the minds of the defence. Although lying outside the realms of formal, national state systems of military organization, the age also produced the phenomenon of guerrilla warfare in Portugal and Spain and the use of semi-independent formations to attack supply lines in Russia. This type of warfare, although striking in its nature, was not so much the result of free choice, but rather the response of countries whose military position allowed them to do little else, and it was not to be a model for any state system of military organization for more than a century.

The most profound change in French military organization resulting from a revolution which, at least nominally, put such a high premium on equality might have been expected in the officer corps, dominated by the aristocracy and therefore seemingly a natural target for social and political purification. The immediate impact of the Revolution on the army was to triple the desertion rate during the second half of 1789. By the end of 1790 the regular army numbered 130,000 and had lost 20,000 men in the previous twelve months, but in the following year the trend was reversed, partly as a result of the decision to increase officers' pay by 50 per cent. In a much smaller officer corps, now numbering 9,406, the prospects of the ranker improved markedly with the reservation of one quarter of all lieutenancies for non-commissioned officers, while the remaining places were filled by competitive examination.

After Louis XVI's abortive flight from Paris in June 1791, many noble officers felt themselves released from their bonds of loyalty to the monarch, and thus able to leave the army and France; the consequent reduction of the old officer corps was increased by the demand made on 11 November 1791 that all soldiers should swear an oath to the constitution. Eighteen days later the Assembly suspended the competitive military examinations, filling half the lieutenancies from the ranks of the non-commissioned officers and the other half from the *Garde Nationale*. An extreme was reached in 1793-4 when officers were chosen by no more formal means than simple selection. These various measures did not, however, represent the letter of revolutionary social ideals being applied to the army, but were designed to create a more able, and therefore a more professional, officer corps. In this they were certainly stimulated by the pressure of circumstances. As a result of some of the reforms of the *ancien régime*, the corps of non-commissioned officers represented just such a reservoir of military talent as was now required, though often devoid of anything more than the rudiments of formal education. A further stimulus to these imaginative measures in officer selection was the fact that drastic steps were necessary to keep up the numbers of the regular army.

By 1793 the structure of the French officer corps clearly reflected a pressing concern for ability and experience. Four-fifths of all infantry officers had served for five years or more, and therefore ante-dated the Revolution, and the same was true of 97 per cent of all artillery officers. There was also clear evidence of utilization of talent from below in the new revolutionary officer corps: more than two-thirds of all infantry officers in 1793 had served in the ranks. The nobility were, however, still well in evidence at this relatively late stage, especially in the higher reaches of the army; two-fifths of all field officers were noble, though only 9 per cent of captains and lieutenants were.

Many members of the French officer corps were new to the higher levels of the profession but were old hands at soldiering. Rather than opening its ranks to the politically loyal or the socially reliable, the revolutionary army was relying heavily on the foundations of Louis XVI's army. This was borne out in the picture presented by the generals of the day. Only five of the 200 generals of 1793 had been generals in 1789, but 79 per cent had served twenty-five years or more in the army, and 70 per cent were of noble background. When on 21 February 1793 the regular army disappeared as a separate entity in the military establishment of France on amalgamation with the levies, its officer corps was in many respects similar to that of the old pre-revolutionary army, though there had been a marked increase in the number of ranker officers. This was the result of a determined pursuit of military efficiency rather than of a determination to implement the wider social tenets of the Revolution, and its outcome was 'probably the most professional officer corps in Europe at that time'.[1] This alone goes a long way towards accounting for the success of the French army during these years.

One reason why the regular army remained relatively undisturbed by the upsurge of the Revolution during the last four years of its existence was the fact that the political movement had thrown up its own unique military expression in the volunteer *Garde Nationale*. Often, and erroneously, presumed to be the most significant military expression of the Revolution, the National Guard was formed in direct imitation of the ideal of the American Revolution that 'all citizens will be soldiers and all soldiers citizens.' The earliest recruits, enthusiastic amateurs from restricted sections of revolutionary society who were chosen on the basis of a property qualification, were given rudimentary training in 1790, and in the following year volunteers were called for from their ranks to reinforce the regular army. Caution evidently outweighed military enthusiasm among the National Guard, for the resulting troops were too few in number to sustain the army at the necessary level and on 22 July 1792 the National Assembly fixed the numbers that each department of France was to provide for a second 'voluntary' enlistment, with the warning that if not enough troops were forthcoming it would have to resort to the ballot.

The poor response of the National Guard to appeals to put their political fervour to practical military use on the frontiers of France was a clear indication that the revolutionary enthusiasm of the propertied classes was far from being a bottomless well from which to draw sustenance and the authorities were forced to resort to the ballot. Nor was the material which was forthcoming of very desirable quality; general Susane wrote to the Convention, 'send us regular troops and dis-embarrass us of the sans-culottes'.[2] Such professional directness was to lead numerous high-ranking officers to the guillotine during these violent years. Incidents which demonstrated the unreliability of the 'voluntary' levies multiplied. Between October and December 1792 they deserted by the thousand in Belgium, while in February 1793 the unfortunate general Casabianca, who had landed an army on Corsica, was forced by volunteers to re-embark to avoid being hanged. Clearly the Revolution could not rely long upon such unruly elements for its defence, especially as it was coming under increasing external pressure. The system of 'voluntary' levies was also causing severe domestic disruption and was one of the main causes of the rising in the Vendée in March 1793. When the first stage of the fighting there was concluded in April 1795, one of the most prominent conditions of peace was that conscription was not to apply to the region until 1803.

The solution to the military problems of the Revolution lay not simply in the large mass of untapped manpower outside the realms of the National Guard, but in the political fervour with which the populace supported the ideals and aspirations of the new regime. This enthusiasm, the equal of which had not been seen before in a European population, meant that the government could mobilize a far wider cross-section of its citizenry without feeling qualms as to its political reliability. On 7 July 1793 Aristide Valcour pointed out to the Assembly that the rich, the merchants and the landed proprietors already had guns, but that the poor, the workers and the artisans did not. Threatened by a federalist revolt from within and by armed incursion on its borders, France and the Revolution needed protection; hence Valcour's demand, which was not without domestic political under-tones, that 'the commanding mass of the people be armed, that a million muskets be handed out'.[3] The concept of an armed citizenry, albeit standing in reserve, was already established in revolutionary thought; a year earlier Carnot had defended mass popular armament as 'the only course of action which can cause our foreign and internal enemies to tremble, as the only means to lay the foundation of a new military system which, by making all citizens soldiers, will deliver the final blow to the spirit of inequality'.[4] Under pressure from this and other demands and faced with a pres-sing military problem, the Assembly decreed a *levée en masse* on 23 August 1793, thereby inaugurating the era of mass conscript armies which marked European military affairs for the next century and a half.

The mass armies of the period after 1793 in France pro-vided some opportunities for social advancement, although meteoric rises from nothing were rare. Of the twenty-five Napoleonic marshals nine came from the officer class, includ-ing Kellerman, Berthier and Marmont; ten came from the ranks, including Ney, Murat, Soult, Bernadotte and Masséna; and six had been civilians, most notable amongst them St Cyr — nicknamed 'the owl' for his preference for living alone — who began life as an artist. Clearly being a successful soldier could produce remarkable rewards, although the fact that out of the entire army only ten rankers reached the position of marshal emphasized the rarity of such advance-ment. A better general view of the ups and downs of military fortune was perhaps provided by the generals, especially during the period of the Convention. Support came from Paris chiefly for those officers who were notable for their courage rather than their tactical or strategical skills, such as Rossignol. During the years 1793-4 attempts to refuse advancement to the rank of general were numerous, and for very good reasons; if their politics or tactics did not suit, there was a considerable risk of the guillotine. More than one unwilling candidate was told bluntly 'il faudra bien que vous acceptez.'

By 1794 France had successfully repulsed the threat to her north-eastern frontier, and the following year her own forces crossed the Rhine. Success, the move on to the offensive, the disappearance of Robespierre and the rise of Napoleon's *armée d'Italie* all helped to make the rank of general more secure and to bring on new men. The *amalgame* of 28 January 1794, whereby regulars, volunteers and conscripts were finally combined together into one military force, further aided the rise of the former regular soldier since one-third of the promotions now turned on the total length of service of the candidate, the remainder being determined by election.

Just as the French Revolution threw into strong relief problems about the social composition of a nation's military forces, so it also produced a conundrum which was, in one form or another, to perplex societies from that time onwards. The replacement of the absolutist monarchical state, whose king commanded its army, produced the need for the political arm of the new state to exercise control over its military servants. The departure from the armies of the Revolution first of Lafayette in 1792 and then of Doumouriez accentuated the problem of reliability and led to the introduction of the Representatives — watchdogs sent by the Convention to accompany its generals up to and onto the field of battle. The Representative was not entirely a figure without precedent: a deputy of the Estates General had been present at the battle of Malplaquet (1709) and had subsequently reported on the conduct of operations. However, the employment of Representatives in considerable numbers demonstrated the seriousness with which the Jacobins, newly arrived in control of the War Department in Paris, took the problem of political reliability.

The Representatives, who were in some ways forerunners of the commissars of the Red Army, made it extremely difficult for the generals to establish and maintain the necessary levels of discipline among the troops since they supported enthusiasm in preference to order and severity. O'Moran was guillotined for objecting to the presence of two Representatives in his army on precisely these grounds; the popular explanation of his fate was that he had been incautious enough as to refuse to drink Marat's health. The Representatives were not, however, an unmitigated hindrance to the military; on the battlefield they could and did help to boost flagging morale.

If the Representatives did succeed in exerting some degree of political control, they also encouraged the most undisciplined and hot-headed elements among the volunteers, and they obstructed military commanders by their assumption of the right to give strategic advice and even, on occasion, orders. The symbol of their influence was the portable guillotine which one corps dragged behind it when it went into action in September 1793. Of more strategic significance was the pressure they put upon Kellerman during the summer of 1793, while he was suppressing revolts in Marseilles, Toulon and Lyons, to remain in the latter city when the Savoyards wanted him with them. It is worth noting that the least successful of all armies in 1794 was that of the Pyrenees, which was also the one most firmly in the hands of the Representatives. Typical of the heights of military thought to which the Representatives could rise was the following declamation: 'What good are generals? the women of our *faubourgs* know as much as they do. Calculations, calm combinations, tents, camps, redoubts? All these are useless. Irruptions, cold steel, that is the only warfare which henceforward suits the French democratic spirit.'[5]

This anonymous Representative had undoubtedly remarked upon one of the most obvious of the military phenomena associated with France after 1789: that the new mass armies had called forth new methods of fighting. Subsequently it appeared to some that the nation-in-arms, first apparent in France in 1793, was a barbarous horde that had in some way depleted warfare by substituting for order and limitation the hideousness of totality, mass, shock, and big butchers' bills.[6] Contemporaries were much more inclined to emphasize the political motivations uniting society into an organic whole. The methods of revolutionary warfare more accurately reflected commitment, politicization and enthusiasm on the part of society at large than the blood lusts of the herd. Arguments about whether warfare was as a result devalued in some way, which depend heavily on assertions of what warfare in the preceding century was like, are fruitless.

Goethe's dictum that at Valmy two ages met should therefore be applied to military matters only with great caution. Valmy actually symbolized the degree to which the Revolution was defended by elements more characteristic of its predecessor. Kellerman's army, which was the one most closely involved in the battle, was not composed of raw levies; all his artillery and cavalry were regulars, as were almost two-thirds of his infantry. Kellerman himself was essentially a product of pre-revolutionary society, so that the Revolution has been said to have been saved by the general who was least its product. In a similar way the methods of fighting adopted by the French armies combined elements of the old regime with a recognition of requirements flowing from the nature of the new.

The belief that the French possessed a special aptitude for shock combat rather than using the fire-power of the musket ante-dated the Revolution, and shock assaults had been written into the drill manuals of 1788 and 1791. The notion that there was a mode of military conduct which uniquely fitted the political enthusiasms of the new France found an early expression in the instructions published by the minister of war in September 1792, ordering that the troops should resort to the method of fighting of 'free and valorous peoples, that is to say, hand-to-hand'. The Revolution also made use from 1792 onwards of skirmishers — *tirailleurs* — who were in themselves physical embodiments of self-reliance and expressions of an enthusiastic spirit of offence. But at the same time use was being made of the structures developed during the preceding forty years. The early actions of the revolutionary wars were fought by independent divisional columns, and at the battle of Montenotte (1796) Napoleon showed what could be done by uniting such columns under a single control. In the same year Napoleon used battalions in columns for manoeuvre and in line for mutual support, an instance of the remarkable flexibility of the French armies of the period.

Conscription swelled the ranks of the French armies and in 1793-4 Lazare Carnot — the 'Organizer of Victory' — created the first mass armies of the Revolution. Carnot's immense feats of organization entitle him to stand beside Trotsky and Kazimierz Sosnkowski — who respectively carved out the Red Army in 1918 and the Polish army in 1920 — in the triumvirate of outstanding military organizers. There was little that his raw groups could hope to perform from the tactical manoeuvres that had filled the pages of the earlier drill-books, and so the military establishment of the day was forced to adopt Guibert's view of the army as something resembling a human steamroller. Patriotism would make up for lack of discipline. The form evolved to utilize the most potent asset of the conscripts, their revolutionary *élan vitale*, was the so-called attack-column: forty men wide and twelve men deep, it still retained enough flexibility to allow it to detach troops or form a square. From sheer military necessity there emerged a fundamental conviction which was to colour the French army's attitude to manpower and training for at least the following century, and which also provided society with a potent argument for avoiding undue military exertion in time of peace. This was that an assailant can achieve the greatest superiority over his opponent not simply by dint of numbers or superior expertise in drill and movement but by 'moral worth'.[7] Needless to say, the French army and the French nation were supposed to be the major repositories of this nebulous quality.

In 1795 the armies of France moved over to the offensive as a result of at least three major considerations. First there was much enthusiasm for the export of the Revolution outside the frontiers of France; then, if the large armies which had been brought into existence were suddenly disbanded severe economic dislocation might well result; and finally, France was coming to exist on an economy of plunder. Military activity now became focused upon Napoleon's army in Italy. Here speed of action was dictated, at least in part, by lack of supply lines, and therefore by the need to keep the army moving in order to prevent it from disintegrating altogether. The impact made upon the peninsula by Bonaparte's troops strengthened the belief in Europe that it was *élan* which lay at the heart of France's military success and which had in some way to be imitated in order to be defeated. An Italian priest who witnessed the sack of Pavia in 1796 best put into words the astonishment of contemporaries at the contrast between the new style of military organization and the old:[8]

> But what is more remarkable still, is, that these men, dying of hunger, generally small, weak, worn out by fatigue and privation, without clothes or shoes — men that one would take for the dregs of a wretched population — should have conquered the Austrian Army, which had everything in abundance, food, clothes, guns, magazines of all sorts, and which is composed of *gaillards* of great height, robust, and innured to war.

The Committee of Public Safety, whose regimen is best known for the domestic terror that marked it, laid down the basis of sound organization for France's military forces under the guidance of Carnot. The Directory, which succeeded it, was a more relaxed ruler, and with it there came a lapse into inefficiency. So low had the much vaunted military spirit run by 1798 that the Conscription Act of that year appealed to patriotism rather than simply to political idealism as had been the case in the past, declaiming 'Every Frenchman is a soldier and owes himself to the defence of France'. Symptomatic of the level to which military morale had sunk after initial fervours died away was the speech made to the garrison of Paris by General Lefebvre six weeks after the *coup d'état* of Brumaire (9 November 1799). Lefebvre informed the troops that the Revolution was terminated and promised them three things as a result: that there would be no more executions, that they would have uniforms made of real cloth, and that they would no longer be shod in boots with paper soles.

The Napoleonic army was probably at its peak in 1805; thereafter it deteriorated. In all, over one and a half million conscripts were raised, of which some half a million became casualties, or roughly 3 per cent of the total population. As the cost of Napoleon's policies mounted, so did the reluctance to serve increase: by 1810 some 80 per cent of the annual quota was failing to appear and Napoleon had to divert 40,000 troops to winkling them out. Also after 1805 there was little time left in which to train troops, and in the last two or three years of the Napoleonic imperium recruits were lucky if they had one week's training. In an effort to compensate for growing inexperience amongst his forces, Napoleon massed ever more artillery to mask their weaknesses.

Both republican and Napoleonic France had been concerned to maximize military efficiency. At a number of points this concern could cut across the new social tenets of the Revolution, and nowhere was the relationship between military force and social requirements more clearly displayed than in the matter of substitution. The hiring or purchase of a substitute to perform military service in one's stead had been permitted in the French army as early as 1774, although it did not become an important phenomenon until after 1789. Then, and despite the voluble assertions that equality was one of the watch-words of the Revolution, both the Declaration of the Rights of Man and the Constitution remained obdurately silent about the principle of substitution; indeed the *levée* of February 1793 made specific provision for it, the clothing and equipment of the substitutes to be found by the men whose place they had taken. An attempt was made to suppress the practice in 1799, but its attractions proved too alluring, and it was reinstated in March 1800.

Substitution did, of course, run directly counter to much of the ideology of the Revolution, but it could be justified by its proponents on a number of social grounds. One argument put forward in its favour by contemporaries was that it gave money to the poorer elements of society. Another was that it provided a useful social filter, allowing the replacement of those 'who would not be able to support the fatigues of war and those who will be of more use to the state by continuing their work or their studies'.[9] Bonaparte was always content to leave the rich with the opportunity to buy substitutes but afterwards he did impose certain socio-geographical conditions, notably that the replacement must come from the same class and the same canton as the man he replaced. The privilege of substitution was not extended to Jews, though

Mennonites continued to enjoy it. It was to survive in France until the latter part of the nineteenth century, and upon it focused bitter arguments over the relative importance of military efficiency and of social obligation.

In assessing the state of the French army by 1814 a careful balance has to be drawn between much of importance that was inherited from the pre-revolutionary era and a little that was both new and cataclysmic. The dominance of the aristocracy in the officer corps was almost as marked after 1789 as it had been before that date. The rise of the non-commissioned officer from the ranks, greatly accelerated by the Revolution's institution of a fixed percentage of junior commissions reserved for rankers only, was, however, to have considerable effects upon the subsequent development of French military society, producing a 'layering' of different types of officer that was unique. It was the direct legacy of a revolution many of whose brightest military talents were not thrown up but advanced by it. On the other hand, the apparent success of the raw levies at Valmy contributed to a deceptive belief that French society contained reserves of military prowess and virtue which were in some way unique to it, and which would always be at the disposal of the military authority, thereby relieving France from having to bother overmuch about the niceties of military training. This in itself was symptomatic of the great social revolution that had taken place in the structure of war as a result of the totality of human effort that revolutionary France could mobilize to support the nation state in its military activity. France had become the first nation-in-arms as a result of the Revolution; all the major European powers were ultimately to be forced to emulate her example to some degree.

In the face of the armies of revolutionary France, the military structure created by Prussia over the previous century revealed serious defects. There had been undeniable social and political advantages in tying the nobility to the crown, but the drawback of such a system, where military virtue was held to derive from a single class and where the sharply hierarchical structure gave those at the base no voice at all, was that it became increasingly impossible to put the machine into reverse and reunite the state with the populace in military terms. Friedrich Wilhelm II was admitting as much when he rejected resort to conscription in 1794 on the grounds that it was 'infinitely dangerous to assemble such a mass of men'.[10] As far as the officer corps went, some of the military talent of the bourgeoisie could be tapped since the middle-class officer could still make his way in arms such as the artillery and the technical units, but after 1763 there had been an insistence on nobility to officer the infantry and the cavalry.

The basis of the Prussian army in its heyday under Frederick the Great had been severe discipline and the use of troops in large formations; the role of the individual soldier had been simply that of an automaton. This official attitude had already begun to change before the impact of the nation-in-arms affected it, the result of the growth of interest in light troops, who required much more in the way of flexibility and individual initiative than did the ordinary infantry of the line. By 1786 such troops had a permanent place in the Prussian army. The death of Frederick the Great in the following year resulted in an amelioration of discipline which further helped to open up the army to ideas of new and unconventional use of troops, thereby paving the way for further changes. However, in Prussia, as contrasted with France, this development was organic rather than revolutionary: the French gave their skirmishers minimal instructions, while the Prussians controlled theirs tightly.

The success of the revolutionary armies and the new welding together of soldier and society did prompt some in the Prussian army to recognize the need for a closer study of war in the light of the new phenomena which were being revealed, and in 1802 Scharnhorst founded the *Militärische Gesellschaft* as a forum for discussion. It lasted for three years only, but many of its members were to be influential during the subsequent 'Era of Reform'. During the same period officialdom gave some consideration to the idea of instituting a national militia, but the idea was soon dropped as potentially dangerous and likely to upset relations between the regular army and the state.

The weakness of Prussia was accentuated by the manner in which she entered the field against Napoleon. In 1805, when both Austria and Russia were fighting against France, the Prussian government vacillated. In the following year, when neither of those powers was engaged in hostilities, she bolted into war. The result of this incautious diplomacy, and of the degree to which the Prussian army had become ossified by the traditions of Frederick the Great, was the catastrophic defeat at Jena-Auerstadt on 14 October 1806. More than anything else, this was the collapse of an outmoded military machine. The Treaty of Tilsit in July 1807 ended the war at a cost to Prussia of half her territory and a heavy indemnity. The appointment in the same month of the Military Reform Commission marked the end of the eighteenth-century military system in Prussia.

Scharnhorst and Gneisenau, who were to be among the leaders of the reforming movement, were appointed members of the five-man commission, which was given wide powers of investigation, recommendation and punishment in an endeavour to set the army on the road to recovery; however, they were outnumbered by its three conservative members until augmented by Boyen and Grolman. Although it made much use of its first two powers, the commission exercised a wise restraint in its hunt for scapegoats: by 1814 only 208 officers had been found guilty of violating the code of honour.

The fundamental problem facing Prussia was the issue of how far the military community should extend. If revenge were to be taken against France, then the essential prerequisites were that the size of the army be increased, its attitude to war brought into line with the new doctrines of mass, and every part of the nation willingly involved in the military effort. All these concepts were foreign to the Prussian military tradition. In order to stimulate the changes which he believed to be essential for survival, Scharnhorst launched an attack on the basic social principle which underpinned the old tradition, namely that the middle classes were temperamentally unsuited to war. This drew considerable opposition, notably from one of the ablest of the Prussian field commanders, Yorck von Wartenburg. Yorck's motive in opposing such an opening-up of the officer corps as would ensue from the acceptance of Scharnhorst's ideas was essentially one of self-preservation: he did not wish to deprive the nobility of a special, though not the sole, claim to officer rank. As a result of his stance on this issue Yorck has been branded a hopeless reactionary, but it is equally possible that he saw the acute challenge such a move would offer to the whole social order.

As a result of its deliberations, the Military Reform Commission began work on the selection of officers on the basis of education and examination rather than of birth alone. However the crown was not to be parted easily from its old shibboleths. The King's Regulations issued in August 1808 affirmed that the 'chief requirements of a good officer are not knowledge and technical ability alone but presence of mind, rapid perception, punctuality and accuracy, not to mention proper behaviour'.[11] The unspoken addendum was that such qualities were to be found rather among the noble than among the bourgeois candidates. The ideas of the commission were further vitiated when, in the following March, a Royal Order reaffirmed the king's right to appoint commanding officers at his own discretion, thereby providing for those whose formal qualifications were not felt to be commensurate with their social worth a means of bypassing educational tests that were too stern. In a similar manner the commission's work on universal military service was stubbornly resisted. In December 1808 recommendations were made that a universal obligation to undergo military service be recognized and that a militia be formed. Both proposals met with strong royal hostility. The king did not want to replace his professional army with a popular one and felt that a militia would be inimical to royal authority, and therefore the notion was rejected. A second rejection occurred in 1810, and when a decree was finally signed bringing the project into effect, in 1813, it was to last only for the duration of the war.

Success in directing the energies of the state upon new objectives was more marked in the civil sphere than in the military. Civil and military reforms were in a certain sense more than merely complementary, they were congruent parts of a single process designed to utilize to the full all the human resources of the Prussian state. As Gneisenau himself pointed out, a 'slavish nation, poor, ignorant, and crude, is no match for one rich in knowledge and resources.'[12] Stein's achievements in abolishing hereditary serfdom and instituting local self-government in the cities were designed to establish a new basis for the conduct of communal relations and a new attitude to class and to social responsibility. At bottom the ideas of the reforming group, whom Metternich referred to slightingly as the 'German Jacobins', were as deeply rooted as those of the French revolutionaries, although in their case in the thought of Fichte and von Kleist. What mattered above all else was the well-being of the community, to which the individual must be subordinated; hence neither the Prussian army nor Prussian society would be quite like those of France. Revolutionary fervour in Prussia did not generate totally new shapes, structures and forms; rather a need to meet and defeat those new methods dictated certain changes in the actions and attitudes of the state. There seems in fact to have been rather more calculation about the process of liberalization as undergone by Prussia, and rather more resistance to it, than was the case in France. As in the case of Stein and Boyen, civilians and soldiers met in seeing the army in this context as an expression of nationalism and patriotism as well as being a purely military instrument.

The military corollaries of the new ideas were too advanced for many, among them the king, and also too dangerous in their practical application. As a result, for some time the military reforms were less eye-catching than were those occurring in the civilian sphere. In March 1809 the powers of a number of separate officials were combined together in the creation of a Ministry of War, an important step in the centralization of military control, but one whose implications were yet to be realized. However no minister was to be appointed to head the new office until 1814, so that the reformers lacked the assistance that might have been forthcoming from that quarter.

At a practical level, much more attention was now paid to the training and tactical doctrine of the army and especially of light troops, whose activities had played a considerable part in the success of the French in the field. In this area the reformers triumphed in substituting caution and detached analysis for emotion and prejudice. The path was long and hard, and on the way explanations had to be produced to counter theories such as that popularized by von der Marwitz to explain the proficiency of the French at open order warfare that 'any Frenchman knows better how to ensure his personal advantage than the German'.[13] The whole thrust of the reformers' arguments was that no such innate distinctions condemned Prussia to military inferiority, but rather that a more enlightened political and social policy towards the inhabitants of the state would of itself improve their military quality. Eventually the Prussians surpassed the French on the field of battle by the expertness of their training, while their adversaries lost their initial dash and enthusiasm.

Diplomacy threatened to undo the patient work of the reformers when, encouraged by Chancellor Hardenburg, Friedrich Wilhelm III concluded a treaty with Napoleon in March 1812 under the terms of which he agreed to supply 20,000 men for the war against Russia and to put their movement under French control. This blow proved an unbearable humiliation for many of those who had been endeavouring to reform army and state, and on hearing the news Boyen and Clausewitz resigned their commissions and led 300 officers into retirement. The king's inept diplomacy thus deprived him at a stroke of roughly one-quarter of the officer corps.

Just as the nadir to which the Prussian army would fall had been the outcome of an act of diplomacy, so too the revival was to come by means of another, but rather more unorthodox, act. On 20 December 1812 Yorck, who commanded the Prussian contingent in Russia, concluded the independent Convention of Tauroggen and withdrew the Prussian units from the conflict. This decisive move spurred Stein to return from exile, mobilize the East Prussian *Landwehr* and force Friedrich Wilhelm's hand. Scharnhorst, who had been forced to leave Prussia in 1809, returned, as did Clausewitz, and with them they brought in their baggage the ideal of a Prussian nation-in-arms. The revitalized Prussia won support from the middle classes despite early defeats at the hands of the French and despite the death of Scharnhorst from wounds. Military leadership passed into the able hands of Gneisenau, assisted by a group of outstanding field commanders which included Blücher, Yorck, Kleist and Bülow.

All this had been brought about by an act which, as well as stimulating the reformers, had great intrinsic significance: Yorck had claimed for the army the title of repository of the values of the state and the role of maintaining them, even if that meant action against the crown itself. Such a revolutionary conception alone is sufficient to explain the reaction against the military reformers which was to follow not long after the defeat of Napoleon.

As far as the ordering of the military affairs of the realm was concerned, the apogee of the Era of Reform came in 1814 with the promulgation of Boyen's *Wehrgesetz*. Its basis was the conviction that the army would be of importance both to civil and military society. By the terms of the law all male Prussians were liable for military service on reaching the age of twenty; they then served three years in the standing army, two years in the active reserve and fourteen years in the *Landwehr* or territorial army, with short annual periods of training to keep up their efficiency. Thereafter they were liable for service in the *Landsturm*, a form of reserve home guard. This system applied throughout Prussia and brought an end to the old method of cantonal recruitment. The comprehensiveness of Boyen's legal enactment took the nation-in-arms several steps beyond the system created first by impulse in France, and in so doing consciously placed new interpretations upon citizenship and nationality. The nineteenth-century nation state would take from Prussia the notion of an absolute right, in return for fulfilling its protective functions, to call upon its inhabitants to lay down their lives in wartime or occupy a good proportion of them in peace-time in defence of the state.

Reforms are seldom accomplished amidst unanimity, and even before 1814 reaction was already beginning to build up in Prussia against the reformist group. Many of the 'Jacobins' were not of true *Junker* origin, some pursued the goal of north German unity — which Friedrich Wilhelm emphatically did not want — and many were critical of the conduct of Prussian diplomacy. Military reform in Prussia was linked to a political ideal, whereas in France it had been as much linked to a set of social aspirations, and the reformers were for this reason both conspicuous and vulnerable. The essential corollary of their military reforms was the introduction of constitutional changes. Pressure from two directions coalesced to prevent such an eventuality and also to isolate and weaken the reformers.

Politically the strength of chancellor Hardenburg and the weakness of von Humboldt ensured the supremacy of the conservatives, a supremacy which was to be enshrined in the famous Carlsbad Decrees published in September 1819. In this climate of political reaction Boyen was unwise enough to launch an attack on the financial stringency of the government, which he felt to be hindering the development of the *Landwehr*. This provided the king with the excuse to demand a closer fusion between regular army and *Landwehr*, a manoeuvre which would have the effect of improving the efficiency of the latter body — which was supposedly suspect — and at the same time subjugating that part of the military forces of the crown which was the symbol of a new and more liberal relationship between sovereign and people. Once the two were yoked together the conservative regular army could destroy the *Landwehr* as a bastion of democratic ideas. In the face of this threat Boyen and Grolman resigned, leaving the reformist wing of the army leaderless.

This defeat for the hard-won military structure was doubled by a social phenomenon: the desertion of the bourgeoisie from the ranks of the new army. The Prussian middle classes no longer wanted universal service now that the war was over. Where once they had seen an avenue to national recovery and self-respect, they now thought to discern the seeds of a militarized society. Conscription and military service would, they thought, lower the moral fibre of society by brutalizing the individual. Though they did not realize it, Boyen's *Landwehr* might have been the instrument of their protection: not a hard-core volunteer army but reservists of the line who yet retained a separate identity from the line regiments and a separate social profile. In the event, as public participation in legislation and administration was whittled away, the *Landwehr* would stand out ever more prominently as the relic of an over-liberal past.

Distanced from the Revolution in France and from the regeneration of Prussia not merely by the comforting width of the Channel but also by the more passive temper of her political and social system, Britain's reaction to the experience undergone by the major European armies was limited to an attempt to emulate their feats by means of a mixture of tactical and organizational reforms. The ranks of the British army were chiefly filled by the Irish, as they had been for more than a decade since the restrictions on Catholic enlistment had been removed in the 1780s. Pay was appalling, conditions of service were wretched and discipline was severe, a thousand strokes of the lash being by no means an uncommon punishment. The officer corps was distinguished by no more demanding requirement than the ability to pay the purchase price of commissions that were trafficked in the open market — or, for a period, by the intervention of the commander-in-chief's mistress.

Despite the relative ease with which they might have invaded it, the wealthy English middle classes did not lay siege to the officer corps as had happened in France a century earlier. As increased parliamentary concern was manifested over the expenditure of public monies, and as the principle of accountability in such matters came to be applied more effectively within the mysterious ramifications of the Horse Guards (the forerunner of the War Office), military position ceased to be a means of generating income and came instead to require the expenditure of sums often well in excess of purchase money if a regiment was to be properly equipped and adequately maintained. Being an officer cost much and offered little by way of material reward. The British army was, and continued to be, officered by gentlemen not only because it required of an intending member no intellectual qualifications whatever, but also because a commission was too poor an investment to attract many members of the monied middle classes, giving little in the way of power, prestige and influence. In Britain the social origins of officers gave the army its importance; in Prussia, by contrast, a commission conferred prestige on a noble and offered some prospect of influence, if not of power.

Under no political or social impetus to change, the structure of the British army during the years of struggle against France was determined by the simple demand not for a larger

45

but for a more efficient army. This was a need brought into prominence by the Flanders campaign of 1793-4, and illustrated in the cartoons of James Gillray. The duke of York — often the butt of Gillray's scornful wit — proved a more effective administrator when installed as commander-in-chief in 1795 than ever he had been previously as a field commander. In the interests of efficiency — and also perhaps of education — he fixed the minimum age for an ensign at sixteen; the frequent absence of officers from their regiments was discouraged; and levels of general discipline were raised. The royal duke also supported and encouraged a new system of drill and tactics devised by general Dundas. Pressure for reform was amplified as a result of the experience of meeting the French skirmishers in the field and led in 1797 to the beginnings of light troops. The distance which separated this British emulation from the generic developments occurring in France and Prussia was clearly demonstrated in the fact that Sir John Moore relied for his early experiments on German manuals.

The need to provide men for the wars against the Directory, and subsequently against Napoleon, produced relatively little change in Britain's military system. In order to raise man-power for the expedition to Holland in 1799, the authorities resorted to a bounty to woo volunteers from the militia, with the predictable result that on the day the troops turned up drunk. By 1802 the military forces of the United Kingdom numbered a scant 151,000 of whom 98,000 were regulars. Short-lived attempts to expand this force and to imitate developments that were occurring on the continent by limiting the length of service in the ranks — a measure designed to permit the army to attract a better class of recruit — met with a withering body of hostile criticism; even Sir John Moore, more usually noted as an enlightened reformer, remarked that only service which was forced from the citizen should be reduced in its duration, otherwise the 'uncommon' quality of British troops might be adversely affected.[14] Attempts to emulate the intellectual adventurousness of the continental armies met with similar lack of success. In 1810 Sir John Burgoyne and captain Charles Pasley founded a 'Society for Producing Useful Military Information' with six charter members, all engineers; it did not survive the end of the Napoleonic wars.

If the professionals were broadly content with the sort of army they already possessed, so too were the British middle classes. From as early as 1803 they demonstrated no significant support for the regular army but went rather to its direct rivals, the militia and the volunteers, both of whom remained firmly under local and not central control. In an attempt to canalize at least some recruits from these organizations into the army a Militia Ballot was instituted, which compelled selected individuals to serve in that body, and from 1806 volunteers went from the militia into the line regiments. However, the public, thinking much the same as Sir John Moore, were willing to go to some lengths to evade service if caught up by the Militia Ballot; a trade in substitutes flourished for those able to pay, one such selling himself to an unwilling victim of the ballot in 1809 for 7s 3d per lb weight.

The British army thus retained most of its attitudes and many of its structures intact over the period of revolutionary warfare, with the happy acquiescence of society at large. Despite this, its professional competence was the equal of any continental army and its discipline probably superior, while its technical services functioned well, especially under the eye of Wellington. The growing recognition of the need for officers to possess some degree of military education was symbolized by the opening of the Royal Military College at Sandhurst in 1802. The isolation of the army from society at large, an isolation exemplified in its attitudes and its structures alike, was not, however, viewed as any bad thing. To many it seemed in 1815 — and indeed for the better part of the century which followed — that a degree of professional inefficiency in the officer corps of the British army would prove a better safeguard of British liberties than military efficiency had proved to be of French ones. Neither France nor Prussia seemed to offer attractive models for the close integration of army and society to a people that wished to remain 'free and unfettered'.

When the wars of Napoleon ended in 1815, the armies of the Revolution had been defeated chiefly, if not entirely, by opponents whose military structure was much more conservative in tone, affording narrower links between the citizen at home and the soldier at the front than had applied in either France or Prussia. The Russian army, where recruitment was by quota and virtually for life, and where officers were automatically ennobled, was the quintessential example of such a conservative military system, whilst among the other victors, powers as disparate as Austria-Hungary and Great Britain shared the institution of purchase of rank. Even Prussia, which had fingered the revolutionary tradition, had maintained intact the notion that high birth was the essential prerequisite and qualification for an officer. Only France had departed from the attitudes towards rank and status, and the phenomenon of a mixed officer corps containing a proportion of non-commissioned officers was to be one of the most durable results of her revolutionary experience.

Those states that had adopted the mass conscript army as their form of military organization had done so in response to the new roles their military forces were being called on to play. Engaged almost from the outset in external conflict in order to defend the Revolution, France had adopted conscription in order to take advantage of the bond which existed between the citizen and the state by converting raw enthusiasm into military power. Prussia, by contrast, had been forced first to develop the necessary inner resources and social harmony before contemplating the outright defeat of Napoleon; for her conscription meant not an expansion outwards but a retreat into herself. The other powers for their part were impelled by neither stimulus, and restrained by forms and traditions which suffered no direct challenge; acting in concert, and aided by the decline of the Napoleonic imperium, the old armies were powerful enough to beat the new.

What had certainly not affected the organization of armies, their size and comprehensiveness, or the notions of what qualifications went to make up a good officer, was technological change. The weapons with which the armies of Europe sought to master one another had changed little since Marlborough's day, a century before. Technological developments had had marked effects upon military organization in the past, and within a quarter of a century of Napoleon's departure from France they would do so again. But in the military revolution, which ushered in the mass army, technology provided no counter-weight to what were essentially social considerations.

After 1815 the armies of Europe relinquished their roles as arbiters of international disputes to adopt instead functions more closely related to the internal needs of their respective states. Although some of those armies were to develop important traditions of extra-European activity which would affect their make-up and attitudes to no small degree, such questions as the proportion of society involved in military activity and the form which that involvement should take came to hinge more immediately on the complex internal priorities of states which were, at least for the moment, at peace with one another if not in conditions of internal harmony. As Europe moved into an era of conservatism the armies of every state demonstrated that, if they were prisoners of their past, they could at least escape from the lessons of their immediate past.

3
The guardians
of order

After 1815 the rulers of Europe sought to erase the new ideas
of social and political order that had germinated in France
and to recreate in their stead the old, stable, conservative
system that had existed before the Revolution. But in at least
one important respect this was to prove impossible. For
France had brought a new element into the military calculations of all Europe when she had introduced conscription,
thereby demonstrating the military potential of the populace
at large to princes who had no wish to admit it to the closed
ranks of the political classes or allow it to upset a social order
based firmly on birth, status and wealth. The conundrum
which now faced most of the rulers of Europe was how to
reconcile military efficiency, which meant a large conscript
army, with reliability, which required a small, elite, professional force. The problem largely resolved itself, for the
politics of all European monarchs became firmly centred on
ensuring the compliance of their own subjects rather than
contesting rival claims with one another. To this conscious
political direction was added the force of economic circumstance, which in many cases simply did not allow the retention of swollen military establishments which would drain
the treasuries of Europe. The princes and the kings were at
the same time security-minded and cost-conscious. So mass
armies became equated with revolutionary politics, and

would remain so until the advent of railways and a mounting concern with external relations raised the conscript army to the fore again in the middle of the nineteenth century. But the immediate concern of all Europe was to make its armies effective agents of domestic repression.

In this task Europe's monarchs were manifestly successful. In the three decades which followed the fall of Napoleon, armies were much employed in support of the civil power all over Europe and all performed reliably. In England troops were used at Peterloo in 1819; they were also used in the Rebecca riots of 1842, and against the Chartists in 1839, 1842 and again in 1848. Success in such activities duly brought social reward; for his part in suppressing disturbances in Bristol and the Forest of Dean in 1830-1, Sir Digby Mackworth was made a knight of the Hanoverian Guelphic Order. In Prussia, the nine commanding generals of Prussia's army corps were given powers to intervene in civil strife to restore order in 1820; thereafter the army was used to crush risings in 1830 and again in 1835. In 1844 Austrian troops quelled a textile workers' strike in Prague, and in 1846 riots were put down in Prague (by an Italian regiment) and in Galicia. In Russia troops were used during the revolt of the military colonists at Novgorod and in the Ukraine in 1831, and again during large-scale uprisings in Perm 1834-5 and at Vitebsk in 1847. Even in France, midwife of the revolutionary tradition, troops were used effectively from the earliest days of the Restoration. In 1817, after a poor harvest, they escorted grain movements and grain riots were put down in Metz and Moselle in 1832 and at La Rochelle in 1839. They were also used to cope with the minor but persistent trouble in the French countryside after 1830 which resulted from the erosion of forest rights. In 1848, the year of revolutions throughout Europe, the French army even proved reliable enough to be used to gather taxes: troops were called into the Dordogne when, by the end of July, the region had paid only 4 per cent of its taxes. Across the face of Europe the reordered armies of the conservative reaction proved effective and reliable, enabling their masters to survive even the turmoils of 1848.

The Napoleonic system did not, however, disappear

entirely, if only because it was too useful. An example of the mixing of traditions which marked the period is the army of Holland; after 1813 the house of Orange revived voluntary recruitment, which included the service of foreigners, on the eighteenth-century pattern but kept Napoleonic conscription. There were thus three elements in the Dutch army: the long-service core, the conscripts and the *Schutterij* or civic guard. With the years, however, the conscript element grew in importance. The neighbouring Belgian army, though under more or less constant threat of Dutch invasion between 1830 and 1839, kept a strong peace-time force on foot by the use of replacements and substitutes, resorting to conscription only if there were not enough volunteers. Thus a population of seven million supported an army of only 40,000 and demonstrated that defence requirements could take second place to domestic social needs.

France certainly seemed at first prepared to retain something of the spirit of the Napoleonic military tradition after the return of a Bourbon king, Louis XVIII, to the throne in 1815. The Charter for the Army published in August of that year decreed that it was to be formed 'according to the principles which constitute a truly national army to form a military force in harmony with the liberal nature of our Charter . . . avoiding the separation of the army from the interests of the country.'[1] The interests of the country would undergo some redefinitions as the political regime of France changed four times in the next thirty-seven years, until Louis Napoleon Bonaparte established the Second Empire in France, but in the immediate future the Loi Gouvien St Cyr (1818) preserved something of the past by introducing a modified form of conscription. Each year 40,000 men were selected by ballot out of a total of 290,000 liable to service, and went on to serve six years with the colours and a further six years in the reserve. Those who drew a *mauvais numéro* in the lottery to don uniform could escape by availing themselves of the services of a substitute, such transactions being sufficiently openly acknowledged to be made subject to the rules of civil contract. The issue of substitution was to provide a reliable indicator of the attitude of Frenchmen to personal military service throughout the period before 1870.

Gouvien St Cyr not only had to create an army, but also to reconcile an officer corps composed of émigrés, royalist volunteers and former Napoleonic officers who had remained loyal to the Restoration during the 'Hundred Days'. This he sought to do by taking promotion out of the hands of the king and by introducing minimum qualifications of age and education. But in 1819 Gouvien left office as minister of war, and the social divisions between *gentilhommes* and *villains* widened thereafter, with the parties sitting on different sides in church as evidence of their social disunity. The experimental 'legions' created in the first years of the Restoration became regiments of the line again in 1820, and in the process the opportunity was taken to do some discreet weeding of the officer corps. A year later the Champeaux company was formed to provide a country-wide insurance service in the face of the ballot by insuring the sons of the wealthy from birth against the need to purchase a substitute — an ill-starred venture which went out of business in 1823 lacking the funds to meet its commitments, but one which none the less bespoke a far-from-military spirit. In the Gironde and Basses-Pyrénées 22.5 per cent of all enlistments were substitutes between 1816 and 1820, and 19.8 per cent between 1820 and 1833. The citizens of France were manifesting their traditional dislike of military service, just as the nobility and gentry were claiming their traditional predominance in the officer corps.

So disparate were its constituent elements that, until 1823, there was no guarantee that the new Bourbon army would fight for anyone. But intervention in Spain in that year proved that the army both could and would fight. In military terms it distinguished itself, in social terms it became an entity, and internationally its success made France once more if not a great power in Europe, then at least one to be reckoned with. However, attempts during the course of the campaign to mobilize the newly constituted reserve resulted in demonstrations against the government and, in some cases, mutinies. The lesson was quickly learned, and in 1824 France sealed her return to military conservatism with a law stipulating eight years' service in the ranks and abolishing the reserve altogether. At the same time 173 officers whose political opinions clashed with those of the regime were dismissed. In 1827 the National Guard was disbanded as a reservoir of republicanism, and France at last had an army fully in tune with a conservative monarchy and similar in almost every respect to all the other major armies in Europe. The Napoleonic tradition seemed dead within the very nation which had brought it forth.

Elsewhere the reconciliation of military structure with social and political conservatism was less difficult to achieve. In Prussia universal service remained and in 1833 the term was lowered to two years to keep pace with the rising population, but the bulk of the reserves — the *Landwehr* — had already been isolated and identified as a liberal relic, socially suspect and militarily inefficient. In Austria the *Landwehr* was dismantled in 1831 in the aftermath of the revolution of July 1830 in Paris. In England there had been no true conscription in any case and therefore no problem of a reserve, reliable or otherwise. By means of regulating their officer corps and their systems of military service the major European powers maintained armies which accurately reflected social and political orders confronted, in varying degrees, with the onset of industrialization and the social tensions which accompanied new modes of political thought.

The retreat into a restrictive military system by a large part of Europe was also, at least in part, the outcome of a need for considerable economies in state expenditure. In Prussia in 1832 men were sent home on unpaid leave after their initial training in order to economize, and an empty treasury continued to exercise its influence until the end of the 1850s; in 1852 of 66,000 Prussians reaching the age for call-up, 28,000 escaped service altogether. In Austria the cost of the wars against Napoleon and the blow of the Congress of Vienna, with its consequent obligation to offer hospitality to half the rulers of Europe, lent a new force to the adage of the previous century that 'au service de l'Autriche le militaire n'est pas riche.'[2] The Austrian army, for reasons of economy, had a smaller proportion of officers than any other in western Europe and from receiving more than half of total state revenue in 1817, its share fell to 20 per cent of what was, in any case, a reduced revenue in 1848. Russia seems to have been alone in supporting a level of military activity at which the army absorbed on average 40 per cent of the annual budget. Elsewhere peace-time meant retrenchment in military expenditure, as it almost always does, which conformed with suspicions of conscription and with conservative fears of mass armies which were also organs of revolution.

Perhaps the most secure bulwark of order, in every sense of the term, was a reliable officer corps, and here Europe's armies quickly reverted to the pattern established everywhere in the previous century, in so far as they had ever left it. In France alone a unique relic of revolutionary tradition survived; by law at least one-third of all first commissions had to come from the ranks of the *sous-officiers*. In practice the military academies were never able to make up the rest, so that over 50 per cent of the French officer corps came from the ranks — a fact which no doubt reinforced its conservative complexion. The immediate result of this practice was to add yet one more source of difference and division to those which already existed within the army: St Cyr versus *sous-officiers* compounded the tensions of *anciens* versus *nouveaux*, and of Royalists versus Legitimists versus Bonapartists.

To a large extent the French army overcame its divisions after 1824, settling down into a state of isolation and focusing on the crown as the source of all senior and many junior appointments and the recipient of the oath of loyalty. Anti-civilian and anti-bourgeois, it turned to an intensive study of the peninsular campaign and of the defeat of Napoleon. The military academy of St Cyr was dominated by the landed bourgeoisie, the Ecole Polytechnique by the professional bourgeoisie of liberal ideals; the business classes were absent from both. For many from the upper levels of French society the choice of a future career seemed extremely limited; until the age of fifteen MacMahon, a future marshal of France and the first president of the Third Republic, was undecided whether to be a soldier or a priest. For others, nothing about a military career held out any attraction; as Julien Sorel remarked in Stendhal's *The Red and the Black* (1830), 'military merit is no longer fashionable.' Dissatisfaction smouldered beneath the surface — with poor pay, with the lowest military pensions in Europe, with antiquated barracks and with poor career prospects. 'Promotion,' remarked Trochu, who would subsequently command the defence of Paris during the great siege of 1870-1, 'was so slow and difficult as scarcely to exist at all.'[3] Beneath an officer corps which was royalist or resigned stood the non-commissioned officers, blocked from advancement by the age to which their more fortunate fellows served in the lower commissioned ranks and susceptible to Orleanist and later republican propaganda.

In Prussia the tradition of aristocratic monopoly of the officer corps continued unabated. This social policy was reinforced by the growing independence of the personnel department of the War Ministry after 1825, when the proportion of bourgeois officers in the army was further reduced. As more and more candidates for commissions came to be chosen by regimental colonels so the level of the educational qualifications of the Prussian officer corps fell. It was in these years, particularly the 1830s, that the cult of professionalism associated with the Prussian army was generated, as the officer corps set itself to study and master the new instruments of the industrial age: the rifle and the railway. This narrowing of focus was encouraged by the future Wilhelm I, who believed that the liberals in Prussia were gradually demolishing the supports of sovereign power and authority. 'It is natural,' he wrote in April 1832, 'that the Army should still be the foremost of these supports; and the more it is inspired by a true military spirit, the harder it is to subvert.'[4] Thus self-preservation appeared to dictate, for the kings of Prussia, heavier reliance upon the aristocracy with its virtues of honour and loyalty, though the Prussian officer corps was becoming noteworthy for the extent to which it was thinking about its job.

In the south German states, unlike Prussia, officers were generally drawn in more or less constant proportions from societies which had, in any case, more civil servants and fewer landowners. Both the Bavarian and the Saxon armies thus acquired marked bourgeois characteristics after 1830 and 1848 respectively, until by the mid-1880s the bourgeoisie were briefly predominant. By the middle of the century this was true even of the Württemburg army, which had initially been more aristocratic than its Bavarian counterpart. The experience of the south German states generally went to demonstrate that the Prussian model was not an iron law of military development and that the supremacy of the nobility in an officer corps was neither innate nor of too firm a standing to be shaken. Rather it was a reflection of conscious policy.

The closest in style of all major European armies to the Prussian was perhaps the Austrian army, which demonstrated to an exaggerated degree the tendencies already marked in Maria Theresa's day. The generals were aristocratic and remained so; in 1815 only 19 per cent were of bourgeois origins, and this figure subsequently underwent a decline. Officers came to their regiments from the Royal Guard, from the schools of Vienna and Wiener Neustadt or from the cadets. The last-named were of three sorts: imperial cadets (the sons of officers or imperial functionaries deemed especially deserving), *exproprius* cadets (who equipped and clothed themselves and applied for entry), and regimental cadets (who provided their own clothing and were admitted by the heads of regiments). It was a system which offered both absolute control over the nature of the officer corps and the power to dispense rewards, enabling the officer corps to replicate itself. The whole organism was both selected and bound together by a complex system of patronage. Every regiment save the frontier troops or those belonging expressly to the emperor had an *Inhaber*, or proprietory colonel: an archduke, a prince or a general of high rank and good birth. The *Inhabern* existed not to exercise command but to dispense patronage, since they controlled regimental promotion up to the rank of captain; thereafter this became the province of the Emperor, with the assistance of an advisory council.

The cadet system and promotion by patronage together ensured a restricted entry into the officer corps with loyalty to the imperial house as the prime criterion. By this means the officer corps became, in the midst of flowering linguistic nationalism amongst the many sub-divisions of the empire, truly a supra-national force. There was throughout the period a perpetual struggle between the *Inhabern* and the Advisory Council on Promotion in which the latter sought to leave the way open for merit; but aristocratic command continued to distinguish the Austrian army, and in Radetzky's army in 1848 two of the twenty-one generals were grand dukes, four were in the Almanack de Gotha, five more were from the greater nobility and the bulk of the remainder were from the lesser nobility. This system, together with the purchase of rank which existed until 1848, bred an army whose leaders were socially cohesive, contemptuous of learning and absolutely loyal to the emperor. They had a high social standing and possessed innate power, but to compensate for this were paid little; it was said in the 1830s that many junior officers were envious of 'salesmen and lackeys, who at least had a full stomach'.[5] They served as the prop of political authority and the symbol of social order, but did not develop their professional function of mastering the instruments of war, a role which was little stressed in any army outside Prussia.

The Russian officer corps took much of its tone from Nicholas I (1825-55) and from his chief military adviser after 1831, prince Paskević. Nicholas, his attitude coloured by the experience of the Decembrist rising in the very first months of his reign, in which army units had been involved, put a high premium on discipline and reliability, and he and Paskević distrusted thinkers and planners. As a result the level of intellectual attainment sank to abysmal depths as the general staff and the military schools languished. Typical of this outlook was the opinion of Sukhozanet, director general of the Military Academy, that learning in military affairs was 'no more than a button on a uniform'.[6]

About half the Russian officer corps came from the hereditary nobility and over one-third were 'personal' nobles; the remainder came from the ranks. There were three routes into the officer corps: via the military schools, by volunteering and subsequently gaining a commission and, for a very few, a commission after long service in the ranks. Of the military schools the best were the Cadet Corps, of which there were five in 1825 and twenty-three by 1855; they were besieged by the nobility in the 1830s and turned away many hundreds of applicants. By far the majority of officers volunteered and served as sergeants (*yunkers*) for two years, or less if they had any educational qualifications. The general intellectual level of the officer corps was very low: during the 1830s only 30 per cent had undergone any form of secondary education at all. The instruction they received in the military schools or the ranks was for the most part harsh, narrow-minded and obsessed with drill, and there was no compulsion to study. The regulations for the educational requirements of intending officers introduced in 1844 were actually less severe than those of 1716, and in any case were not met.

Low levels of intellect were matched by low levels of pay; by 1855 the pay of ensigns and colonels was less than it had been in 1801, and during that interval prices had risen. A Russian colonel was paid half what his Austrian or French equivalent earned and one-third of a Prussian colonel's salary. Commanded by bullying and corrupt generals, faced with the boredom of winter quarters in some distant and semi-civilized province and divided by internal rivalries with Baltic Germans, Poles and Caucasians, the Russian officer corps slumped back into idleness and apathy, relieved only by the hope of promotion which would enable its recipients in their turn to exercise their greed and pettiness on their inferiors.

In its own way the British officer corps was as resoundingly aristocratic as any to be found on the continent, and as a result of the financial basis of its selection displayed faults which were almost the equal of its European fellows. A system of purchase had existed since 1681 and by the following century it was well-rooted enough for George I to introduce a general tariff of prices which were to be paid for each step up to a colonelcy and for an illegal stock exchange in commissions to flourish throughout the century. The last full tariff before the abolition of purchase, which was published on 11 August 1821, set an upper limit for every step from ensign (£450 in an infantry regiment, rising to £1,260 in the Life Guards and Horse Guards) to lieutenant colonel (£4,500 for an infantry regiment, reaching £9,000 for a regiment of Foot Guards). These were, however, notional prices since illegal payments were unavoidable in the hunt for promotion in rank or a step sideways into a better regiment; the highest sum paid for a colonelcy seems to have been £57,000. Once purchased, a commission was an investment which, unlike land, brought no income but which had prestige and could be realized when the holder wished to move or retire.

The purchase system had many defenders, and its defence was usually couched in social terms. The duke of Wellington warned in 1828 that the gentlemen who composed the officer corps made 'from their education, manners and habits the best officers in the world, and to compose the officers of a lower class would cause the Army to deteriorate.' The necessity for an officer to be possessed, before all else, of good social standing was expanded upon twenty-nine years later by Sidney Herbert:[7]

> In despotic countries, the strong military feeling induces military obedience . . . here . . . military obedience would be impossible, were it not that the soldier comes from the class that is accustomed to respect and obey the class from which the officer comes.

Many of the leading military and political figures of the age shared these views, Palmerston among them. Purchase was held to attract into the army men of fortune and character who had some disinterested concern in the country's progress. A system decided by wealth had the added advantage, in a constitutional monarchy, of avoiding the need for selection (since the rich selected themselves — or one another), a procedure which many feared would open the army to political jobbery. Below these rationalizations in defence of purchase lay the deep-seated fear that an army of professional soldiers could prove to be a focus for radical discontent, as it had in France at the end of the previous century.

Behind all the sophisticated arguments put forward in its defence, purchase was accepted because it functioned as a successful mechanism of selection, and in this it was not unlike the systems operating on the continent. It was designed to ensure that only the right people attained position and rank in the army, which could then be trusted to support and sustain the existing order. In this respect it fulfilled its task.

In 1830, 53 per cent of the officer corps came from the aristocracy or landed gentry, and forty-five years later that figure had only diminished by 3 per cent. Nor did the system ease the path of the ranker; of 1,197 transactions between 1834 and 1838, only three represented purchase from the ranks. The wealthy middle classes who chose to commit their resources to the purchase of commissions were largely content to fall in with the attitudes of the aristocracy and to ape their betters in every respect.

The Victorian army was in essence one link in a three-way relationship with the landed interest and public service. This goes far to explain why its political history was so different from that of many continental officer corps, although its make-up was at least superficially similar. In the first place a commission represented only one step in a clearly defined process of socialization, an interlude before returning to the responsibilities of the landlord or entry into the House of Commons to pursue a political career. In this context it may be noted that military experience was distinctly useful for justices of the peace in the first half of the century, when they had considerable law and order functions. The result of this general situation was that, unlike their *confrères* in any European army, a large part of the English officer corps regarded themselves as only temporary inhabitants of the military world. The army occupied a less central place in their lives and was not seen as the basis from which and through which to achieve a change in social or political status. Secondly it was possible to effect a transfer from the army, often by way of the Commons, to the material rewards of a civil career or to administration and a role in the development of the empire. Former officers governed, surveyed, constructed or became chief constables in the newly emerging county police forces. The English officer corps thus had an important double safety-valve. The French army which moved into North Africa after 1830 and the Russian army which expanded into the Caucasus and Central Asia between 1852 and 1855 were the only ones with comparable possessions to absorb the energies of individualistic or ambitious officers. And the British officer developed much closer links with government: between 1784 and 1832, one-sixth of the members of the House of Commons had a military background.

Military ambitions in England were not, however, the sole prerogative of the well-born. On 12 May 1859, in the aftermath of the Orsini plot and anti-English agitation in France, and in the year which witnessed the launching of the world's first steam-powered battleship (*La Gloire*), a government circular authorized the lords lieutenants of the English counties to raise volunteer corps. Under the patronage of the wealthy and the titled, the middle classes sprang smartly to arms. The expense of enrolment fees and high subscription rates (half a guinea to one guinea a year), the machinery of proposing and seconding members and the often considerable expense of uniform and equipment (twelve guineas in the Exeter and South Devon Corps) all bespoke a determination that the Volunteers should be the resort of professional men and the middle classes. And so they proved to be, at least at the start and outside London and Scotland. Their character gradually changed as they were taken over by artisans and clerks, but they remain a unique piece of social history and a demonstration that, in England at least, patriotism and dedication to military service did not reside in the upper classes alone.

In maintaining, extending and demonstrating the distinction between the officer and the civilian in Europe at this time one of the most powerful factors was the duel, the instrument by means of which notions of corporate behaviour were maintained which were increasingly out of tempo with civilian life and manners but which preserved the old notion of the separateness of the warrior from society. The duel reigned in every European army save Britain's, where in 1843 the duke of Wellington, newly returned to the post of general officer commanding-in-chief, moved to block the practice after an unseemly meeting between colonel the earl of Cardigan and one of his subalterns. Subsequently a British officer could be cashiered for being concerned in, or merely conniving at, the fighting of a duel. Elsewhere duelling was an integral part of the notion that the officer belonged to an order which stood separate from ordinary society. In France it was illegal under civil law, outside military regulations, proscribed by the church, but imposed by custom and tradition. The lengths to which officers were prepared to go, or see others go, to avenge imagined or real slights verged on the absurd. In 1825 at Brest two *sous-officiers* fought one another seven times, each affray ending with one of the two participants being carried to hospital gravely wounded. In the end the matter was settled, in the presence of the regimental colonels, with a brace of pistols (one of which was unloaded) at five paces. Whilst duelling was continually enforced by habit and custom, the Restoration (1815-30) witnessed perhaps the high point, when duelling fever would grip whole regiments; regimental champions fought one another, and in some cases teams of five, six or eight men were fielded. Where officers did endeavour to inflict punishment on duellists and witnesses, higher authority frequently intervened to reduce the sentence. Unofficially a fairly strict code of rules existed, under which generally only officers of the same grade were allowed to fight one another.

In Prussia duelling had been outlawed by the Great Elector in 1652, and again by Friedrich II in 1688 but by 1749 Frederick the Great was prepared to be lenient in affairs of honour. The notion of the collective honour of the regiment, in addition to the individual honour of its members, appeared in 1808 but was replaced thirteen years later by Tribunals of Honour which judged an officer's behaviour and its impact on his class. The notion of the officer corps as collectively bound to a separate and defined code of behaviour was one means by which the military ethos of Prussia could be further cemented. In 1841 Boyen toyed with the idea of extending the system of tribunals to other organizations besides the army and in 1843 the complex regulations which governed them demonstrated that the system of collective ethics had finally supplanted personal ones. This was in outright conflict with civil law, where such practices were illegal.

The duel was a device which accentuated the division between the social attitude of the officer caste and the civilian and also reinforced a sense of identity. Both were modes of reassurance which were becoming increasingly necessary as the industrialization of Europe and the impact of liberal and socialist ideas began to extend the gap between soldier and civilian. Duelling, in short, was a distinctive behaviour pattern which both identified the officer and bore evidence of his fitness for membership of the military elite by reason of his readiness to accept and participate in the process. In Britain, where officers were primarily wealthy gentlemen temporarily in uniform, such corporate identification was unnecessary since it already existed by virtue of birth and breeding and was something with which military occupation had little to do.

Aristocratic dominance of the officer corps across the face of Europe ensured the loyalty of the upper levels of the armies to their conservative masters. There was still, however, the congruent question of determining the loyalty of the rank and file. In France the first serious test of the army of 1824 came six years later with the July revolution and the dethroning of the last Bourbon king, Charles X. One month before the revolution broke out 37,000 troops had left France to take part in the campaign just beginning in Algeria, and their absence may well have had a hand in determining the course of that brief revolution. Those who remained adopted a 'wait and see' attitude to the change of authority being effected around them, expecting a lead from their monarch which never came. Where the civil administration resigned, as in Lyons, Marseilles and Cherbourg, the army stepped in to take over the day-to-day running of affairs, thereby tacitly associating itself with authority whatever — or whoever — that authority was. Soldiers used the opportunity offered by the upheaval to protest against unpopular officers, and a number of non-commissioned officers led their regiments in declaring for the provisional government, aspiring to promotions which the existing regime had denied them. The general feeling of the army was perhaps best explained by Canrobert:[8]

> The soldier dreads civil war. He does not know if the cause he is defending will be victorious, or if perhaps tomorrow he will be serving the insurgents . . . he becomes restless, manifesting a lethargy and mistrust which sometimes leads him to desert, to disobey and panic.

Desertion was indeed widespread during these weeks, and many conscripts went home in the serene conviction that revolution meant liberty.

It meant, of course, no such thing in that or subsequent revolutions. But the pieces of the French military structure were skilfully put back together by the July monarchy. An amnesty for deserters decreed on 28 August 1830, and another for those condemned for insubordination on 21 October, were recognitions by those now in authority of the exceptional nature of recent events. Legitimists unwilling to serve under Louis Philippe and the house of Orléans left the army and were replaced by veterans who had themselves decamped from the army fifteen years earlier, and who now returned in a motley collection of uniforms of defunct regimes dating back to 1792. One side effect of this influx of *anciens*, together with the use of considerable numbers of non-commissioned officers to fill out the officer corps, was that the proportion of old officers to young increased after 1830. Casimir-Perier doubled pensions while Soult dismissed officers with strong political views and led a movement to put the army above politics. The detached, and somewhat dogged, professionalism of the French army was formed in the same decade and a half that the Prussian army was focusing on technical problems to the exclusion of politics.

After 1830, capital ruled in France. A new bourgeoisie appeared, an industrial middle class fearful of a proletarian revolution. Lacking anything in common with the old revolutionaries, they disliked the army as a relic of less civilized ages: politically dangerous, unproductive, expensive and a potential prop to the independence of the monarchy. Thus the army law of 1832 made provision for the size of the contingent inducted into the army to be voted each year by the representatives of a middle-class electorate of 170,000 who feared that a large, lower-class army might be less than reliable. While this measure safeguarded the civilians from the army, it did make the task of planning somewhat difficult since the army was never sure how large, or small, it would be the following year. For similar reasons of reliability service was to be for seven years, and there was to be no reserve.

The July monarchy created a force of detached, long-service professional soldiers, whom it then isolated from the rest of society. The influence of French social attitudes on the shape and structure of the army was also clearly apparent in the use of substitution, which by 1835 was increasing noticeably. This worried some in the army, since substitutes tended to be less well disciplined than conscripts, more often punished, and more frequently rendered *hors de combat* by bouts of venereal disease. Yet when general Janin attacked the cupidity which lay at the root of substitution as destructive of the military spirit, Bugeaud — the hero of the North African campaign — defended it as a social necessity for the man who had been prepared for another social destiny than that of the army. Bugeaud was especially alarmed lest the experience of 1830 might lead to an over-valuing of enthusiasm as against the sober virtue of the long-service professional, and complained to the Chamber of Deputies in 1834: 'we have been told until we are sick of it that the battalions of volunteers at the beginning of the Revolution conquered Europe thanks to their enthusiasm'. This, he emphasized, was false. 'In the first two campaigns . . . [they] . . . were almost indisciplinable, because they contained men who had brought to the army the spirit of the political clubs, incompatible with discipline and military strength.'[9] France was now in the process of creating the sort of army that the political nation and many of the soldiers themselves seemed to want.

As the army moved into the 1840s, visible signs of opposition to this order of things appeared, and debate over the army began to mount. The army had proved relatively unsusceptible to republican agitation, and uprisings at Lunéville in 1834 and at Strasbourg in 1836 had proved stillborn — an indication of the success of the remedies applied to the army by the July monarchy. Now the spread of railways and the increasing frequency of leave brought the army firmly back into society's field of vision. Pressure began to mount for a large army with a large reserve, democrats arguing that any system which permitted the purchase of exemption was profoundly socially unjust, and patriots that a truly national army was in any case both a good and a desirable thing. Saint-Simonians wanted to use the army as an instrument with which to reform society, mixing rich and poor together and possibly undertaking such works as railway construction. The future emperor of France, Louis Napoleon Bonaparte, contributed to the debate in 1843, publishing a tract in which he strongly supported the Prussian system of conscription. The bourgeoisie preferred to believe that to be defended by an army containing elements of the proletariat rather than one selected from the peasantry was to be placed in a position of some danger, and they continued to argue for long service as essential to provide military education as distinct from mere military training. This distinction boiled down to the belief that only a long period under arms could allow of a recruit being exposed to the opiates of discipline, *esprit de corps* and the ethos of service which together would dull any errant social or political convictions.

In Prussia, where shortage of money dictated that although universal service remained the letter of the military law it was not strictly applied, the future Wilhelm I was manifesting a conviction — based on similar grounds — that three years' military service was essential not merely so that a soldier might be well trained but also, and more importantly, so that he would absorb the spirit of professional soldiering for life. In the long run his obstinacy over this issue was to lead to the appearance of Bismarck as chancellor of Prussia and to the *konfliktszeit* of 1862-6. In the immediate future it was the *Landwehr*, the symbol of a civilian army imbued by military spirit and more at home out of uniform that in it, on which the prince focused his attentions. Of it he wrote in 1841:[10]

> It must learn to use its weapons and move in the field like the line army from which it has learned such skills. What this means above all is obedience, discipline and subordination . . . . To encourage the idea among the Landwehr that its members are to be treated differently under arms from the soldiers of the line marks the first step towards a revolutionary force.

Wilhelm's objective was that of most of the princes of Europe: blind obedience as a counter-force to the revolutionaries and liberals who were everywhere growing more vociferous.

On the face of it, these sentiments were completely at odds with those of the new king of Prussia, Friedrich Wilhelm IV, who on his accession to the throne in 1840 promptly recalled to the War Ministry the old liberal war-horse, von Boyen. Yet at heart the new king seems to have hated liberalism, and the army to have remained unaffected by it. The Prussian army had entered an era of technical specialization in 1835 when a special commission had been set up to examine the future of railways. Despite its conclusion that the new phenomenon would never replace roads, a keen interest and concern in railways soon developed, and an alliance quickly grew up between liberal Rhenish industrialists and the army which was based upon a common recognition of the need to build railways and build them quickly. Though an unlikely alliance at the time, it foreshadowed the partnership of east and west — rye and steel — which became the basis of the Second German Reich after 1878.

The military soon sought and then gained the influence over the pattern of Prussian railway development which was their prime concern, since military lines did not always run in the same directions as commercial ones. The industrialists, for their part, were more than willing to use the army to further their own interests, and in 1841 major Helmuth von Moltke — the future chief of the German general staff — joined the promoters of the Berlin-Hamburg railway; soon von Moltke was pressing for state ownership and control to secure an adequate network of lines against purely commercial interests. German troops were first moved by rail in September 1839 — nine years after the British army had been the first in Europe to take train — when 8,000 Prussian Guards were moved from Potsdam to Berlin after troop manoeuvres; in 1840 Saxony followed suit, and in 1846 Bavaria.

The concern of the Prussian army with railways was dictated by a mixture of strategy and economics; purely technical considerations dictated their concern during these years with the rifle. Sporting guns made by Hugo von Dreyse had already been used by prince Wilhelm and the crown prince (Friedrich Wilhelm IV) for some time when in 1835

their gunsmith produced his first breech-loading 'needle' gun
— so called because the self-contained cartridge which it fired
was detonated by means of a needle striking the base of the
round. Though having a much shorter range than muzzle-
loading rifles — effectively only some 200 yards — the
needle gun had two clear advantages over them: it had
approximately three times their rate of fire, and it could be
loaded whilst lying down. By 1840 Dreyse's rifle had been
tested and accepted for use by the Prussian army. It was not,
however, put into service; instead it was to be stored away
until there were enough for the whole army or until an
emergency demanded its use.

In the 1830s and 1840s the Prussians had set themselves to
master two of the tools of the industrial revolution which
were to shape war for the next sixty years. It was this process
which inaugurated the era of concentrated professionalism
more commonly associated with the German army of the
1890s, a type of professionalism not yet being generated in
any other major European army. The importance of technical
capacity was reflected in Friedrich Wilhelm IV's ordinance of
February 1844 which recognized — albeit with some reluctance — the value of educational qualifications for an officer
corps. While France's military structure was the subject of
public debate, Prussia had changed far less markedly, and the
role of the army and the place of the citizen-soldier had not
come into an arena of discussion: political quiescence and
social stability had seen to that. So the Prussian army
developed its own role — the mastery of new technology —
to accompany its social and political ethos.

The nature of the Russian army was governed by the social
characteristics of autocracy under Nicholas I, and in any case
lacked any reforming impetus. It was simply impossible to
implement anything approaching conscription since by law
anyone entering the army ceased to be a serf, so that any
attempt at the introduction of universal military service
would have undermined the whole social structure of the
state. The commune could send off as a recruit anyone who
proved troublesome and unreliable in paying taxes, while
the landowner could send any serf at his own discretion;
these provisions, together with exemptions from the draft

through class status and bribery meant that the burden of military service fell upon the very lowest levels of Russian society. Service was for twenty-five years, reduced in 1834 to fifteen years for those with good records, who then went on indefinite leave and entered a form of reserve for five years. Between 1826 and 1850 some 80,000 men were inducted a year, of whom on average 10,000-12,000 were substitutes, known as 'hirelings'.

Once in the army, the recruits were treated with great harshness and brutality, though there was some amelioration in punishments after 1830 when the Tsar intervened to forbid the use of the knout and branding, and set a limit to 'running the gauntlet' of six times through a ring of 1,000 men. The Russian army was almost constantly in action — more so than any other army save that of Great Britain — and its losses were enormous, largely through sickness; during the Polish campaign of 1831, 7,122 men were killed in action while wounds and sickness carried off another 85,000, and during the Hungarian campaign of 1849, 708 men were killed in battle while another 7,414 died from cholera alone. Indoctrination which made skilful use of Orthodox religion and adoration of the Tsar, coupled with fatalistic soldiers' proverbs ('The bullet will find the guilty man') maintained what was, on the whole, an effective instrument for internal repression, but a sorry force when confronted with a major western European foe.

The situation faced by Austria-Hungary was unique in kind and quality since military service was an issue tightly bound up with the means by which the polyglot empire was to be held together. Differences of race and language dictated regional recruitment, but the needs of internal order and reliability demanded that regiments be stationed far from their districts of origin. To resolve this dilemma, units were divided into two portions, one allocated to the centre of recruitment whilst the other did garrison duty outside that region. At the same time geography and the need to maintain internal order among disparate peoples without constant reference to Vienna resulted in the creation of six great military commands — Vienna, Bohemia, Galicia, Hungary, Lombardy-Venetia and the Turkish borders. This was Austria's equivalent of the Prussian regional commanding generals.

As a result of differing historical origins, liability to serve was almost as varied as race and language within the empire. In the Austrian Tyrol there existed a general and personal obligation, and intermittent call-up; and Lombardy and Venetia operated a variant on the form of service of the old kingdom of Italy. In Hungary the Diet voted each year the size of the annual class to be called up and the length of its term of service, up to a maximum of ten years. Always short of volunteers, the Hungarian local committees had to make up the numbers required, which they did by drafting those social elements the great landed proprietors wanted to be rid of. In Lombardy, Venetia and the Tyrol service was for eight years; in Bohemia, Moravia, Austria, Styria, Carinthia and Carniola it was for fourteen years. Everywhere in the empire before 1827 the well-to-do were automatically exempted and local authorities arbitrarily selected recruits; after that year a more regular system was established by which selection was made from eleven classes aged nineteen to thirty, starting with the youngest. As in almost every army in Europe, substitution was permitted, with the assent of the corps commander. In 1845 an attempt to bring order to this welter of complex regulations resulted in a uniform term of service of eight years being prescribed throughout the empire.

By means of this complex system Austria provided herself with a reliable, conservative, long-service army whose functions were essentially to support the imperial dynasty against threats from any quarter and to repress outbreaks of civil disturbance. The army performed its tasks effectively, surviving and triumphing over the strains which might have split it into fragments as they threatened to split the very empire itself. Nationalist ideas did percolate into elements of the military forces, especially in the Hungarian regiments between 1832 and 1836 and again in 1840, and there was some ethnic friction between Germans and Czechs in Bohemian regiments. And Italian and Polish regiments were always under a cloud of suspicion regarding their loyalty. But the organizational system adopted by Austria-Hungary minimized these weaknesses and when the test came in 1848 the army remained steadfast and thus saved both empire and dynasty.

The revolutions which spread through Europe in that year tested every military structure that had been constructed in Europe since 1815. They all had in common the notion of the long-serving professional soldier as the guardian of order; in this era the soldier was something more than the armed civilian he was to become by the close of the nineteenth century. The armies of Europe sprang from differing social, political and national conditions but yet they all behaved in a similar manner. This was not always likely from the outset, perhaps most markedly in the French army where republicanism sputtered fitfully below the surface after 1836 and where there were considerable professional tensions over conditions of service. Facing the revolutionaries in the spring of 1848 the French army, like an animal attempting to resolve equally strong instincts to fight and to run, stood still; all that could be discerned of its reactions by an outside observer were signs of indifference. The revolution was the signal for various manifestations of discontent at regimental level, but the army's basic principle in these months was not to compromise itself too much in any direction. Thus on 15 May the insurgents dissolved the Assembly and busied themselves at the Hôtel de Ville in establishing a new government, watched impassively by a general and two regiments of infantry. When asked why he had taken no action to intervene, the general explained, 'Je n'ai pas d'ordres.' It would not have been possible to plead that the army did not know what to do, since in Roguet's *De la Vendée militaire* (1833) it had what was perhaps the first manual of counter-insurgency warfare in Europe.

The change of regime in France did not produce a wholesale departure from the officer corps such as that of the legitimists in 1830, and in the purge of April 1848 only 84 senior officers were dismissed, most of them being reinstated in August of the following year. Gradually, however, the army turned against the Second Republic in the belief that it was against them. Loyal in crushing the socialists and restoring order, they saw in Arago — the only civilian minister of war since the revolution — the expression of a civilian reaction against the army. Louis Napoleon offered them expectations of promotion and glory which the Republic did not; therefore, acting in accordance with what they saw as their corporate interests, they were prepared to subscribe to an oath to the future emperor as president of France on 9 March 1851. When, nine months later, Napoleon executed his *coup d'état* he deemed it advisable to train three pieces of artillery on the gates of the Ecole Polytechnique — always the most liberal of those institutions which provided the army with its officers — in case of dissent. There was none. The era of turbulence ended in January 1852 when the new emperor dissolved the *Gardes Nationales* (which Louis Philippe had revived), a move apparently greeted with relief by the bourgeoisie. Saved from disturbance at home and free to adventure abroad, army and nation sank back into what they hoped would be an age of comfort and well-being.

The Prussian army lacked any theoretical work on which to base their reaction to their insurgents; the fire-fight followed up by the decisive attack on close columns, which were the basic manoeuvres prescribed by the infantry regulations of 1847, were of little use in such circumstances. In any case their posture was set for them by that of their king. After revolts had broken out in Paris and Vienna, Friedrich Wilhelm IV agreed to summon a diet and grant a constitution — which was what the liberals of 1848 all wanted. In this time of tension the troops were not withdrawn from Berlin and when, on 18 March, a nervy soldiery faced a jubilant crowd firing soon broke out. In a state of confused leadership, and finding street fighting difficult, the garrison commander, von Prittwitz, withdrew his troops to their barracks. Temporarily deprived of the support of his army, the king gave way to demands for a civilian defence force (*Burgerwehr*) to replace the regular army, earning for himself the derisory epithet of *Pflasterkönig* ('King of the Streets').

In several parts of central Europe democratic military organization now seemed briefly the order of the day. In March 1848 the armies of Saxony and Württemburg swore oaths to a constitution, an act which conformed with the increasingly bourgeois characteristics of their officer corps. Yet, as if to disprove what would otherwise be a neat sociological generalization, the Bavarian army did not follow suit: despite having displayed clear signs of liberalism in the previous two decades they did not now succumb to it. Nor did the Prussian army, which liked neither the proposed civilian defence force nor the news that they would have to take an oath to the new constitution. They were not, however, to confront the most testing of choices, that between loyalty to the crown and loyalty to the traditions and spirit of the army itself. The election of a bourgeois parliament in Frankfurt, the loss of revolutionary ardour and a noticeable political shift to the right reinforced the supremacy of the regular army, as did the demonstration in June 1848 that the civilian *Burgerwehr* was incapable of preventing the radicals from storming the Berlin armoury and laying their hands on the new needle gun — which they did not know how to use. Order was restored by the city battalions of the *Landwehr*. The bombardment of Vienna stimulated the suspension of the Assembly in November 1848, and von Wrangel re-entered Berlin at the head of his troops — 'hailed by the solid mass of the middle class, long weary of the insecurity and discomforts of a people's revolution.'[11]

Thereafter the Prussian army gave clear demonstrations of its loyalty and its efficiency, giving their new needle gun its first large-scale test against Saxon insurgents at the four-day battle of Dresden in May 1849 and then defeating the army of Baden and a collection of assorted sympathizers under the command of Mieroslawski at Rastadt in July. The new weapon proved its value during these months, notably in Saxony. The *Landwehr*, however, proved somewhat more suspect; it had by and large stood loyal in 1848, but it did not acquit itself well in Baden the following year; this was to give some measure of empirical support for prince Wilhelm's disregard of it. The crushing of the remnants of the German revolution was a valuable testing ground for the Prussian army in another respect also; its smooth-bore artillery fared badly throughout the period 1848-9, outranged as it was by the rifles of the insurgents in Baden and elsewhere. A rifled piece would solve the problem of lack of range, though its low rate of fire and high muzzle-velocity made it in other respects unsuitable for use in a counter-insurgency role. It was chiefly this problem — of what the gun was to be used for — which explains the very considerable delay between Krupp's unveiling of his steel six-pounder piece at the 1851 Exhibition and the order finally placed by the Prussian army in May 1859 for 300 of them.

Like the Prussian army, the Austrian army was successful in achieving its military objectives during 1848. Save for some Viennese, Hungarian and Italian units, the army remained firm in its loyalty to the emperor. Those troops who did go over to the rebels tended to come from the fixed portions of regiments which remained in their recruiting districts; hence while the fixed elements of one Hungarian regiment went over to the insurgents, the remainder of the same regiment fought loyally and successfully against Italian and Piedmontese revolutionaries. All the armies of Europe in fact bore witness to the success of the military systems adopted to ensure their reliability; even the French army, which was in an unusual position in this respect, supported what it saw as established authority. But no other army tested its weapons and drew technical lessons from the experience to anything like the same extent as the Prussian. In this respect, if in no others, they were already on the path to greatness.

Having survived and triumphed over the revolutions of 1848-9, Europe's armies seemed to have justified the social and political criteria on which they were founded, so that for the next decade there was little to be seen by way of reformist tendencies. In February 1852 Lord Hardinge, newly installed as master general of ordnance to the British army, discovered that there were only some fifty guns fit for service in the whole of the country, not one of which had been constructed after the time of Waterloo. When, in September of the same year, Wellington died, Hardinge took his place and during his brief reign did introduce some material reforms — chief amongst them the introduction of the Enfield rifle to replace the Minié. But individual initiatives apart, the truth was that there existed absolutely no pressure to reform anything about the British army, which fought seventeen major campaigns between 1814 and 1852 in places as far apart as New Zealand and Canada and fought them successfully. Lacking a minister of war to exert a controlling influence, six separate government departments vied for authority in a situation which masked the true effects of such bureaucratic inefficiency. England's eighteenth-century army was not to meet its test until the Crimea.

In France, Napoleon III repaid the army for its support, or at least its lack of opposition, by placing it in an important and symbolic position. The early years of the Second Empire were spangled with reviews, parades, the creation of the *Garde Impériale* and the distribution of new decorations. Yet the army of metropolitan France remained in essence routine-ridden and poor. Regimental officers, their manners and comportment studiously noted by their superiors, married nearer forty years of age than thirty and, far from continuing their education, forgot what they had learned as young cadets. Intense competition and rivalry developed for one of the very limited number of places in the African regiments — the Zouaves, Turcos and Spahis whose colourful uniforms glamorously signalled danger, action and promotion. Two separate traditions thus grew up in the French army as a result of its division into 'European' and 'colonial' segments, each with its own attitudes, experiences and traditions. The campaigns in Algeria and Morocco, and later in Indo-China, also provided a form of safety-valve, like that which England possessed in her Indian empire and Russia in the Caucasus. Prussia totally lacked such an outlet, a fact which goes some way towards explaining the greater homogeneity of her army in outlook as well as in make-up. Alone of all the major armies of Europe, it could play politics in one arena only — its own continent.

In Prussia, however, an important institutional legacy of 1848 remained which was to exacerbate the tensions between soldiers and civilians. A written constitution of a sort was granted by the king, although the army remained outside it and subject only to the crown's control. This did bring with it, however, as part of the trappings of a parliamentary system, the notion of ministerial responsibility, destined to conflict with royal responsibility where the army was concerned. It also brought the notion of approval by parliament of all state expenditure, including the military budget. Within a few short years both king and army would grow to resent these parliamentary restrictions upon a freedom of action which had hitherto been absolute.

The social and political convictions which still governed the Prussian army, and which were, if anything, strengthened by its experiences in 1848 were clearly apparent two years later when the elector of Hesse fled to Austria after popular demonstrations against his absolutism, and appealed for help in regaining his throne. Those who were pursuing the goal of north German unity under Prussian leadership wished at all costs to exclude Austria from Hesse and were eager to respond to the Hessians' appeal for support against their erstwhile ruler and his ally. However, when the Prussian army was called upon its mobilization was deliberately retarded by officers who did not want to fight for the rebellious Hessians against their monarch. Wilhelm I subsequently blamed the defective organization and training of the *Landwehr* for his defeat, but this was merely another manifestation of his conviction that the soldier, to be effective, must be separated from society by the possession of a truly military attitude. Thus when, on 21 July 1858, von Roon submitted his famous memorial arguing that the achievements of the *Landwehr* had been over-estimated, that it was politically unwise to maintain it since its existence tied the hands of the government, and that the *Landwehr* man was not really a soldier, these thoughts caught and amplified the echo of the regent's own convictions. On the eve of the constitutional crisis which was about to break out there were some who felt reservations about the elimination of the *Landwehr* – Bonin among them – but they were faced by two generations of professionals raised in the long years of peace since 1819 and strangers to the brand of patriotic fervour which had inspired the great reformers. Roon's call for cadet schools and narrow specialization fitted precisely with the exacting technological needs of the age as the army turned its face resolutely towards its monarch.

In Austria too the years between 1849 and the outbreak of the Austro-French war of 1859 were marked by little in the way of military reform. By a statute of 1857 the over-all command of the army was split into four: Vienna, Buda, Lemburg and Milan. Service was for eight years with the colours and two with the reserve with, in theory, a general obligation to serve; in practice there were many exemptions, soldiers serving for three and a half years or less and then being sent home on leave as financial shortage began to bite. In common with almost every other state in western Europe, Austria showed a marked aversion to civilian soldiers, abolishing her *Landwehr* in 1852. No one in the empire had any desire to recruit a new army of potential insurrectionaries in Hungary or elsewhere.

The first severe test faced by any of Europe's armies after the end of Napoleon's wars, the Crimean War (1854-6), was in its origin more akin to the seventeenth century than the nineteenth — it blew up from a dispute over who was to hold the keys of the Holy Places in Jerusalem — so that it was appropriate that its weight fell on one of the least modern of the armies of western Europe, the British army. Unreformed in attitude, outlook or structure, it associated professionalism with utilitarianism and regarded both as middle-class. When the war broke out there was a deep and widely diffused expectation of national unity as aristocratic spirit and aristocratic leadership guided the nation to victory. Moderate liberals hoped, in fact, exactly what advanced radicals feared — 'that the coming war would demonstrate beyond dispute the moral and practical benefits of vigorous, aristocratic institutions.'[12]

The reality turned out to be rather different, a fact which was soon to be impressed upon the public's mind by the reports of William Howard Russell in *The Times* and by the photographs of Roger Fenton. In the Crimea the French were astonished to find as their ally an army which had no over-all infrastructure by which to distinguish it from a collection of privately-owned regiments — which is what essentially it was. An eye-witness, of whom there were many, graphically described the depths to which Britain's class attitudes had allowed professionalism to sink:[13]

> The English arrangements at Varna are as bad as can be — all is confusion. Every department appears overworked but does nothing — indeed with such entire want of arrangement, the simplest piece of business becomes difficult in execution. People

> are referred from one office to another, but can gain no
> information or assistance from any of them, even after having
> overcome the difficulties of discovering them in that maze of
> lanes and blind alleys.

By the first winter of the war, with the supply system in shreds and gloves selling at the front for 33 shillings a pair, the defects of England's military system were at last beginning to become obvious to everyone.

Within a few months aristocratic survival came to be seen as the factor that had condemned the Crimean expedition from the start. The attack upon it was launched by the middle-class reform associations which rapidly sprang into existence on the grounds not that privilege had existed but that it had failed to justify its existence. As Nathaniel Hawthorne remarked: 'At this moment [3 January 1855] it would be an absurdity in the nobles to pretend to the position which was quietly conceded to them a year ago. This one year has done the work of fifty ordinary ones.'[14] The cry arose in England that both army and state should be run by businessmen. It was not to last.

In time distinctions came to be drawn in place of these crude generalizations, particularly as scandals among the civilian contractors were revealed. Order slowly made inroads upon chaos as Florence Nightingale organized the army's nursing services and Alexis Soyer left the kitchens of the Reform Club to do a similar job for its catering. But a great question mark still hung over the army, and it was one which the antics of captain Nolan and the earl of Cardigan at Balaclava did little to dispel. Belated and long-overdue reforms split the secretaryship of state for war and the colonies into two in July 1854, and the following year the office of secretary at war was merged with that of secretary of state for war. But there remained questions about purchase and the consequent lack of professionalism in the officer corps, about military organization and military administration and about the essential unfitness of the Victorian army for war which would have to be answered.

Of the other parties to the war, only Russia experienced a comparable shock to her military system. Her army of grey-clad automatons fought bravely but was revealed as incapable of standing up to even a third-rate European army. The need for a mass army composed of reliable conscript troops with which to face the west was to be one of the major impetuses which moved the Tsar to emancipate the Russian serfs in 1861. The tiny Piedmontese army had performed creditably, establishing its credentials to be the basis of an Italian army, and Piedmont's to be the basis of an Italian state. But out of it all the French emerged best. It is possible that prolonged campaigning might have tarnished their image, but they had at least the rudiments of a supply system, and an army which was efficient and moderately professional in outlook. Moreover, the French Minié rifle had proved greatly effective against the masses of Russian troops, so much so that in December 1854 Friedrich Wilhelm IV ordered that the needle gun be reconverted to it. Against opposition of Russia's calibre, a sober careerist army could do well. It remained to face the test of a more advanced opponent.

A decade of violent military activity was about to begin in 1859. On its eve the armies of Europe were still essentially the long-service professional forces they had become after Waterloo. Europe's internal social and political order rested on her armies, and they were themselves reflections of that order. But policemen do not necessarily make good combatants. As states began to measure their strength against one another, social reliability declined as the dominant factor determining the scales of military efficiency.

4
A decade
of violence

In the years between 1859 and 1870 the armies of all the major states in Europe clashed in four wars which tested the value and flexibility of their military systems, and which forged the nationhood of Italy and Germany. Out of these experiences were to come new ideas about the size, organization and structure of armies all of which had at bottom a common intention; a peace-time army ready for war. For as the rivalry between the industrialized nations of Europe mounted, the experience of this decade stood to demonstrate that force, and force alone, could maintain national independence. Yet there were compromises which had to be made in the interests of societies which were becoming more complex both in terms of structure and beliefs. All the calculations which had later to be made to balance the interests of defence against the many competing concerns of the modern industrial state were, however, coloured by the experiences of wars which demonstrated all too clearly that small, long-service armies of regular soldiers officered by gentlemanly but unprofessional aristocrats might reflect the internal dynamic of a society, but that they could not preserve that society against the onslaught of mass armies controlled by intelligent professionals who put at their service the instruments of the new military technology — the railway, the rifle and the cannon.

The first of the four great conflicts, between France and Austria, occurred in Italy and demonstrated the weakness of three armies all of which, in separate ways, were relics of the age of European conservatism. The Piedmontese army had born the hallmarks of a repressive force since 1832: service, determined by lot, was for eight years and because of Charles Albert's acute suspicion of bourgeois elements there was a chronic shortage of officers. The result of such restricted horizons was apparent in 1848 when Charles Albert moved to declare war on Austria, in the wake of the insurrection of Milan, with an army of 55,000 which totally lacked support services and had given little attention to the problems of supply. Old fears ran deep, and despite vague public pronouncements to the contrary the Piedmontese authorities showed a marked reluctance to enlist the aid of students, the professional middle classes, veterans of the civil wars in Spain in the 1830s and 1840s and even *Garibaldini* — anyone, in fact, who might conceivably be tinged with republicanism. Support from Rome and Naples was quickly withdrawn, the high command displayed a marked lack of unity and Charles Albert refused to impart the necessary stimulus to his army. As a result it was soundly defeated, but not destroyed, by the Austrians at the battle of Custoza on 25 July 1848, and defeated again during the second brief round of Charles Albert's attempt to win Lombardy at Novara on 23 March 1849.

In the early 1850s the Piedmontese army was remade by La Marmora on the French model. The army law of 1854, which contained provision for selection by lot and exemption, divided those selected for service into two categories, the first serving five years with the regular forces and six in the reserve whilst the second performed forty days' training and then went into the reserve for five years. In an attempt to encourage a more professional attitude among the officer corps, La Marmora also made promotion by merit more common than it had previously been. The weakness of this system, in purely military terms, was precisely that displayed by the French army on which it was modelled: excessive concern to save the bulk of the citizenry from the unpleasantness of military service resulted in an army that lacked reserves. In an attempt to remedy this defect, the *Legge di sangue* ('Blood Law') of 1857 required that all those exempted from call-up on grounds other than medical should go into the second category of the reserve. What seemed a reasonable compromise was balked by lack of money. Piedmont was already spending some 28 per cent of her annual revenue on her armed forces and could afford no more; as a result these reservists were only fully called up in the summer of 1859, after the Austro-French War had broken out.

The French too had done little to reform their army, made complacent in part by its comparatively effective service in the Crimea. Administrative chaos had not been eased by the creation in 1858 of five great regional commands (Paris, Nancy, Lyons, Toulouse and Tours) and the system on which the army was organized 'made no provision for permanent divisions or corps, organized for field service, with supporting arms and services attached.'[1] In 1855 substitution had been replaced by 'exoneration' by which the holder of a *mauvais numéro* paid a fixed sum into a central fund which was then used to provide bonuses and encourage the re-enlistment of veterans. At a cost of between 1800 and 2800 francs this was a service well beyond the reach of the average French peasant's pocket. Nor was the officer corps changed in character. The Crimean campaign had been a financial catastrophe for many officers, and those without a patron still languished in small provincial garrisons. There was considerable competition to serve in Africa, but none to serve on the staff at home: the staff examination had been re-established in 1858 (having been suppressed in 1853) but only three years later the selectors had to go as low as the 137th place on the list of pass-outs at St Cyr in order to fill thirty-eight staff places. Intellect figured decidedly low down on the list of attributes of the French army, as it did for the Austrians and the Piedmontese.

The war which broke out in Italy in 1859 was compounded of Piedmontese determination to dominate northern Italy and French determination to remove Austrian predominance there, reinforced by Napoleon III's desire for an active and successful foreign policy. This imperial enthusiasm for war was not, however, shared by the populace at large and the

Bourse fell at the rumour of war and fell again when prince Napoleon married the daughter of Victor Emmanuel II, king of Piedmont-Sardinia. When war broke out on 26 April 1859, precipitated by Austria's demand for unilateral Sardinian disarmament, the Piedmontese army was spared from an early defeat only by the fact that the Austrian command was so riven with internal disagreement as to make rapid co-ordinated action impossible. Victor Emmanuel at once took over supreme command of the army, making Della Rocca his chief of staff, but was given little opportunity to display his military talents. When the French landed at Genoa, Napoleon III and his commanders rapidly took over all the military decisions and the Austrians, who greatly feared extending their forces, took the opportunity to withdraw into their famous defensive quadrilateral.

The military geography of the ground on which the war was fought centred on the presence of a spider's web of rivers and a large number of fortified towns. The first essentials for conducting the campaign were therefore bridging materials and a siege train of some sixty batteries. The French possessed neither of these assets, even though the war had been a distinct possibility since 1856. Nor did they possess a supply system, nor a medical service worth the name. Their command system was characterized by confusion and a lack of communication with headquarters, on which reefs French dash and *élan* foundered at Melignano. There was no clear French strategy and the major battles were accidental encounters during which the French took the brunt of the casualties. Only one battalion of Bersaglieri fought at Magenta on 4 June and no Piedmontese took part at all at Solferino on 24 June, though 21,000 were fighting that same day in the battle of San Martino. In all, the conduct of the war did the French military system no credit.

Paradoxically, French experience was seized upon by most of the major armies as a model in the light of the 'lessons' they seemed to have taught their opponent during the Italian war. For the French had made a virtue of necessity. Their long-service veterans, with a high proportion of officers among them, were equipped partially with smooth-bore muskets and partially with Minié rifles which were markedly inferior to the Austrian Lorenz rifle in range and accuracy. Recognizing that his troops could not hope to compete with the enemy in a fire-fight at long range, Napoleon III determined that they must get to close quarters as soon as possible. This they did, advancing on their opponents in two lines of battalions *en masse*, preceded by skirmishers. The Austrian army, operating according to field regulations first issued in 1806, were cautious and defensive; their poorly trained troops opened fire at ranges which were too great and wasted their ammunition. French successes at Montebello, Magenta and Solferino led many military observers to believe that the defensive had been overrated and bayonet-charges rapidly became the order of the day in Austria and the south German states, and even in Prussia, where only von Moltke believed that poor Austrian leadership had simply allowed the French to get close enough to their enemy to use their weapons properly. He accordingly began to develop the theory of forcing one's opponent to take the tactical offensive by means of superior strategy and then using the needle gun. The second lesson of the war appeared to be that the style of army produced by France was as militarily effective as it was socially desirable.

The French, who had had the largest hand in the war, not unjustly determined when it should end. Although the armistice signed at Villafranca on 7 July surprised everyone, it had been presaged by a demand for peace on the part of the French populace after Solferino and by a concern for the position of the pope once deprived of Austrian support. The threat of a Prussian mobilization also helped Napoleon III make up his mind, although in point of fact the troops never left their cantonments. The threat, however, was enough and in the process von Moltke observed the deficiencies of the Prussian railway system and became alerted to the importance of the factor of time in the mobilization of a country's military resources. Over the next decade he was to perfect his mastery of this element of war. The slaughter which two relatively inefficient armies had managed to inflict on one another helped to speed a peace by which the two external participants settled Italy's political shape for at least the immediate future: as Franz Joseph remarked after

Solferino, 'Rather lose a province than undergo such a horrible experience again.'[2]

The war had two decisive effects upon the military structure of Italy. First, the Piedmontese army was swamped as it absorbed the army of Lombardy and subsequently those of Tuscany, Modena, Romagna, Emilia and finally the Two Sicilies. In all there were seven armies and the *Garibaldini* to weld into a single national force. This was achieved by means of the admission of a number of former officers of the once-hostile armies, a process by which ex-Bourbon officers did markedly well and former members of Garibaldi's politically dubious southern army conspicuously badly; and by reorganizing the structure of the army in such a way as to require fewer senior officers and more junior ones, thereby allowing the Piedmontese aristocracy to dominate the upper reaches of the army. This process, which helped to earn its initiator Manfredo Fanti the title of 'Founder of the Italian army', reached its symbolic culmination when, on 4 May 1861, the new force took the title of *Esercito Italiano*.

From the first the new army was regarded as having a definite social and political function as well as a military one. Its role in this respect lay in overcoming the past deficiencies of Italian society. 'Italy, scarcely unified, felt a strong and perhaps exaggerated aversion towards the regionalism to which for many centuries had been attributed the nation's misfortunes.'[3] To overcome this the army was to foster and create *Italianità*, and to this end Fanti began the process of mixing brigades of men from different regions and moving them from place to place to prevent their coming unduly under the sway of local feelings. The effectiveness of this policy, which continued until the end of the century, is still the subject of debate. What is beyond debate is Italy's intention to avoid anything that smacked of a 'nation-in-arms'. When the Tuscans had formed a militia in 1859 anyone receiving a daily wage had been automatically excluded as socially unreliable, and when the *Guardia Nazionale* was created in the wake of the Italian army on 4 August 1861 its membership was restricted to volunteers who had no obligation to serve or who had already done so. In evincing such concern over the social reliability of her new armies Italy was at one with every other major army in Europe. The military efficiency of the new army was yet to be put to the test.

As the Italian army was being born in response to needs which were not all purely military, the Prussian army was undergoing a process of transition so profound as to be rather a refounding than a mere reform, and one which was based entirely upon military criteria. In 1858 the increasingly frequent bouts of insanity manifested by the king of Prussia, Friedrich Wilhelm IV, finally resulted in his brother Wilhelm taking over the reins as regent. Wilhelm found Prussia's humiliation at the hands of Austria in 1850 profoundly disagreeable and wished to increase her influence in Europe by reforming her army. On this point German liberals, who wished to see a united Germany under Prussian leadership as a force for progress, agreed emphatically with the regent. Wilhelm was already firmly convinced that the minimum period of military service in which it was possible to provide a conscript with a military education was three years, and his suspicion of the *Landwehr* was reinforced by the mobilization of 1859 which appeared to reveal that it had fallen into disarray and was quite incapable of fulfilling its theoretical role in fighting alongside the infantry of the line. In the summer of 1859 Wilhelm called for immediate military reforms which should include three-year service, reduction of the independence of the *Landwehr*, the creation of more battalions to deal with an influx of recruits and greater expenditure on cadet schools to furnish the army with more officers. Although everyone seemed to agree that the situation with regard to military service was inequitable, Wilhelm's proposals evoked uproar among the Prussian liberals who were particularly hostile to the cadet schools and viewed further expenditure upon them as subsidizing the nobility and creating a militaristic and anti-social attitude. The liberal minister of war, von Bonin, opposed Wilhelm's plans on various grounds — not least the considerable increase in military expenditure they required — and was promptly replaced by the conservative von Roon.

The looming clash over military policy in Prussia was accentuated by the pattern of Prussian politics, which was manifesting an increasing shift to the left. The number of liberals in parliament rose from 116 in 1855 to 286 in 1858 and 333 in 1861, whilst the number of placemen shrank from 236 to 15. The so-called 'Old Liberals' were not unfavourable to military reform though they disliked the attack on the *Landwehr*, and voted provisional funds for one year with which to increase the army. Wilhelm and von Roon, who found the liberals incompatible with his concept of the Prussian monarchy and was ready to supplant them, created the new regiments before they had been given the provisional grant and Wilhelm's first act on becoming king in 1861 was to present them with their new colours. By this time the 'Old Liberals' had been supplanted in power by the Progress Party, which had determined upon parliamentary sovereignty at full speed, and thereupon refused to co-operate with the crown. There was no prospect of their voting further provisional funds for the army in 1862; instead they were prepared to offer two-year military service in return for abolition of all the reforms effected by von Roon and the king after 1860. The scene was set for a bitter constitutional conflict in which Prussia's army was both a symbol and a central practical consideration for both sides.

While von Roon was enough of a politician to be prepared to compromise with the progressive liberals if that were possible, the general stance of the army was perhaps closer to that of von Manteuffel who, as head of the Military Cabinet, had the responsibility of selecting officers for the army. A fanatical reactionary, he had done his best to purge the officer corps of bourgeois elements and now saw himself as the king's Strafford, prepared to see Wilhelm rule by force if necessary. Opposing any compromise with parliament, he issued sealed orders for a *coup d'état* in 1862, believing that for security reasons the army must remain the province of the king alone. In the event, when parliament cancelled all provisional grants in September 1862 and demanded what amounted to the disbandment of the new regiments, it was von Roon who suggested that the king send for Otto von Bismarck, the one man who might find a way out of the deadlock.

Bismarck did indeed come up with a compromise shrewdly calculated to appeal to the liberals. He offered two-year service and the opportunity to evade service by substitution payments, the monies from which would be used to support a larger number of regular soldiers. In return he asked that the size of the army be fixed at the constant proportion of 1.2 per cent of the population and that the money to support it be fixed at a given sum per head. The latter provision would have had the effect of permanently freeing the army from the control which parliament could exercise over it by means of manipulation of the size of the military budget — which the military conservatives wanted. But Wilhelm refused it because it did not contain three-year service, and was supported by von Manteuffel on the grounds that fixing the size of the army in such a manner would infringe the sovereignty of the crown. So Bismarck devised the ingenious theory that there was a gap in the constitution where no budget had been voted, that the crown must in such circumstances continue the administration and that it could for these ends legitimately collect its own taxes. In the summer of 1863 parliament was dissolved and there followed the ferocious civil repression of the *Konfliktszeit* which lasted until 1866.

Though the pattern of military organization envisaged by Wilhelm and von Roon had proved domestically divisive, Bismarck soon realized that it would be possible to break through the crust of suspicion and touch genuine national support for the army if it were to be used imaginatively in order to raise Prussia's standing in Europe. The first step in this policy was the Danish War of 1864 which had as its objectives the Elbe duchies of Schleswig and Holstein. The minute Danish armies were soon beaten to their knees by the combined forces of Prussia and Austria, and the disputed territories were subsequently shared between them — thereby providing Bismarck with an irritant which he could use at will to provoke Austria into an act of hostility should the need arise. The Danish War did not provide a thorough test of the efficiency of Prussia's new forces but it did demonstrate the growing influence and efficiency of the general staff, transformed after 1857 when Helmuth von Moltke the elder became its chief. As well as possessing strategical genius, von Moltke was aware of the political values of the use of force, and was himself thinking of war first against Austria and then subsequently against France as early as 1862. As yet, however, few inside Prussia or outside it recognized the qualities of Moltke or his army.

From the moment that the Danish War ended, Prussia's demands for a vast share of the spoils made it apparent to the Austrians that they were being confronted with a demand that they yield supremacy in the north German confederation to Prussia. A provisional partition was recognized by both sides as no more than a truce and by the spring of 1866 the Austrian government had accepted the inevitability of war and begun to call up its reserves. At that moment the Austrian army had the finest reputation in Europe, won by Radetzky's exploits in Italy in 1849, and by an effective performance alongside Prussia in 1864, and of the two Engels had no hesitation in declaring it the finer. But beneath the polished surface which the army of Austria presented to foreign observers, exemptions, lack of a reserve and an acute shortage of money which had resulted in small annual contingents serving for no more than six years combined to riddle Austria's military structure with weakness. While the cavalry and the artillery were both superior to those of Prussia, the infantry were armed with an inferior rifle and committed to outmoded tactics of mass assault; and the officer corps, while devoted and courageous, lacked intellectual appreciation of the magnitude of the tasks confronting them. The Austrian staff had shown little interest in the *Kriegsspiel* ('war game') as a device by which to improve their techniques of leadership once they had discovered that it was not a game at which they could win money; and at their head as commander stood Benedek, his position not dissimilar to that of Radetzky, to whom Francis II remarked after Wagram 'Your character is a guarantee that you will not deliberately make mistakes; as for the usual blunders, if you make them I am quite used to it.'[4] Perhaps the gravest of all the weaknesses which flowed from the social and political priorities which had determined Austria's military structure was the fact that, as a result of the severance of regiments from their districts of recruitment, it took the Austrian army seven weeks to mobilize. When they did so they could only

90

field an effective fighting force of 320,000 men.

Whilst the popular impression of the Prussian army was that it was not the equal of that of Blücher's day, nor even Frederick the Great's, the truth was that it was strong at just the points where its opponents were weak. The reforms initiated by Wilhelm and von Roon had taken as their starting point not social reliability but military efficiency. As a result the peace-time Prussian army was organized into the corps, divisions and regiments in which it would take the field and — most significantly — army corps were stationed in the same districts from which they would draw their reserves in wartime. The result of this was that in 1866 the Prussian army mobilized in less than half the time taken by its opponents and fielded a force of 254,000, despite having a population only half the size of the empire. The staff was highly trained and had made some study of the role of railways in modern war, and at their head stood von Moltke, the possessor of the finest strategical mind of the nineteenth century. The Prussian infantry based their tactics upon the fire-power of the needle gun and upon flexible, open order advance in small units.

Austria began her mobilization on 21 April 1866, and Prussia followed suit twenty-one days later. Moltke strung out his armies along the borders of Saxony, Bohemia and Silesia, intending to concentrate them not before the campaign began but at the moment of decisive battle; this also enabled him to take advantage of Austria's hesitancy and confusion to occupy Saxony, Hesse and Hanover and thereby bring them under Prussia's dominance. The three Prussian armies then moved into Bohemia to meet at Gitschen, fighting a series of preparatory engagements which demonstrated the slackness and lack of co-ordination of the Austrian staff and the efficiency of the Prussian needle gun. Benedek, gloomy from the outset (he had been the only person to object to his own appointment to the field command), telegraphed the Emperor on 30 June urging him to make peace at any price and stating that otherwise catastrophe for the army was unavoidable. The Emperor's reply, which ran on the lines that Austria's position as a European power depended upon her selling herself dearly and ended querulously 'Has a battle taken place?', decided Benedek that he must fight. Moltke, meanwhile, was dominating Prussia's war councils with his plan for an encirclement when, on the evening of 2 July, one of his army commanders bumped into the bulk of the Austrian army and decided to fight them the next day. Moltke's task was now limited to arranging for the arrival of his second army to support Frederick Charles, a task which he accompanied with a fervent 'Gott sei dank.'

The battle of Königgrätz (known also, confusingly, as the battle of Sadowa) which took place the next day was the largest encounter of its kind in modern history; some 450,000 troops contested the field, 20,000 more than had met at the 'Battle of the Nations' at Leipzig in 1813. Fought over broken ground by troops fed in as the day progressed, and with little central control as the Royal Headquarters remained largely in ignorance of what was happening, it was in reality a series of separate but related engagements, swirling eddies which swept up battalions, scattered them and drew them from the sight of corps commanders, army commanders and chief of the general staff alike. In these circumstances the sheer military quality of Wilhelm's army came to the fore and nowhere more obviously than at Swiepwald.[5]

> The companies had all become mingled together as the fight swayed backwards and forwards in the dense wood: no unity of guidance was possible on ground where hills and wood shut out all the surrounding country, and all that the commanders of the different detachments could do was to lead their men by their own personal example. In all parts the officers rallied around them whatever men were in their neighbourhood, no matter to what regiment they belonged, and led them forward again and again.

Here, as in most of the other engagements which comprised the battle, one of the most important factors in enabling the Prussians to claim the day was the initiative displayed by their corps commanders who frequently marched towards the sound of guns without awaiting von Moltke's orders.

The day was won by the Prussians at a cost of some 9,000 casualties, against the losses of their opponents which totalled

44,300. Some three weeks later the preliminaries of peace were signed. Prussia did not profit by the war to the extent of a single foot of Austrian territory, but her dominance of a centralized German state was assured and at the same time those elements of Prussian liberalism which might have restrained an irresponsible use of Germany's enhanced military power were severely weakened by the success of Wilhelm's armies. The war had also revealed considerable defects in the handling of Prussia's artillery and railways, both of which were well remedied by 1870. The needle gun had given a demonstration of its deadly efficacy so striking that many contemporaries ascribed Prussia's victory chiefly to it, though other commentators were equally prone to discount it and to explain victory rather as a demonstration of the superior merits of the Prussian system of military organization which made effective use of large armies of short-service conscripts as against Austria's small, long-serving and supposedly more 'professional' army. In this sense the war was most certainly a test between two sorts of military systems which had arisen after the defeat of Napoleon, and General Bonnal had no hesitation in ascribing the victory of the Prussians to their superior human attributes rather than to their technical paraphernalia.[6]

> Their generals, their officers, and their soldiers were infinitely superior to their adversaries in character, energy, professional efficiency, and intelligence . . . from subaltern to General, a thorough military education had developed in them the reflexes necessary for the proper exercise of command in war.

The very nature of the system of military organization with which Prussia had bested what was widely held to be Europe's most proficient army carried with it two corollaries which were to assume mounting importance from this time onwards, and which in 1914 became critical factors in the military calculations of all Europe. In 1866 the official mind of Prussia had been convinced that if the whole army were called up then it could not be dismissed unless it had fought a war. The war machine was already beginning to seem like a juggernaut of uncontrollable proportions. Also the technical mastery of Prussia's general staff made it seem possible to harness the mass armies to fight a quick war which could produce diplomatic gains without inflicting undue strain upon society. This was an important calculation since Prussian society was then no more bellicose than any other: a highly placed staff officer recorded in his journal on 9 May 1866: 'It is truly remarkable with what tenacity the man in the street clings to the idea that there will be no war. Nobody wants it; in fact they all dread it.'[7] Mass armies, railways, and the strategic plans which co-ordinated the two seemed to offer an effective means by which to circumvent the restraints which civilian society might otherwise impose upon intense military effort.

Whilst Austria's military system had crashed to defeat in six weeks against the armies of Prussia, she did markedly better in the simultaneous campaigns she fought in Italy. Wooed by Bismarck, the Italians had sent general Govone to Berlin in the spring of 1866 to conclude an offensive-defensive alliance with Prussia, his parting instructions from La Marmora supposedly having been 'Parli il meno possibile'. The Italians duly declared war on Austria on 20 June, four days after Prussia had begun operations but one day prior to her own declaration of war on Austria. The Italian army, which had been fighting a gruelling campaign against brigandage in the *Mezzogiorno* for the previous five years, could field only something like 200,000 men (authorities vary between 145,000 and 250,000) and the army was in any case much less homogeneous than it had been in 1859. For one thing, the guerrilla war had strengthened the traditional dislike felt by the northerners for the southerners, and for another the high command was marked out by fierce internal squabbling. Ricasoli confided to his diary on 3 June 1866 'The fleet and the army are rent in pieces by jealousy and by rival cliques' and La Marmora, Della Rocca, Pianell and Sirtori were all — rightly or wrongly — suspected of disloyalty, political ambition or treason.[8]

The Italian forces were split into two parts: the army of the Mincio under Victor Emmanuel II and La Marmora, and the army of the Po under Cialdini. The question of who was in over-all command was left extremely vague, the supreme command was poorly organized and there were no up-to-date and co-ordinated war plans. On 24 June 1866 the army of the Mincio blundered into an Austrian army which was numerically superior, more mobile and better led. The battle of Custoza which took place might have been little more than a reverse for Italian arms — the Austrians lost 1,170 dead against 1,714 Italians — had Cialdini been prepared to support La Marmora, but he was not. Instead he initiated a retreat to which his sorely pressed colleague had no option but to conform. In a day, La Marmora's military reputation, built up over twenty years, disappeared and the army suffered a defeat which still weighed on it like a 'leaden cloak' twenty-seven years later. It was perhaps some odd sort of consolation to the Italian army that one month later, on 20 July, the Italian fleet was similarly crushed at the battle of Lissa. By now events had been decided far to the north in Bohemia and the Prussians signed terms with their opponents without bothering to consult the Italians.

The events of 1866 gave every major army in Europe pause for thought, though none so much as the defeated. It was unfortunate for Italy that her self-analysis soon descended to the level of *ad hominem* abuse and self-justification as La Marmora and Cialdini fought over their reputations. A commission of six generals was established to study a new form of organization for the army bearing in mind financial exigencies, the defence of the frontier and the requirements of public order. It produced a scheme in which for the first time a comprehensive system of reserve troops figured, but its recommendations were never even discussed, let alone acted upon. The pressures for economic stringency were so strong, and the costs of the wars of the Risorgimento had been so great, that strict financial retrenchment became the order of the day. The postponing of call-up for the class of 1846 was a measure of how deep financial concerns bit into Italy's military fabric. Unwilling — or unable — to reassess the whole question of military organization in relation to social responsibility, the army turned back to tinkering with the existing machinery to try to improve its efficiency, a policy which resulted in seven complete transformations of infantry regulations in the decade 1860-70, 'creating professional uncertainty, hardship among personnel by reason of the incessant transfers and little faith in the authorities.'[9] Nothing changed in the Italian military system as a result of Custoza and when in 1870 an army was required to capture Rome after the French garrison had relinquished it, it was only with the greatest difficulty that a force of 50,000 was mobilized for an operation which, though of very great political importance, was hardly a demanding military test.

For Austria-Hungary the direct result of her defeat at the hands of Prussia was the *Ausgleich* of 1867 whereby the empire was split for administrative purposes into two constituent parts. The regular armies of the empire were still under the central control of the Imperial War Ministry, however, and the advent of field marshal Kuhn as minister of war in 1868 heralded six years' military reorganization during which the Prussian system was modified to fit into a national army with regional recruitment. Certain regional privileges were suppressed, provoking an insurrection in Dalmatia, and so were the great army commands which were replaced by territorial commands linking regiments more closely to the districts from which they drew their reservists in wartime. Reasons of finance and politics prevented the empire travelling the full distance along the path that Prussia had marked out, and this hesitation was embodied in a system which stood short of a general obligation for equal service: Austria's contingent was split into two portions, the first of which served three years with the colours, seven with the reserve and two in the *Landwehr* whilst the second served twelve years in the latter force only. As if to symbolize the completeness of the break with the past, Kuhn also replaced the famous white uniform of the Austrian army with a less obvious dark blue.

Prussia's success on the field of Königgrätz had revealed the value of reservists recalled from their day-to-day civilian occupations in order to swell the size of the regular army and to augment its fighting power. Austria was now attempting to build herself a larger army, but was caught in a political dilemma not faced by Prussia in Germany. For whereas the regular army and the reserves came under the orders of the imperial war minister, the *Landwehr* did not; its two distinct portions — Austrian and Hungarian — depended on their respective Ministries of National Defence. The *Landwehr* was therefore of immense political significance to Hungary since it represented the only military force which could remain independent of Vienna. In 1848-9 Hungary had raised its own battalions of infantry — the *Honved* — and these were now revived. Hungarian political intentions determined that the *Honved* would have different characteristics from the Prussian *Landwehr* which, though at first sight narrowly technical, had far wider implications. Unlike the German model, the *Honved* kept reduced cadres in existence in peace-time instead of only coming into existence in wartime, and it also had assigned to it in war not merely the older military reservists but also new recruits. These arrangements reflected the Hungarian wish to have a permanent army on a peace-time footing composed of young men taught and officered by Hungarians. Austria was forced, somewhat reluctantly, to follow the Hungarian example and in the last two decades of the century a race was to develop between the two forces in terms of size and standards of equipment which was finally won by the Austrians in 1906. But for Hungary the *Honved* always had a political symbolism which transcended its obvious military importance.

In 1867, as a result of the *Brüderkrieg* which von Moltke had viewed with some distaste, the north German confederation was refounded and its military provisions were modelled on those of the reformed Prussian army. The Law for Liability for Military Service of 9 November 1867 set out the new obligations: every north German was liable to serve, with no possibility of exemption or substitution (a return to the ideas of 1814), and had to undergo three years with the colours, four years in the reserve and five years in the *Landwehr*. Behind the technical provisions lay the philosophy that the army was the training school of the whole nation for war. Moreover, the *Landwehr*, whose role was now defined as that of home defence or a reserve for the army, ceased to be a separate organizational structure embodying the tenets of the old liberal tradition; run by regular officers and non-commissioned officers and brigaded with regular army regiments, it was no longer a bourgeois preserve. Von

Roon's ideas had come triumphantly to fruition.

The second great change in the military organization of the north German confederation was won by Bismarck. His earlier attempts to fix the percentage of the population which would be inducted into the army had failed, but now under paragraph nine of the terms of the Convention he gained that freedom of military organization from the democratic control of parliament which he had sought earlier. It was agreed that the army should permanently consist of 1 per cent of the population, and that it should be given a budgetary allocation to cover the whole of the five years 1866-71. It is impossible to minimize the social and political significance of these concessions, for they were to convert the traditional social distinctions between aristocratic army and bourgeois population that had been in existence for a century and a half into a rigid institutional separation. They also ensured a series of regular confrontations between parliament and army whenever the budgets came up for re-allocation, and as parliamentary democracy grew the army would come to symbolize the struggle against the independence of the crown and the alliance of 'rye and steel' forged by Prussian *Junkers* and Rhenish industrialists later in the century. Bismarck's victory was in the long run to be perhaps his most damaging legacy; but in the immediate future it seemed to offer only the prospect of further Prussian glories.

The new system would permit the north German confederation to put into the field forces totalling 955,000 men in 1870 — more if the south German states joined them. As yet, however, the sheer numerical size of the new German armies impressed few minds. Military opinion in Europe rested hitherto on the historical proposition that the larger the army the less efficient it was, and maintained as an article of faith the inherent contempt of the professional soldier for any but professional soldiers. Even the Prussians felt doubts about ranging their troops against an army such as the French, which had displayed in 1859 *élan*, high morale and the capacity to move quickly. This comforting assessment of the military virtues of their own army was something many Frenchmen shared, although the perceptive French military observer in Berlin, Baron Stoffel, sought in a number of reports to demonstrate the strengths of the Prussian military system, based on the twin pillars of compulsory education and compulsory service, and to point out that if it came to war between the two powers Prussia would prove a redoubtable adversary.[10] In peace-time the Prussians possessed merely size; it would take a war to demonstrate that the Prussian staff system was the touchstone which could convert that size into strength.

The threat which the armies of the north German confederation posed to France after their victory at Königgrätz was soon obvious. Marshal Randon, the French minister of war, calculated in August 1866 that against Prussia's 800,000 men he could field some 454,778 and in the light of this and similar calculations the Emperor himself put forward a plan for the total reorganization of France's military structure the following month. Napoleon III's object was an army with a war establishment of 1,000,000 and he proposed to obtain it by introducing six years' regular service and three years in the reserve for an annual contingent of 100,000 men and by forcing all those enjoying the protection of a 'good number' into the *Garde Mobile* − a form of untrained *Landwehr*. There would be no more exoneration and it would be impossible for any Frenchman to buy his way out of military service in at least some form.

The principle of universal obligation to serve − which was literally revolutionary − threatened to change the whole social basis on which the French army had been built up since 1824 and it ran into widespread opposition. The prosperous members of the community resented the loss of the privilege of purchasing full exemption from service and the workers and peasants reacted against the ending of their chance to win freedom by the possession of a *bon numéro*. Though Napoleon's requirements were scarcely demanding in comparison with those to be undergone by any citizen of Prussia, and though the *Garde Mobile* would in truth have been less than an onerous resting place, the latent interests of almost every section of society seemed to be − or were felt to be − threatened by Napoleon's new ideas. As one *procureur général* wrote, 'This semi-barbarous system is incompatible with the customs, the education and the wealth of a great nation.'[11] Randon himself opposed almost every part of the scheme, supporting instead a small long-serving regular force and a small reserve. A commission was duly set up to examine the relative merits of what were by then six rival proposals, and not long afterwards dissolved in disagreement. Most of its military members had favoured increasing the citizen's liability and ending exoneration but all three civilian ministers on the commission were acutely hostile to any change in the existing law.

Realizing that Randon alone was an insuperable obstacle to any reform, Napoleon replaced him with Niel on 20 January 1867. There followed a great public debate over the nature and extent of the Frenchman's obligations to military service in which many individual soldiers put up schemes. Opposition came from legitimists, republicans and Bonapartists alike and cut across traditional party lines. The right did not relish the idea of increasing conscription or arming the *Garde Mobile* as it meant putting weapons in the hands of those elements which represented a threat to social stability and the class system. The middle classes wanted to retain exoneration or replacement, landlords feared that conscription would result in a loss of labour or rural depopulation. There was some merit in the argument that a system of military service which intended, among other things, to forbid marriage to recruits and to reservists would have adverse effects upon the rural populace; in Basque territory the very announcement of a change in military service had increased the already heavy stream of citizens departing for the quieter reaches of Argentina.

What finally emerged from the complex and vigorous debates, in a law dated 1 February 1868, was something of a hybrid between the new Prussian and old French models. The contingent due to perform military service was split into two portions, the first serving five years with the colours and four with the reserves whilst the second did five months' training and then served out the remainder of the nine years in the reserve. Exemptions continued and replacement was re-introduced. All those — and they would be many — escaping regular or reserve service were to serve for five years in the *Garde Mobile*, during which they were to undergo fifteen days' training each year; however, in order to preserve France's sheltered and fortunate civilians from the vileness of the *caserne*, those fifteen days were to be served separately so that no *Garde Mobile* had to spend a night in the company of the regular soldiery. The powerful interests in France's political society had worked to shred away Napoleon III's original plan for an army with a real and effective reserve standing behind it until what remained was little more than the old traditional structure which had adequately protected France's interests prior to 1866. In the spring of 1870 the army numbered 380,000 and had no reserves. From the standpoint of its structure alone it was ill-fitted to try a passage at arms with the force created by Wilhelm and von Roon.

In political terms Napoleon III probably lost more than he gained by his vain attempt to alter the nation's military stance. There were disturbances at Toulouse and Bordeaux when the first intake was called upon to appear before examining councils for enrolment into the *Garde Mobile* in the spring of 1868, and in the elections which were held the following year the republicans made striking gains. These were not unconnected with the military policy of the empire, for the army measures were vigorously attacked on political platforms as burdensome to agriculture and finance. Even the blind partisans of the empire now began to criticize it. In sum, by introducing a comprehensive scheme and then allowing it to be modified almost beyond recognition Napoleon had neither produced an effective force nor mollified public opinion. Rather than copy Prussia's taxing system of egalitarian military service the French preferred to live in comfort.

If the structure of the army changed little as a result of Königgrätz its composition altered not at all. It still lacked social status and suffered from poor pay — in 1868 it enjoyed the first general pay rise for thirty-one years. There was little in the way of tactical study and no single body had over-all responsibility for strategic planning; in 1861 Napoleon had suggested a Committee of Defence to rationalize frontier defence but nothing had come of it. Among the officer corps obedience was thought more worthy of merit than intelligence, and advancement to the higher ranks was determined largely by the rank achieved by one's father, membership of the nobility and the influence which could be wielded to support a claim to promotion: between 21 and 45 per cent of all divisional generals were recommended for their position at ministerial level. And in the more rarified levels of the French army, as in its English counterpart, wealth was as necessary as was influence. Without money it was not easy to be a general in the French army; as Niel reported in July 1868, 'there are generals of division ... who ask daily as a favour (*'grâce'*) that they be relieved of their commands because they are unable to support their position.'[12] This was a far cry from the brand of military professionalism being nurtured by von Moltke and the *Grossergeneralstab* in Berlin. It is a measure of French *insouciance* in these matters that it made no attempt to imitate the institution which trained the German general staff — the *Kriegsakademie* — whereas the Italians had learned enough to appreciate the value of such an institution and had set up the *Scuola superiore di guerra* in Turin in 1867.

France's army was fast becoming the least professional in Europe on the eve of the Franco-Prussian War; for even the British army was facing up to the need to use criteria other than birth and wealth to secure military efficiency. In the aftermath of the Crimea a royal commission had been set up to enquire into the system of buying and selling commissions and during its proceedings the institution of purchase had been violently attacked by Trevelyan and his associates as wrong in principle and harmful in practice. The crux of Trevelyan's argument was that purchase and professionalism were incompatible and that the army needed the drive and ambition which were held to characterize the middle classes. In response to this and other pressures the Royal Military Academy at Woolwich, which trained the army's engineers and artillerymen, had by the early 1860s made entry fully competitive. Examinations were to be based on general subjects rather than specialist military-related ones. Sandhurst later followed suit.

The specifics of the new examinations were to be determined by consultation between the military authorities and the headmasters of the older public schools. This provision was to effect a major change in the composition of the British officer corps which has lasted, broadly speaking, up to the present day. The disappearance of specialist subjects for examination such as fortification obviated the need to remove an intending candidate from one of the older public schools, which understandably could not provide such tuition, and send him to a 'crammer' in order to fit him to attempt the examination. Any public school could provide for the teaching of general subjects at a modest level if no more, and those schools such as Cheltenham, Marlborough, Rossall, Wellington and King's College School which rapidly established 'modern sides' were especially able to prepare candidates for entry into the army, the civil service and the professions. As a concomitant of this change, entrants to Sandhurst and Woolwich were now older (sixteen to seventeen years of age) and had had a wider education. Not unnaturally they resented the restrictions imposed on them by those bodies, which had retained the notion that their role was to act as an inferior form of army public school and treated their pupils accordingly. In 1868, after sporadic rioting at Sandhurst, a royal commission was set up to look into military education; in view of the obvious deficiencies which prompted its creation, general Lord Paulet's remark in the same year that 'when I commanded a regiment, I would rather have taken an Eton boy, from choice, than a Sandhurst boy, to make an officer' looks less bone-headed than when it is taken out of context.[13]

Though purchase was still the predominant characteristic of the British officer, attitudes to army education were changing and were bringing with them an appreciation of the sort of professionalism applied to the law, medicine and the civil service. Profound change awaited Gladstone's first ministry of 1868. It contained pupils of Peel and Jeremy Bentham who were inspired by the principle of utility which was to be applied to all institutions and from which not even the army would be exempt.

Though the Franco-Prussian War of 1870 was not the first great war to be fought with the tools and weapons of the industrial revolution — a distinction which belongs more properly to the American Civil War — it was the last and greatest of a series of tests between the major armies of western Europe which had begun eleven years earlier and the one which had the most profound political and military effects upon Europe. Yet for a war in which many 'modern' characteristics were manifested its origins had about them a flavour that was decidedly not of the nineteenth century, for the war began as a dynastic contest over the throne of Spain, vacated by Queen Isabella II in 1868 when revolution had forced her to flee the country. Although one of the candidates was a Hohenzollern, Wilhelm I was reluctant to press a claim to the vacant throne. The French council of ministers, backed by vociferous public opinion, were however determined to oppose the candidacy up to and beyond the point of war. Bismarck's doctoring of the Ems telegram triggered off the conflict.

Bismarck's version of the Ems telegram reached Paris on 14 July and the following day, amid mounting war fever, France voted war credits. Both sides began to put their mobilization programmes into action later that same day, though it was not until four days later that France formally declared war on Prussia. Von Moltke had been preparing for a war with France ever since November 1857, and under his guidance the armies of the north German confederation swung smoothly into their deployment programme. Although the French had the advantage of a standing army of 142,000 the total numbers they could mobilize amounted only to some 300,000, rather less than they calculated the Prussian forces to be. In an attempt to make speed count for more than mass they therefore changed their plans and endeavoured to mobilize and concentrate their troops at the same time. The result was an absolute fiasco; reservists lost their units completely, one long-suffering Zouave travelling from his home in Strasbourg to his regimental depot in North Africa only to discover that his unit was by then concentrating in Strasbourg; and in one case a desperate divisional commander threatened to ship 9,000 men from Marseilles to Algiers because he did not know what else to do with them. In the midst of this chaos an advance guard of French troops crossed the frontier at Saarbrücken on 2 August and the war had begun.

The imperial army was defeated in exactly a month. After early set-backs at Spicheren and Worth one portion of it, under Bazaine, fell back on Metz and then began a leisurely retreat westwards. The Prussians, who for some ten days had lost their opponents, raced westwards and overshot Bazaine's army. An encounter battle at Vionville-Mars-la-Tour on 16 August, begun by a Prussian corps commander under the mistaken assumption that he had caught the French rear-guard when in fact he was facing the bulk of the army, halted the retreat westward, and a second battle two days later at Gravelotte-St Privat blocked any move north. Bazaine retreated into Metz and there he stayed until he surrendered on 28 October. The other part of the French army, in acute confusion over who exercised ultimate military authority and under very strong and misguided pressure from Paris to relieve Bazaine, was pushed north and west away from Metz and penned in at Sedan. There, on 1 September, it was obliterated. The Prussians had learned the lessons of Königgrätz and St Privat well and surrounded their opponents with a ring of a thousand guns. The remnants of Napoleon III's army were blown to pieces while they stood all day awaiting an infantry attack which never came.

The immediate effect of the collapse of France's armies was to bring about a political revolution. On 4 September 1870, three days after Sedan, the Third Republic was proclaimed and it was to last seventy years until an equally resounding military disaster ended its life in 1940. The Government of National Defence, dominated by Léon Gambetta, its foreign minister, at once set about registering all citizens between the ages of twenty-one and sixty for military service and enrolling volunteers and men without family responsibilities under forty years of age. Meanwhile on 20 September, German advance units joined hands at St Germaine-en-Laye and Paris was under siege. The defeat of the French imperial army had not signalled the end of the war; rather von Moltke and his commanders were faced with two separate military campaigns which threatened to last for months. The war was already providing a pointer towards the future in its demonstration that a nation's power to resist had to be measured by more than just the strength of its formal military forces.

The command of Paris during the siege was vested in general Trochu: Catholic, Orleanist, defence-minded and respecting only regular troops, he was totally out of sympathy with the political regime with which he had to deal. He also lacked supplies and munitions and had for the most part to depend upon *mobiles*, who were frequently drunk, and National Guards who were reluctant to fight. Internal conditions within Paris thus dominated Trochu's conduct of the siege — 'strategy' would be too strong a term to use in this context, since as Trochu himself afterwards admitted he had never had a single tactical or strategical idea throughout the siege. One of his subordinates, Ducrot, put the military position with brutal clarity: 'almost the whole of the defence turned on one thing only: the fear of a riot'.[14] Harried by left-wing agitation and hindered by a press which contrived to publish full details of military plans in advance of their being put into operation, there was in truth little that Trochu could do to save the city; that was a task which could only be carried out by Gambetta's provincial levies.

Whilst they waited for rescue, Parisians settled down to a life which was for many one of harsh deprivation but for others weirdly exotic. Whilst the members of the exclusive Jockey Club ate their way through menus composed of the former exhibits in the Paris Zoo, Trochu was bombarded with wild-cat schemes to lure Germans within range of French machine-guns by playing Schubert and Wagner to them or to crush the German headquarters at Versailles by means of a giant sledgehammer fifteen miles in circumference and weighing ten million tons which would be floated out from Paris by balloons. An infinitely more serious note was struck when on 5 January 1871 the bombardment of Paris commenced. Urged by Bismarck for political reasons and opposed by von Moltke for military ones, it proved to strengthen rather than weaken civilian morale, thereby providing yet another pointer towards the future.

The armies built up on the Loire by Gambetta and de Freycinet, the minister of war, won their only victory at Coulmiers on 9 November. Poorly trained, ill-armed and never amounting to their target figure of 650,000, they could defeat the Bavarians but not the better organized and battle-hardened Prussians — though in Aurelle, Bourbaki and Chanzy they had generals of considerable ability. Aurelle's army of the Loire was split into two parts: one under Bourbaki was smashed on the Lisaine on 15 January 1871 and driven into Switzerland by the end of the month (its commander having attempted suicide sooner than live with defeat and disgrace), whilst the other under Chanzy was destroyed at Le Mans. By the end of January the republic had nothing left with which to hope to relieve Paris, and on the 29th an armistice was signed. Exactly a month later peace terms were agreed and the German army marched into Paris. By the Treaty of Frankfurt France lost Alsace, Lorraine, Metz, Strasbourg and had in addition to pay an indemnity. Whether that was an unduly heavy price to pay for the military policy France had followed since 1824, and for the complacency with which she had viewed the defeat of Napoleon III's attempts at reform, is debatable.

The French did not lose the war of 1870-1 because everything about their military system appeared on the debit side of the balance sheet; the French infantryman had fought at least as well as his Prussian or Bavarian opponent and the *chassepot* rifle had proved its superiority at St Privat. But at almost every other level the French military structure had displayed flaws which were to prove fatal. The over-all political and strategic direction imparted by the French to their war, where it existed at all, was immeasurably inferior to that of their opponents — and it is worth remembering that the Prussians made their share of mistakes and suffered from sulphurous disputes between the civilians and the military. The flexibility and initiative encouraged by the Prussian general staff system contrasted dazzlingly with French reliance on orders; time and again, from the very first battles of the war, Prussian corps commanders marched to the sound of the guns while their opposite numbers sat and waited for instructions. Moreover, the Prussians had proved that it was possible to mobilize and control huge armies of reservists, who had themselves proven their ability in combat. The Prussians had won not one but two wars — a dynastic war against Napoleon III and his professional army and a national war against the Government of National Defence and its levies. The Prussian system seemed invincible. The symbol of the change in attitudes which had been brought about as a result of the war was very soon visible to any observer of the military scene: the armies of Europe stopped dressing like Frenchmen and donned instead the victor's *Pickelhaube*. More profound imitation was soon to follow.

5

Armies and international rivalry

In the years between 1871 and 1914 every major state in Europe, and many minor ones, first adopted and then adapted the institution of general military conscription to meet a variety of needs determined by factors which were both domestic and foreign in origin. The single impressive lesson of the Franco-Prussian War had been that mass armies composed to a considerable extent of civilians in uniform could dominate and destroy so-called 'professional' long-service armies, though the essential concomitant was that their control depended upon a highly articulated general staff which acted as the brain or nervous system to co-ordinate the movements of the separate corps making up the huge armies now deemed essential for survival. By 1873 even Japan had adopted a system of conscription which brought her into line with European practice. A universal obligation to undergo a period of training under arms also brought with it the opportunity to exert influences of both a political and a social variety. To many in authority in Europe military obedience and political submission seemed to go naturally hand-in-hand when considering the advantages to be gained from imitating the Prussian system.

A further range of considerations was added to these calculations as the century drew to a close and political instability and tension mounted in Europe. The political

alliances and military agreements which by 1914 had
enmeshed all the great powers, severely circumscribing their
freedom of action once a commonly perceived situation of
general crisis occurred, represented the degree to which brute
military force had shouldered its way to the fore in diplomatic calculations over the forty-six years since it had so
manifestly proved its efficacy in France. By 1914 Europe had
grown neurotic over its birth-rates and the numbers of men
it could put into the field. In most countries legislation had
been passed with the sole object of getting as many men
under arms as quickly as possible and diplomats, increasingly
a prey to the delusion that the use of force could provide a
rapid and effective solution to apparently intractable problems of international relations, came to accommodate the
practice of their craft to an ever-mounting content of force.
Industry too grew increasingly geared to the production of
armaments — most easily visible in the race to build battleships which began in 1889 — and a general integration began
to take place between military factors, politics and economics. Europe was, it has been well said, in the process of
creating a war machine.

The most profound change came about in France, where
defeat at the hands of the German armies had destroyed not
one but two military traditions; those of the Second Empire
and of 1792. Theories about the value of the long-service
regular soldier had been conclusively disproved at Metz and
Sedan whilst radical doctrines of the effect of levies had been
swept away on the Loire. The Third Republic embarked
upon a quest for moral regeneration and hoped for a new
nation with the support of an army whose sole success had
been against fellow Frenchmen in its suppression of the
Paris Commune in 1871.

For the first seven years of its life the republic was dominated by conservatives, and it was a measure of the primacy
with which it viewed the role of the army in society that the
National Assembly did not turn to devising a constitution
until it had first passed laws on conscription in 1872 and on
military organization in 1873 which were designed to maintain a period of moral order. This ordering of priorities
clearly indicated where the cornerstone of the new France

was to be located. The Assembly, which was strongly right-wing and was at first dominated by monarchists, expressed its military conservatism by arguing that long military service was essential for three reasons: it would produce discipline and obedience, it would act as a moral antidote to the decay of the Second Empire and enable the different orders of society to develop 'mutual esteem', and it was in any case necessary to produce a good soldier. These considerations conformed with the convictions of Thiers, the first president of the republic, whose ideal was the army of the July monarchy. He was reported as saying of the levies raised by Gambetta's Government of National Defence 'Your numbers are nothing; if the armies had been well led and constituted, as they should have been, we would have beaten the Prussians.'[1] Some leading military figures, Trochu among them, supported a three-year term of service *à la Prusse* even though it was doubtful whether the budget would bear the amount of expenditure that such a policy would inevitably entail. In order to ensure the triumph of his views Thiers busily lobbied the 'Commission of 45' which had been charged with drawing up a conscription bill and persuaded some of the generals who sat upon it to change their minds and support the long service which he favoured.

Attempts were made to question the concept of military discipline which underlay the attitude of the right towards the army and to give soldiers some opportunity to exercise their own judgment, but they were doomed. Denfert-Rochereau, a deputy and former officer, dedicated a book to Gambetta in which he extolled the high state of discipline of the captive troops during the siege of Belfort and drew as a consequence the response that this type of free discipline was only possible 'in a corps of officers of an eminence equal to that of the Engineers, and in a situation as exceptional as that of a *place forte* in wartime'. Moral discipline, explained Gambetta, could not activate the mass of the people since they had only a rudimentary knowledge of scientific concepts and of their duty to the *patrie*.[2] Denfert-Rochereau put forward his ideas during the debate on the conscription law, challenging the concept of passive obedience as making the army an instrument for violating the law (here he cited the

111

coup d'état of 1851) and arguing that the failures in 1870 had been due to the lack of initiative at all levels. His rehearsal of these somewhat advanced ideas was continually interrupted by Ducrot, Chanzy and Changarnier and a subsequent speaker reflected the feelings of many in the chamber when he referred slightingly to 'les baionettes intelligents'.

The law on conscription passed in 1872 was a measure of the success of the conservative views of Thiers and many of his generals. The principle of compulsory military service was established, for a term of five years, but was immediately eased by a variety of exemptions — which could no longer be bought — and by the drawing of lots to determine whether service would be for the full term of five years or for one year only. In imitation of the Prussian system, a category of one-year volunteers was also established to cater for upper-class young men who paid for their own lodgings and equipment and were given in return officers' training. Total exemption was permitted to all those intending to follow the so-called 'liberal careers' in education and the church. This was hardly an egalitarian sharing of the burden of arms among all elements of the populace, but to have expected a stance of that sort from the conservative Assembly would have been excessively sanguine. In the event the most significant feature of the law was to be the principle of universal service which, having once been established, the government seemed at such pains to undermine.

An examination of the army's structure in the light of the defeat inflicted upon France by Prussia, and of the part which rapid mobilization had played in Prussia's initial successes, naturally led on to the problem of the organization of France's army in such a way as to enable it to perform comparable feats. Thiers at once spoke out in opposition to the Prussian system of regional organization, arguing that France's political and social structure differed from that of her neighbour and that regionalism would not suit France. In essence he offered the military authorities a choice between annual manoeuvres and a large standing army, with the argument that the budget would not support both. Prompt mobilization he deemed in any case unnecessary since he intended, he said, to keep three-fourths of the army stationed on the north and north-eastern frontier at all times. The core of Thiers' hostility to anything approaching a regional system was not, however, to be found in any of these military calculations but in the profound conviction that a regional system would be a veritable counter-revolution. It would, the president felt, be a reversion to the trends which had existed in France before 1789 and would evoke a dangerous political spirit in regiments; in sum, it would mean re-establishing the provincial armies of Bretons and Picards and other sub-national groups. MacMahon disputed almost every point of Thiers' analysis and under his lead military opposition proved too strong for the president to enforce his political calculations on the army; by the law of 1873 provision was made for the French army to be divided into eighteen corps, each of which was to be seated in a military region.

If the organization of the French army demonstrated that a spirit of reform was abroad, in most other respects the army of the new republic bore more than a passing resemblance to its imperial predecessor. Nowhere was this more true than in the officer corps. Swollen to almost grotesque proportions by the promotions made by the Government of National Defence, it had now to be slimmed down, a course of action which was combined with a thorough and careful weeding to exclude all those officers who had broken their parole and escaped from German hands during the war and others deemed equally undesirable. The officer corps of the Second Empire was restored almost intact, and it was clear from the criteria adopted by Changarnier's examining commission that its watchword was to be 'honour'. Bound together in this way, it was not required to take an oath to the republic — a recognition of the diversity of opinions it contained and of faith in the ideals of loyalty and service to legally established authority which it had already abundantly demonstrated.

Considerable efforts were however expended to reinforce the French soldier's natural delicacy with regard to active politics. The terms of the law of 1872 forbade soldiers undergoing regular military service to vote in elections — a provision which had the added effect of excluding regular soldiers from the political process until their retirement —

and in 1875 they were debarred from sitting as members of the Chamber of Deputies. Nine years later all but the most eminent were likewise barred from the senate. None the less there was clearly some lingering doubt about where the loyalties of the army might lie in the first years of the republic, and Gambetta had dossiers made up on the political opinions of the officer corps between 1876 and 1878 — a remarkable forerunner of what was to occur under the regime of general André after the turn of the century.

The army had been remade in its own conservative social image and proved loyal during the political crisis of 16 May 1877, when it seemed possible to some that a military coup might be instigated to support the conservative president of the republic, MacMahon. None the less to many republicans the new military system seemed a sell-out, debased by inequality of service, the privilege extended to the clergy and the threat of the political dangers inherent in a long-service army. Despite the republican victory in the election of 1879, the 'Opportunists' who came to power operated a tacit alliance with the army which did not begin to show signs of strain for almost a decade. All Frenchmen united in seeing in their army the unique instrument for *révanche* against Germany as well as for moral restoration at home. Accordingly the social prestige of the army rose to unexampled heights. To conservatives the officer was priest, to republicans he was schoolmaster; to both he was to be the instrument of national retribution. The new popular fervour and growing excitement over military affairs was crystallized in 1886 around the flamboyant figure of general Boulanger.

In Germany there was after 1870 considerable popular enthusiasm for an army which had been victorious in three wars in less than a decade, and this helped to establish a new social cachet which the army retained for more than twenty years. The possession of a reserve commission enhanced a civilian's status in the world outside the barrack walls, as did an invitation to dine in the mess — both representing a situation unique to Germany. Moreover, since an infantry regiment could bring a garrison town a million and more marks a year, there was a considerable economic gain to be made out of association with the army as well as a social one. Gradually, however, the army began to lose its popularity as it retreated into a self-enforced isolation. This was exacerbated by its tendency to call people up without regard for their civilian occupation: the Ministry of Justice made frequent formal representations to the War Ministry about the lack of notice given to lawyers who were recalled to the colours in the midst of cases. Perhaps most noticeable to the man in the street was the immunity of the soldier from the law; soldiers committing civil offences could be tried only in military courts, where they tended to get off with lighter sentences.

This change in the position of the soldier in German society was a reflection of — and perhaps in part a reaction to — the change in the position of the army within the state which was also taking place during these years. The prospect of collision between *Heer* and Reichstag loomed almost immediately after the success against France, for the law of 1867 fixing the size of the army at 1 per cent of the population was due to expire in 1874, when it would undoubtedly signal a revived attempt by the deputies to exert their control over the military machine. To counter this the military sought to win their independence not by coups but by a two-pronged strategy: vital military matters were gradually withdrawn from the province of the War Ministry (and therefore from parliament) in favour of the Military Cabinet and the general staff, whilst the Military Cabinet itself followed a careful policy of officer selection by which it sought to maintain the officer corps as the bulwark of royal absolutism.

Between 1874 and 1880 there was little serious trouble — despite the 'War in Sight' scare of 1875 and the Russo-Turkish war of 1877-8 — though the army clearly signalled its intentions in 1874 when an attempt was made to fix a permanent figure for the size of the army which no one would be able to vary, von Moltke pointing out that fluctuations inflicted by changes in military legislation disrupted and complicated planning. In reply the left-wing opposition pointed out that the army already took 90 per cent of the federal budget, which they not unnaturally regarded as a large burden to bear in perpetuity. In the event the army was fixed in size for a term of seven years. However, in 1878

Bismarck broke with the National Liberals and began the refounding of the Reich on the basis of the alliance of interests which existed between the landowners of East Prussia and the conservative industrialists of the west. In 1882 he combined with the military conservatives to force the war minister, von Kameke, out of office and in the process lowered the ministry to a level no higher than that of the Military Cabinet or the general staff. In the following year the loss of the personnel section and of the right of military command further diminished the minister's power.

While the Reichstag increasingly feared that the army would escape into financial independence, the army seems genuinely to have feared that parliamentary influence over military matters might increase to a detrimental degree. The achievement of military autonomy was made more difficult by the embarrassing fact that the three chief military agencies were hopelessly at odds with one another in their objectives. The general staff wanted more money and an expansion in the size of the army; the Military Cabinet maintained that any expansion would lead to an irreversible adulteration of the quality of the officer corps; and the minister of war thought in any case that the army's demands were too large. This conflict of interests might result in a balance so long as all three parties retained positions of strength, but by 1888, with the emasculation of the war minister's position, with the arrival of a new and — in one sense — ineffective emperor and without a chief of staff of Moltke's vision, the army found itself in a position of some autonomy but no little internal confusion.* When the post of chief of the German general staff was occupied by a technician rather than a soldier who was aware of and attuned to the world of politics, as was the case after 1891, the structure of the German military machine would contribute to a widening gap between the army and the people and would help to generate a military

---

* Germany had four chiefs of the general staff between 1857 and 1914: von Moltke the elder (1857-88), von Waldersee (1888-91), von Schlieffen (1891-1905) and von Moltke the younger (1906-14). Italy and Britain had four each also, but for much shorter periods, 1882-1914 and 1904-14 respectively. France had seventeen between 1874 and 1914.

policy which ignored any considerations other than purely professional ones.

By the mid-1880s the Reichstag was beginning to become alarmed at the extent to which the army appeared to wish to foster its own interests, though at this stage those interests were seen to relate to the army's place in peace-time society rather than its support of war as would later be the case. Members of the German parliament began to look closely at the aims of the Military Cabinet and concluded that, by its policies of officer selection, the army was engaged in a deliberate plot to thwart political and social progress in Germany. If this was not entirely true, then only the structure of German society seemed to be preventing it, for the army's need for officers was quite simply beginning to outstrip the capacity of the *Junker* class to supply them. The army was caught between the need for social reliability which seemed to dictate a small army, and the necessity of adequate military defences which demanded a large one. Only in 1890 would Wilhelm II recognize and encourage the trend of middle-class entry into the German officer corps. Meanwhile the power of the Social Democrats grew in parliament, and in 1887 they tried to replace the Septennat with three-yearly military budgets. Sooner than consider this Bismarck dissolved the Reichstag, thereby exposing himself to a house even fuller of Social Democrats after the elections, and the army responded by demanding even larger grants to meet the needs of an arms race against Russia and France, aided by the bellicose utterances of general Boulanger.

The success of the Prussians in 1870 placed Italy in a considerable military dilemma. She had to a large extent modelled her military system on that of the Second Empire, and after Sedan the cry arose that she should rid herself of the Piedmontese system and of the generals associated with it: La Marmora, Cialdini, Della Rocca and Menabrea. Finance was — or was made out to be — a dominant factor in any considerations of military reform, for the wars of the Risorgimento had placed a heavy burden of debt upon the nation and it was not until 1876 that it succeeded for the first time in balancing its budget. Liberals, clericals and socialists were united in wishing for military economies but

French hostility, Prussia's example and France's evident military renaissance provided counter-pressures to those exerted by the economy. All the schemes put forward shared two characteristics: they involved as little expense as possible and they followed the Prussian model not the French one. The shape of Italy's future military forces was not determined wholly without opposition, however, for there was a current of opinion which both questioned and opposed the principle of military subordination which would thereby percolate through society, with a Prussian — Rodecker von Rottek — as its chief protagonist. Against this was set the view expressed by general Bertolè-Viale and others that obligatory service would integrate the different classes which composed Italian society, would instigate a sense of patriotic obligation and would thus level out rich and poor.

The argument in favour of disregarding the Prussian system of regional recruitment and mixing conscripts together was put by Italy's foremost military thinker, Niccola Marselli, who was prepared to recognize the advantages of the Prussian system but who pointed also to Italy's youth as a nation, to her administrative decentralization and to the reform of the spirit which animated the army as the first priority; as he pointed out in a celebrated and widely read study of the significance of the war of 1870, 'the army is the great crucible in which all provincial elements come to merge in Italian unity.'[3] This was to be a recurring theme over the next three decades, though its logic was somewhat undermined by the fact that of a population of 32,000,000 only some 110,000 a year underwent military service. If conscription was to be the sole, or even the chief, means by which an Italian nation was to be created then the process was going to take some time.

During the last years in which the right dominated in Italian politics a spate of laws was passed under the direction of the reforming war minister Ricotti Magnani, designed to put into operation a military system which could both create Italians and provide some form of security. Laws of 1871 and 1873 reduced the service of conscripts in the first category to four years, with a further nine in the reserves, copied the Prussian system of one-year volunteers, and set the wartime strength of the army at 800,000, divided into ten army corps. The number of different grounds on which a potential recruit could be exempted from military service were reduced and the law of 1873 — like that passed in France a year earlier — established the principle of general obligatory personal service. Finally, a law of 1875 reduced service to three years. Further changes of significance were to occur during the first years of the rule of the left, among them the development of a territorial militia as a further form of reserve and the expansion of the army to twelve corps, but Ricotti's reforms, together with his concern to improve the standards of education at the military schools and academies, served to raise his status to equal that of La Marmora and Fanti. 'There was no branch of the military organism', wrote a subsequent historian, 'in which Ricotti did not leave some trace of his valuable work and of his wise innovatory spirit.'[4] His efforts, and his successes, were considerable but the army which resulted was not one which could be used as an effective lever by Italy in the conduct of her diplomacy; in 1880 almost every European state had one army corps for every 2,000,000 inhabitants and by this formula Italy should have possessed an army of sixteen corps, whereas she had only ten. The consciousness of her own military weakness which this brought about was to be one of the main factors which propelled Italy into the Triple Alliance shortly afterwards.

It was largely by coincidence that Britain found herself sharing in the experience of reform and reorganization which all the other great powers of Europe — and many which were not so great — were experiencing in and after 1870. In one sense this was the effect of the culmination of a period of intense pressure to reform the military system; between 1815 and 1854 there had been only a dozen committees on military reform, whereas in the next fourteen years there were seventeen royal commissions, eighteen select committees of the House of Commons and thirty-five officer committees. External stimulus and domestic social and political concerns combined in generating the reforms effected between 1868 and 1872 by Edward Cardwell which were designed to alter the shape of Britain's army as markedly as anything which was happening on the continent. Britain's situation in the world made it virtually impossible for her to ape those foreign powers which had introduced large, short-service armies, for her troops had to cope with the garrison duties and the almost incessant procession of expeditions and small wars which were a part of the toll exerted upon her resources by her possession of an empire. Nor was there a tradition of conscription in Britain, and no likelihood either of its being introduced. To increase the size and improve the quality of the army in this environment Cardwell set about making soldiering a respectable occupation for the British ranker. The Army Enlistment Act of 1870 reduced service from twenty years to twelve, half of which time was spent with the colours and half in the reserve, bounty money was abolished and bad characters rejected and, as a result of the improvements in pay and conditions, the private soldier was at last brought out of the eighteenth century.

The abolition of purchase — Cardwell's other great reform in a ministry marked by great energy — came about almost by accident. A proposal in 1869 to reduce the size of the officer corps by abolishing the lowest commissioned rank created uproar in army and parliament since it made no provision to recompense officers for the illegal over-regulation prices they had been forced to pay to gain the rank at all. A royal commission officially introduced these payments to the government's notice, and since Cardwell was prepared neither to permit them to continue nor to overlook them he had recourse to the only other alternative which existed — to abolish them altogether. When he revealed his intentions to Gladstone, the prime minister gave his fullest support not because purchase was unworkable — the reverse was the case — or because he felt it lacked moral foundations, or even because it acted as a hindrance to the more professional development of the officer corps, but because he feared that if the government did not act against class immediately 'the time is approaching for what may be termed a rather strict settlement of account'.[5] Publicly Gladstone declared that the abolition of purchase would not alter the aristocratic nature of the officer corps, though this was not what some of the reformers intended.

For British aristocrats seeking a commission the situation

was in some measure analagous to that which had obtained in France a century earlier. There were grounds for believing that purchase actually kept the poor aristocracy out of the army while it allowed entry to the sons of rich manufacturers. The implications of this argument were obvious; abolish purchase and the army would become more and not less aristocratic. This subtle argument did not convince opponents of the change, who were perhaps more concerned about property rights and investments, and a bitter debate followed. In the end it became apparent that a bill would never carry the House of Lords no matter what the appeal of abolition and Cardwell was therefore forced to by-pass the parliamentary system and abolish purchase by Royal Warrant.

The result of this act was to exchange one set of restrictions on entry into the officer corps for another. The increasing prevalence of examinations served to restrict entry to a net of public schools who could prepare candidates to pass them, so that shared educational experience to some extent replaced shared breeding as the characteristic of the British officer corps. But money still remained an essential qualification for a commission, which required that certain standards be kept up — extra uniforms, hunting and polo ponies, mess expenses — and raised expenditure well beyond the levels of pay. By the end of the century it was calculated that an infantry officer needed a private income of £200 a year and a cavalry subaltern at least £700 a year in addition to pay and allowances, and a report of 1903 concluded that expenses were so great that 'suitable candidates are precluded from entering the Service by no other consideration than the insufficiency of their private incomes.'[6] Despite reforms which seemed to contemporaries spectacular, Cardwell had not after all wrought great changes upon the social profile of the British officer corps.

The experiences of the Crimean War had done much to stimulate the moves for reform of the British army, and they acted in a like manner upon Russia, who also felt the need to respond to the pressures which international rivalry was exerting upon the military organization of all the states of western Europe and which were inexorably forcing them to abandon their suspicions of large conscript armies in order to strengthen their positions in an increasingly hostile world. In 1861 Dimitrii Miliutin had become war minister and he at once proposed a conscript army based on military districts. The following year four such districts were created (Warsaw, Vilno, Kiev and Odessa) and they successfully survived the test of the Polish insurrection of 1863. By 1865 the army corps had been replaced by the new Great Military Districts — nine in Europe and five in Asia. European Russia was also divided into twenty-two recruiting districts to handle reservists. Miliutin also revived the general staff and raised the standards of the military academies, enabling the *Genshtabistyi* ('general staff men') to ride the wave of reform which he had begun. The Franco-Prussian War resulted in pressure being put on the minister of war to adopt the Prussian system, and in 1874 military legislation replaced the old term of fifteen years by periods of six years with the colours and nine in the reserve.

The experience of the Russo-Turkish War (1877-8) soon demonstrated what the military history of both Austria and Italy would show; that crippling disadvantages now faced every state whose military organization was not designed to accommodate the rapid mobilization and deployment of large units in war. Accordingly the army corps reappeared in Russia — at first sixteen, they had risen in number to twenty-six by 1899 — and in 1878 'reserve units' were created in the regions to receive reservists on mobilization. This system, which was roughly in line with western European practice, crumbled during the Russo-Japanese War (1904-5) when reserve units did badly. Shortly afterwards the system was scrapped and service reduced to three years for the infantry and four for the cavalry and engineers. In the long run the abandonment of the second-line system of incorporating reservists was to have effects which were of considerable strategic significance for Russia. Whereas before 1904 fifteen army corps were massed in the districts of Vilna, Warsaw and Kiev and eight in the interior, by 1913 fourteen were in these districts and thirteen had to be stationed in the interior in order to be in a position to incorporate the reserves now that the separate second-line units had gone. This meant that general Russian mobilization could only be a slow, ponderous process — a fact of considerable importance in determining Russia's reactions to the military crisis of late July 1914.

By the 1880s almost every army in Europe, major and minor, seemed to be in the throes of reform or at least to be contemplating reform, and the army of Austria was no exception. Severe weaknesses had been revealed in her military organization during the war for Bosnia-Herzegovina (1876-8). Kuhn had designed a system whereby three battalions of each regiment could fight as soon as war broke out, while the fourth and fifth battalions remained in the recruiting districts in order to incorporate reservists before adding them to the campaign. The war revealed quite clearly that regiments could not fight without their reservists, and since these often had to travel long distances to rejoin their units the Austrian military machine would be alarmingly slow in mobilizing for war against Russia. Accordingly in 1882 the war minister, Bylandt Rheidt, inverted the Kuhn system and stationed three battalions of each regiment permanently in the recruiting districts whilst the fourth could be detached for occupation duties. The demand for military efficiency was breaking down the traditional antipathy in the empire towards too close an association between regiments and particular geographical areas as demands for external security began to outrun pressures for internal reliability.

The Austrian half of the empire was also forced to emulate, somewhat belatedly, the Hungarian *Honved* and there developed a race between the reserve forces of the two halves of the empire during the latter part of the century. Both were expanded to include infantry as well as cavalry; both were organized into regiments, then into brigades, then into divisions; both decreased their periods of service and came to take on more of the appearance of regular army units. In one respect only was the Austrian *Landwehr* superior to the *Honved*: it had artillery by 1913, whilst its counterpart did not. In terms of the efficiency of the reserve forces of the empire, therefore, the division of Austria-Hungary in 1867, by creating competitive conditions, did little but good. As far as the regular army was concerned a law of 1912 reduced service to two years and raised the size of the annual contingent from 103,000 to 159,000. On the eve of the First

World War, however, there were doubts about how far the army and the reserves were united in their loyalty to Vienna as racial tensions mounted in both the German and the Magyar portions of the state, and doubts also about whether the shared experience of military training was enough to hold together national minorities, some of whose interests might be better served by Russian overlords. It was a tribute to the success of the system of recruiting the officer corps, and to the effectiveness of the body of regular non-commissioned officers, that when war broke out in 1914 they were able to sustain the *schwarze-gelb* spirit of loyalty to the emperor for as long as they did.

Europe's concern to develop a sizeable and well-trained reserve army and to divide the country into effective working military units rather than administrative ones was even experienced during these years by Turkey. A series of reforms effected between 1880 and 1888, inspired by the German example, provided for six years' service with the *Nizam* or regular army, followed by eight years in the *Redif* (reserves) and six in the *Mustahfiz* (or territorial militia); Turkey had in practice suppressed exemptions long before France did so. In 1904 the regular army and reserves were reinforced at the cost of the territorial militia, and in 1912 the military division of the Ottoman empire into seven *Ordù* (each containing one corps of regular troops and one of reserves) was replaced by a system of centralized inspection over fourteen army corps. In this way military organization reflected both the German influence and the concern of the 'Young Turk' regime for a more efficient and centralized state.

Everywhere in Europe armies were conforming to a common pattern which put a premium upon scale and upon systems of military organization designed no longer to support local political control but to mobilize as many men as possible and as efficiently as possible in the event of war. Perhaps the most striking example of the dictates made upon societies by the need to possess the highest possible level of military efficiency was to be found not in western or central Europe at all, but in the armies of the Balkan states. They shared one fundamental characteristic — a remarkable disproportion between the size of their populations and the military forces they sought to maintain — and since they were poor they maintained large armies by reducing service to a minimum and endeavouring to achieve a rapid turnover of trainees. They also kept their male inhabitants under military obligations to such an advanced age that their efficiency must have been in some doubt.

By 1913 French military missions had brought order to the Greek army and a system was finally settled on by which service was for two years in the regular army, twenty-one years in the first reserve and a further eight years in the second reserve. This was not as impressive an achievement as it appeared on paper since on average less than half the annual intake of 25,000 was ever inducted into the army, but it did represent an attempt to maximize military power in the face of massive obstructions.

Montenegro, whose army until the war against Turkey in 1877 had consisted of little more than the *Perianiki* or Royal Guard, found herself thereafter wooed by Russia, Austria, Hungary and Italy alike, a process which seems to have consisted for the most part in giving the Montenegrins modern arms. In 1896 a form of brief military training was instituted for those aged eighteen to twenty, and by the law of 1913 this was regularized at two periods of sixty days, after which Montenegrins served in the reserve until the age of sixty-two. By such means as these a tiny state with no industrial resources to speak of maintained its military capacity during an era of acute Balkan competition.

The kingdom of Rumania, created in 1881, found itself from the first more deeply involved in European affairs than any other Balkan power and felt a commensurate need to ensure its own independence. Squashed between Austria and Russia, its concern was always to maintain its territorial integrity and the *status quo*. When the kingdom was created it inherited a curious system of dual service whereby one part of the annual contingent served continuously for two or three years whilst the other, under a system termed the *Cuschimbul*, served by turns in regiments after a brief preliminary instruction. The details of this sytem were embodied in a law of 1880 which remained the basis of Rumania's military organization and under which permanent service was for three years with the colours and seven with the reserves, whilst men in the *Dorobanzi* or semi-permanent infantry served five years in each; there then followed six years in the militia and a further ten in a territorial reserve. By these means Rumania managed to support under arms a force of 100,000 men, double the size of the Belgian army although the two countries had comparable populations. Gradually military efficiency dictated that semi-permanency be converted to a more orthodox system until by 1912 it existed only in certain cavalry regiments.

Serbia and Bulgaria lacked both a sizeable noble caste and a cultural and intellectual class, and the officer corps of both armies suffered as a consequence. The Serbian army, after a disastrous campaign against Bulgaria in 1885, was reformed in the following year on the basis of two years' regular service followed by eight years in the reserve and then ten years in each of two 'bands' of the National Army. This did not provide enough trained manpower, however, and on the eve of the First World War military service was reduced to eighteen months in an effort to expand the military forces still further. The Bulgarian army, by contrast, was by far the healthiest of all the Balkan forces for two reasons: its military structure was thoroughly organized by the Russians on sound German lines, and it had no pre-existing military institutions which had to be modified or incorporated into the army. A military law passed in 1889, after the acquisition of Roumelia, established the framework of its military system: two years in the active army, eighteen in the reserve and a further six in the territorial reserve. Apart from an exemption granted to Mahommedans, military obligation was universal, and Bulgaria inducted 35,000 men a year into her army.

So widely did the pressure to emulate the German system extend across Europe in the last quarter of the nineteenth century that it was even felt by the peaceable Scandinavian states. Sweden extended her period of military obligation in 1892 from five years to twenty, during which time recruits underwent thirty separate periods of training each lasting ninety days. However, after its separation from Norway in 1905 the need for strong military forces increased and in

1913 the *Beväring* was divided into two sections in which recruits served a total of twelve years, followed by eight more in the Home Guard. Service was for 180 days — lengthened in 1914 to 250 — followed by recall for a month every second year. Norway for her part operated a similar system from 1909, requiring that her citizens pass twelve years in the line and reserves, followed by eight in the *Landvern*. By such means the two countries, both poor by the standards of Germany and France, implemented their own variants of the German system, though since Sweden inducted 43,000 men a year and Norway only 10,000 there was a considerable disparity in their size.

The case of Belgium was an interesting example of the gradual extension of the idea of general conscription in a country which was neutral by its foundation treaty, and went against the grain of its ruling parties. During the Franco-Prussian War mobilization and a move towards the frontier at Sedan revealed the defects of the Belgian army all too clearly: it took two months to mobilize 80,000 men, and they were short of many accessory services. In the face of the refusal of politicians to do anything about this situation the generals went on strike and refused to accept the portfolio of war minister, compelling the president of the council to take it *ad interim*. The conservative Flemish Catholic governments which succeeded one another during the rest of the century were in a sense anti-militarist and refused to introduce conscription since they did not wish to open up the opportunity for Catholic youths to be corrupted by associating with socialist Walloons. However the war scare of 1905 changed the order of Belgian priorities somewhat, and in 1909, a few days before his death, Leopold II signed a law which introduced the principle of universal compulsory service with exemptions for clerics, and for any sons in a family if one was already serving. Service was for eight years in the active army and five years in the reserves, and by 1913 the Belgians could field an army of 100,000.

As conscription strengthened its influence upon all the armies and states of Europe, and as a wider social spectrum came to be incorporated into the ranks of the major European armies, the distinctions between the social origins of officers and men began to grow more marked. This was especially the case in the French army where conservative monarchists increasingly lost ground to republicans in provincial politics and left industry, commerce and administration; only in the officer corps could such men be sure of a place. The continuous decline in wholesale agricultural prices, symbolized by the collapse of the Catholic *Union générale* bank in 1882, helped force the gentry off the land and into the only occupation left open to them. The increasing diminution of the social spectrum from which officer candidates were drawn may have had a detrimental effect upon its intellectual quality: after 1900 it was certainly much easier to get into St Cyr, because of the decline in the number of applications, and the non-commissioned officers' schools turned no one away. Even Jean Jaurès, the great socialist leader, talked openly of 'radical mediocrity' in the French officer corps. What is more certain is that the officer corps developed a heightened political attitude of detachment and rectitude, perhaps the product of the gulf which was opening up between it and the political classes of France, and felt a strong responsibility for preserving French institutions. The army saw the nation as being separate from the state and saw its task as being to safeguard the values of the nation in trust, though for what it would not say. This stance of silent and embattled rectitude earned the army the soubriquet *la grande muette* ('the great mute') in French society at large. In the political life of the republic the army maintained a privileged position; the minister of war was almost always a general, regarded by his colleagues as an ambassador from another nation. As yet that nation might be deemed friendly, but two great politico-military scandals were to tarnish its image of disinterested service.

In 1886 general Georges Boulanger entered office as minister of war. At forty-nine the youngest general in the army, he already had a high military reputation and was popular for his unrestrained nationalism. He at once established his flamboyance and exuberance, proposing among other measures to abolish promotion by seniority and to dispense with St Cyr and the Ecole Polytechnique. His intrigues to remove the conservative and highly respected military governer of

Paris, general Saussier, earned him the disdainful label 'this Bolivian-type general' from Jules Ferry. During 1886 and 1887 Boulanger used his position and his arts to campaign for a greater degree of military preparation against Germany, thus providing Bismarck with a current of *révanchisme* with which to manipulate domestic German politics. In July 1887 he was dropped from the War Ministry and picked up in the world of politics by the radical republicans and Orleanists. The Opportunists, then the dominant faction in French politics but already in decline, heartily disliked Boulanger and began to spread stories of a military conspiracy against the republic, for which there was no real evidence.

After leaving Paris Boulanger did enter politics, though the ends he had in view were far from clear. He campaigned against the appeasement of Germany and against corruption in public life, and later for revisions of the constitution. Dishonourably discharged from the army in March 1888, he was charged by the government with plotting against the state and found guilty *in absentia*, having prudently removed himself to Brussels. The support he enjoyed during his brief and pathetic foray into public life has aptly been called 'the disease of the protest vote', and the public seem to have been interested in his constitutional proposals chiefly as a vehicle for social reforms, their apparent readiness to express support for him probably being fuelled by economic discontent. With his departure from France, Boulanger's 'party' shrank and swung to the left; its figurehead died by his own hand on 30 September 1891, an ambitious general who had had a penchant for playing at politics.

On this somewhat fragile basis Boulanger's political opponents built a legend of caesarism, of the 'man on a white horse' — a more familiar figure in Latin American politics than in Europe — who had sought to put the army at the head of the political life of the nation. Within a very short space of time a second and much greater scandal would shatter the trust many Frenchmen placed in their army and demonstrate that the military's pursuit of their own interests could never be divorced from their place in the political and social fabric of France. The Boulanger affair had provided something of a foundation for this, and produced the sort of bitter division between families later to be associated with the Dreyfus case: general de Gallifet, who was later to become involved in *l'affaire Dreyfus*, remarked at the time to his cousin the duchesse d'Uzès 'When you were a duchess, you were my cousin; now that you have become Boulangère I can no longer know you.'[7]

The Boulanger affair proved of no small value to Bismarck in his campaign to maintain the Septennat, keep control of the army out of the hands of the Reichstag as far as possible and increase the proportion of the budget devoted to military expenditure. In 1887 the chancellor dissolved the Reichstag when it attempted to reduce the seven year period of budgetary immunity to three years, itself both a symptom and a product of the increasing influence of the social democratic party as political power was gradually shifting in Germany. The army responded to the crisis by demanding even more money to meet the needs of a new arms race with France — for which case Boulanger had provided almost indisputable support — and with Russia. In this it proved successful, and such was the impact of the affair in Germany that in 1888, after the passage of another Septennat, Bismarck actually managed to extend the age up to which Germans were liable for service in the *Landwehr* from forty-two to forty-five. Ironically the issue of international security which in 1888 had saved the Bismarckian system of military organization would alter it five years later.

In France a new law of conscription was enacted in 1889 reducing military service from five years to three and raising the proportion who served the full term from 50 per cent to 73 per cent. The belief that technology had ushered in the age of mass and therefore demanded of every nation that it put into the field the largest possible number of troops certainly contributed to this change in France's attitude to her soldiery, as did the advance of a more left-wing republicanism with its egalitarian ideals. However, it is important to remember that the law of 1889 was passed in the aftermath of the Boulanger affair by a parliament which thought that the republic had been threatened by a clique of monarchists, anti-semites, clerics and high-ranking officers. Its objectives were to counter this trend and to spread the burdens of military service more widely and more equably, and at the same time to lessen the distinction between the soldier and the civilian. This was a laudable aim, even though the outcome was to be a further advance in the pace of international military competition.

At a time when the French army was becoming the object of some concern its officer corps was growing ever more sharply differentiated from society at large in terms of its social origins. Many of France's landed estates were broken up as Canadian wheat flooded into Europe in the last quarter of the nineteenth century, so that the aristocracy could not turn back to the impoverished countryside for a livelihood. At the same time the officer corps was increasingly set apart from the growing anti-clericalism of the left by its bias towards catholicism: from 1865 to 1886 between 25 and 35 per cent of the annual intake at St Cyr came from Catholic schools, and by 1898 a quarter of the general staff had been educated by Jesuits. Many French officers who shared this background viewed with some distaste the rise of the anti-militarist socialist party, which by 1893 had some eighteen members in parliament. Some recognized that the officer, whatever his social origins or predilections, had a role to play in educating Frenchmen to patriotism and at the same time undoing the work of the lay schools. Foremost amongst such officers was the future military governor of Morocco, Hubert Lyautey, who, having fallen under the influence of the social catholicism of Albert de Mun, published in the *Révue des deux mondes* an article on the social role of the officer which adopted just this line. However the openness with which he professed views privately shared by a number of brother officers was so disturbing that he was hastily whisked off to Indo-China in 1894. Once there he celebrated his happiness at being 'far from the falsity of the *salons de lettres* and the dinners of Paris, and from the mummification of our moribund, idle, routine-plagued army'.[8] The army of metropolitan France remained largely undisturbed by advanced ideas of the role of the officer, and unaffected by imaginative minds such as that of Lyautey.

Into this atmosphere there erupted in 1894 the celebrated Dreyfus case. Alfred Dreyfus, a Jewish officer serving in the statistical section of the general staff, was arrested on suspicion of espionage on grounds which amounted to little more than that he was reserved, ambitious and unpopular, convicted on what turned out to be the flimsiest of evidence, and sentenced to hard labour for life on Devil's Island. This miscarriage of justice gradually came to attract attention, partially as a result of the efforts of one or two conscientious soldiers, and in 1897 evidence came to light which pointed to another officer in the same section as Dreyfus, Esterhazy, as the guilty party. The following year a court martial acquitted Esterhazy, and the whole case might well have died had not Emile Zola chosen it as a means to revive his flagging reputation and published his famous open letter *J'accuse* in which he charged the army with incompetence and corruption. Scenting political advantage, the socialists moved in to attack first the French army and then armies in general and *l'affaire* rose to its height.

As the movement to free Dreyfus gained momentum in French society the attitude of the army changed from bewilderment to annoyance. Reassured by its commanders, and ignorant of the industry displayed on its behalf by major Henry in forging evidence with which to ensure that Dreyfus remained where he belonged, it saw the issue as one in which the honour of the army became more important to France than mere matters of guilt or innocence in law. The suicide of major Henry, which was taken to purge his guilt, further strengthened this attitude. It was based on the understandable conviction that at a time of acute international tension nothing should be done — or undone — which might shake the confidence of France in her army and thereby impair its military efficiency; nor should anything be undone which seemed to demonstrate the army's exemplary efficiency in speedily detecting and thoroughly punishing those who weakened France's defences. This attitude was based on what seemed an increasing threat from Germany: in 1893, learning of the Franco-Russian *entente*, the Reichstag had accepted legislation reducing the budgetary period from seven years to five and at the same time reducing the period of military service from three years to two. As international tension mounted France's birth-rate was falling ever farther behind

that of Germany and this, together with a more rapid turnover of recruits in the German army, would dictate defeat in
a future contest unless France could keep intact her military
morale, which she regarded as the basis of her military
superiority. The Dreyfus case thus had for the army implications which ran far beyond plain domestic politics or even
the loftier questions of law and justice.

Moderates proved acutely reluctant to re-open the issues
of Dreyfus's guilt or innocence and in this they were supported by the president of the republic, Félix Faure, who
shared their attitude. But on 16 February 1899 Faure died —
although in his bed, in circumstances delicate enough to
savour of yet another political scandal — and his successor,
Waldeck Rousseau, proved ready to re-open the question.
The army, however, was not. Five generals passed through
the portals of the Ministry of War in a single year (1898-9)
before one could be found with sufficient disregard of his
fellow generals and of the military implications of finding
Dreyfus innocent to see the trial through again. Dreyfus was
found guilty once more but this time with 'extenuating
circumstances', and was sentenced to ten years, of which
he had by now already served five. President Loubet then
remitted the remainder of his sentence and Dreyfus was
released. At a final Court of Appeal in 1906 he was declared
innocent and reinstated in the army.

Throughout the twists and turns of the sorry, and extremely
complex, affair the army had always taken the line of the
primacy of national greatness; it was not in the nation's
interest to question the character of the force to which it
owed its independence, nor had it the right to interfere in
the inner workings of an army which it had largely disregarded
in the past and which had served it loyally and impartially —
Boulanger notwithstanding. In striking this pose the army
had been cruelly misled by many of its generals who knew
the truth of the Dreyfus case, or at least knew enough not
to want to know more. Honour, the watchword of the army,
lay shattered and the case for military autonomy was undermined. An era of active political intervention was about to
open.

As the nineteenth century ended many of the great powers

of Europe were witnessing widespread anti-military feeling as the democratic parties grew in strength. In Italy the sociologist Guglielmo Ferrero published his celebrated study *Il Militarismo* in 1898 and gave a basis to the belief that interested parties existed in every state who not only did not believe that war was disappearing from the modern world but who saw positive benefits to the state in encouraging such military virtues as discipline, obedience and nationalism. In France Jean Jaurès published his study *L'Armée nouvelle* in which he advocated national defence by means of a militia system .with a period of service of only six months as the ultimate expression of the concept of the nation-in-arms born during the Revolution. Such a system, he argued, would not only be an effective means of national defence but would also check aggressive foreign policies. Yet the turns of international rivalry were bringing military strength ever more to the fore in the diplomatic actions of the great powers as France concluded a military convention with Russia in 1894, Germany concluded railway conventions with Italy in 1896 and 1898 and in the latter year began to build the High Seas Fleet, and Britain and France moved hesitantly towards an *entente* in 1904 and military staff conversations two years later. As the rivalries among the great powers began to crystallize into two separate power blocs the need for large military forces grew more pressing; yet at the same time the pressures of democracy threatened to make armies less efficient by reducing their periods of training, and many states faced considerable problems of reliability in contemplating either the expansion of their officer corps or the increase of their ranks. Domestic and external demands were pulling in opposite directions.

In France, as military patriotism and intransigent nationalism waned, politicians turned from the problems of political legitimacy and structure which had preoccupied them for three decades, and which had led them to look to the army for loyalty rather than for ideological soundness, to the question of whether an authoritarian army could exist alongside a democratic republic — an issue which suited the temper of the radicals who were by now in power. In 1900 they brought to the War Ministry general André, a positivist who was determined to republicanize the army by judicious use of promotions. Using prefects, sub-prefects and especially freemasons, he gathered detailed information on the political views of every officer in the army and lodged it with the masters of the masonic order. The system had grave effects; officers spied on one another and the internal cohesion of the army broke down, while the competition for promotion which André's system generated, and which was something quite novel to the army, raised the value of political connections to a premium. By the time that the *fiche* system was made public knowledge in October 1904, the French officer corps was in complete disarray.

André's machinations, though clumsy, were not ill-intentioned. He realized that the army had a domestic role to play and that before it could hope to do this it had to be purified. The objective towards which his efforts were directed was the implementation of some of the ideas put forward a decade earlier by Lyautey. 'The regiment is more than a big family,' he remarked. 'It is a school. The officer is the extension of the teacher, the nation's instructor.'[9] The time when the army could live apart from society was over, in his view fortunately so. In concrete form his ideas resulted in the introduction of courses at St Cyr and the Polytechnique on the social role of the officer, and in regimental officers having to lecture their men on economics, hygiene, morality, patriotism, agriculture and trades. The year after his departure French military service at last reached that egalitarianism towards which it had been moving, at least in theory, ever since 1871: the law of 1905 introduced two-year conscription with no exemptions whatever, a move brought about chiefly on social and political grounds and one which the military viewed with acute disquiet since they felt it gave them too brief a period in which to hope to train men for modern war.

In Italy the actions of the left were viewed by the government with as much suspicion as they were by the aristocratic officers of the French army. Italy had been in the hands of the generals since May 1898 when general Bava Beccaris broke the revolt at Turin and Pelloux, another soldier, took over as president of the Council of Ministers. The Italian general staff was at the time convinced that it was being called upon to contain an international revolt of anarchists, radicals, republicans and socialists with links extending to France and Switzerland. The higher levels of the army remained acutely distrustful of anything which smacked of the left, and viewed with disfavour the rise of the 'Neo-Modernists' who called for military discipline to be based not on regulations but on reason. A parliamentary commission of enquiry was set up to examine the state of the army in 1907, and while it was undertaking its lengthy deliberations Giolitti, the premier, was moved to order an enquiry to detect the presence of freemasons in the army, with small result, since there were none to speak of. By 1911 the commission, together with Spingardi the minister of war and Pollio the chief of the general staff, had laid the basis on which Italy might have built up her army to a level comparable with the needs of the state and the advances of the other great European powers. In her case the design was thwarted not by internal difficulties but by an ill-advised war against Turkey in Libya (1911-12), from which her forces had by no means recovered in 1914.

In Germany the pattern of aristocratic dominance over the officer corps remained dominant, though it was more muted by the eve of the war: the proportion of aristocrats fell from 65 per cent in 1860 to 30 per cent in 1914. But behind these statistics lay the fact that the exclusive cavalry and guards regiments remained the preserve of the *Junkers* and that the general staff was growing more and not less aristocratic. Two arguments were raised against a self-perpetuating clique which was, for social reasons, neglecting the German middle classes: that the army could not do without the technically qualified middle-class army officer, and that if the army were to expand in size to meet growing international threats then it would have perforce to draw its officers from a wider segment of society. Wilhelm II was quite willing to strengthen middle-class representation in the army, partly because by these means he thought to present a united front against the social democrats. However classical theories of the social composition of the army, which went back to Yorck and beyond, continued to have great influence upon debates over its size. Schlieffen, a 'technician' *par excellence*, who was concerned only to secure the best possible means of defence for Germany, pleaded for an expansion in the size of the army in 1899 and was opposed by Gossler and von Einem, successive ministers of war, since his *Millionenheer* would have necessitated abandoning the social elitism of the officer corps. His successor, von Moltke, attempted the same expansion in 1911, influenced by Ludendorff and aided by the revelation that the army was short of some 1,200 lieutenants. Despite the alarums signalled by the second Moroccan crisis that year the war minister, von Heeringen, put up the standard case that not enough officer material of the right class was available, with support from the chancellor. 'We would not be able to meet these greatly increased requirements', wrote Bethmann Hollweg, 'without lowering our standards by using men from unsuitable classes to increase the officer corps and this, quite apart from other dangers, would expose the army to democratization.'[10] Moltke did win an increase in the size of the army of 90,000 men between 1912 and 1914, but this was less than one-third of his original demands and was achieved at the cost of removing Ludendorff, who was a commoner, from the ranks of the general staff.

The army's distrust of its left-wing opposition took two further forms in the years up to the outbreak of the war. In a programme which bore a superficial resemblance to that introduced by André in France, it sought to combat the growing influence of the social democrats by the use of organized religion and educational programmes, and by compulsory instruction in mowing, milking and ploughing every Saturday afternoon. These bucolic temptations proved to be less seductive than the skilful left-wing propaganda being disseminated among recruits by Rosa Luxemburg and others, which the army proved powerless to arrest. More ominously, it began to take practical steps to develop a knowledge of counter-insurgency techniques after the Russian Revolution of 1905. The historical section of the general staff gave close attention to the events of 1848 and of the Paris Commune, and in 1907 produced as a result *Fighting in Insurgent Towns*, a manual which urged that in any such situation the army must act fully, quickly and without parliamentary interference. In an attempt to ensure loyalty to conservative notions of authority and hierarchy, the army drew some two-thirds of its recruits from rural areas, although only two-fifths of the population lived on the land, an imbalance which reflected the growing problem facing the German army as it sought to find a way to increase its size without decreasing its reliability.

Even Britain experienced hitherto unexampled problems as she sought after 1906 to produce a military force more in keeping with her growing obligations to France as well as to the empire. Haldane's army was designed to be able to meet any one of a number of threats which might present themselves to Britain in various quarters rather than simply to fight against Germany on the continent as its creator subsequently claimed, and behind it lay the Territorial Army which was the closest that Britain could hope to get to conscription on the continental model in time of peace. Fears about putting arms into the hands of unreliable groups who might one day use them to do the bidding of socialist county councils were voiced at the highest levels of government, but Haldane was alive to that problem and well aware of the need for a reservoir of future officers who were socially reliable. 'We saw', he admitted,[11]

> that there was only one source from which we could hope to get young men of the upper middle class, who are the usual source from which this element is drawn, and that was the universities and the big public schools, like Eton and Harrow, and other public schools of that character, which at present have larger cadet corps.

When John Ward, a Labour MP, subsequently charged Haldane with attempting to fashion a national army on a class basis he was simply recognizing that despite the advent of the Territorial Army the social composition of Britain's military forces had changed little since Cardwell had abolished purchase. In this respect at least Britain was manifesting a concern shared by most major continental powers about social reliability.

At a time when almost every major army in western Europe was alive to the problem of altering the social basis of its officer corps and constructing the mechanisms by which to reconcile itself to an increase in the middle-class element, one army was showing quite a different attitude to class, status and a commission. In Russia by the latter quarter of the nineteenth century the army had become an accepted vehicle for social mobility. In the 1870s the background of one-third of the officer corps was so poor that they had not even completed their primary education; correspondingly their status was low, with extremely poor pay and second-class railway travel as manifestations of their country's attitude towards them. The influx of non-aristocratic officers continued and expanded, so that between 1900 and 1914 some two-fifths of the officers ranking as colonel or below were of peasant or lower-middle-class origin and many more were only one generation removed from it. Together with a sizeable number of 'hereditary' soldiers — foreigners and their descendants — they made up a large and distinctive proportion of the officer class.

Pressure to reform the ramshackle system of military organization in Russia, and particularly to institute a modernization of the general staff, grew rapidly after Russia's defeats at the hands of the Japanese during the war in Manchuria (1904-5), and was supported by the aristocratic wing of the officer corps who saw in it a means to dominate the army, since very few of the non-noble officers would be able to afford the high fees required to attend the General Staff Academy. A strong general staff would also serve something of the function it served in Germany: the autonomy of the army was threatened by the creation of the *Duma* (parliament), another of the legacies of the Russo-Japanese war, and a powerful chief of the general staff would be a means to by-pass the control of parliament exercised through the minister of war. By these means, and by controlling the promotion committees and thereby determining the senior appointments in the army, the aristocratic wing of the officer corps protected its hold over the senior appointments in the army and over its general development until 1908. In that year Sukhomlinov became chief of the general staff.

Temperamentally on the side of the infantry and against the artillery and cavalry (where most of the aristocrats were to be found) in the debates over the technical reorganization of the army, and in favour also of the lower- and middle-class officer, Sukhomlinov used the War Ministry to control the army, getting himself made minister, controlling promotions and downgrading the importance of the post of chief of the general staff, which had four incumbents down to 1914. In peace-time the non-aristocratic central military administration could dominate the army and the regional and corps commanders could do little more than squirm and complain, but the advent of war reversed the currents of power. Authority and control slipped from the *Sukhomlinovsty* to the general headquarters of grand duke Nicholas. The clash between non-aristocratic 'modernizers' and noble traditionalists split the Russian command once war began and contributed in no small measure to its defeat.

In the decade between 1905 and the outbreak of the First World War mounting tension between the two alliance groupings began to bring about changes in the pattern of social composition of many of the armies of Europe as the likelihood of active military engagement grew. In France Catholic officers flooded back after a period in the wilderness under André's regime; Foch took command of the influential Ecole de guerre in 1908 and de Castelnau (nicknamed 'the booted friar') co-operated with Joffre in devising Plan XVII with which France went to war in August 1914. The republic swallowed its fears of a strong army leadership and appointed Joffre, a *petit-bourgeois* republican, to head a centralized military command in 1911. In 1913 France signalled the extent to which she was prepared to go back on the left-wing ideal of the briefest period of military service that was possible by extending the term from two years to three, a measure which owed little or nothing to domestic social or political considerations but one which international circumstances, and particularly the growing threat from Germany, made imperative. In Germany von Moltke the younger won an increase in the size of the army despite severe doubts about the wisdom of such an expansion from the social point of view, and in order to dissuade the *kartell* of industrialists and agrarianists from opposing the measures necessary to finance expansion in the army Bethmann Hollweg shrewdly permitted the army to dominate the Zabern incident and pose as the defender of order and patriotism in Alsace — a move which rather misfired due to the absurd and overbearing conduct of the military and produced a vote of censure in which social democrats, centre and right combined to defeat the government by 293 votes to 54. This was such an uneasy coalition that it could not long hold together but it did reflect some of the social tensions within Germany, tensions for which many soldiers and civilians saw only one solution — a preventive war. Ludendorff, who may stand as their spokesman, complained querulously on 2 February 1913 'I think it is this everlasting peace which is responsible for all the political and military confusion.'[12]

The concern being manifested at this time by France and Germany over military expansion was not, however, solely concerned with the issue of numbers but also with the question of armaments, for by the turn of the century, if not before, superiority in armaments was every bit as important as superiority in manpower in weighing the balance of military advantage in any prospective war. Advances in weapon technology during the years after 1870 began to place enormous financial burdens on all the major states, and never more so than after 1894, during which year two French officers, colonel Deport and captain Ste Clair-Deville, developed the famous '75' field gun based on a recoil-less gun-carriage — an advance of such immediate significance that president Faure at once authorized its production without waiting for parliament to grant the necessary credits. Every army had immediately to contemplate re-equipment on the basis of the French innovation, a prospect so costly that Nicholas II of Russia issued his Imperial Rescript on 24 August 1898 in an attempt to slow down the armaments race which Russia could ill afford. The attempt was doomed to failure, though a dozen years later king Victor Emmanuel III of Italy toyed with a similar idea, and for a similar reason.

Russia reluctantly adopted a quick-firing gun between 1898 and 1900 and Italy began hesitantly to do the same. Germany expended enormous sums on artillery, with the result that she entered the war in 1914 equipped with new 77 mm, 105 mm and 150 mm guns. French military finance, however, was restricted to approximately one-third of what was asked for, with the result that she went to war with only her by now ageing '75'. Strategic railways were the other main consumers of funds during the period, and all states poured increasing amounts of money into them; Russia alone, the most backward country of all in this respect, built 7,000 miles of new railways between 1904 and 1914 alone. Together the two areas of armaments, along with others of less over-all significance, occupied mounting proportions of productive capacity and, at the same time, produced interested lobbies within states.

By the opening of the twentieth century a very great deal of money was required to keep up the pace of armaments development. In 1904 France was expending 36 per cent of her national budget on the army, Germany 20 per cent of her budget; in real terms, however, the imbalance ran quite in the opposite direction for the sums involved amounted for France to 38,000,000 francs and for Germany to the equivalent of 99,000,000 francs. Moreover, money was also necessary to stockpile reserves and prepare for the outbreak of war; the German war reserves in 1913 amounted to 240,000,000 gold marks.

Expenditure at these levels placed massive financial burdens on the states of Europe, which some could not hope to meet. One way of resolving the conundrum was by the use of diplomatic means: thus France and Russia formed their *entente* in 1894 partially because they were in this respect ideal complements to one another since France had capital but lacked numbers whereas Russia had spare manpower but lacked capital. Large French loans were advanced for the construction of strategic railways, although they were not fully utilized and by 1914 Sukhomlinov had unspent credits amounting to 250,000,000 roubles. Germany for her part poured money into Turkey from 1899. In her case the problem of raising the money for such activities was particularly acute, for the armaments race could in the end only be financed by a measure calculated to arouse the hostility of the conservative alliance of agrarianists and industrialists

— a tax on increases in wealth. This was the most striking example of the general truth that the armaments race caused political reactions of which civilians had somehow to take account. Competition in armaments, like the expansion of armies, contributed to rising feelings of tension and instability in Europe for the resolution of which war was deemed an effective agent; it may also have led in some cases to a political pressure to act in order to justify the heavy financial costs which had been borne by the state.

At the moment when Europe's diplomats were about to turn to the soldiery to resolve international tensions the very mass armies which had been the hallmark of late nineteenth-century military organization were, however, coming to be regarded by some as of little military worth. In Germany the influence of social democrats on recruits was proving impossible to check and the Zabern incident had produced a wave of hostility towards traditional Prussian militarist attitudes. In France the army had been employed against strikers in 1906-8 and again in 1911-12, and it too had grown less than popular as it fired on demonstrators. Of the Austrian army it was said that in no European country west of Russia had the workers been so readily and so often fired upon by the soldiers. Set against this background of somewhat inchoate unease about the reliability of citizen soldiers who were becoming the objects of some derision, and possibly a prey to doubts about their role, there now existed a very real concern about their military value. The Germans, under the terms of the Schlieffen plan as revised by the younger von Moltke, calculated on winning the war by a rapid forty-day campaign in Belgium and northern France or even a series of earlier battles of encirclement near the French frontier in order to put as little strain as possible upon their forces. The French pinned their faith to a blind *sortie torrentielle* under the impetus of which they would surge irresistibly across the frontier and into Germany, chiefly because they believed that with conscripts who had had no more than two years' training they could do little more complicated than dash towards their enemy (a conviction which may have become rooted in the French army as a result of the supposed intellectual inferiority of its officer corps on the eve of war). Broader

143

social considerations also dominated the military calculations of both sides in the coming conflict: the blow must be struck quickly in order to avoid any lengthy strain upon economy and society, under which it was all too probable that either or both might give way. Norman Angell had in any case warned in *The Great Illusion* (1909) that war could bring no economic gains, only losses. War was thus in many senses a gamble in 1914, and was often recognized as such. Every social consideration dictated speed as essential for decisive and successful action: 'On the eve of 1914, the offensive torrent in its most simple form reigned everywhere, and the example of the Balkan wars was ignored.'[13] By Christmas 1914 the plans of Europe's soldiers lay in ruins and the states of Europe were about to enter precisely that situation they had sought to avoid — the long war.

6
The First
World War

————◄◄◄◄◄◄◆►►►►►►————

When, in August 1914, Europe's diplomats handed her fate over to the soldiers the consequent shift of authority out of the hands of civilians was for some of the participants an alteration in the ordering of national affairs which was scarcely detectable. East of the Rhine, Berlin, Vienna and St Petersburg were already military courts whose monarchs rarely appeared out of uniform and who regarded themselves as ruling over military fiefs, though all were plagued to varying degrees by mounting pressures for political reform. The soldier had played a central role in preserving both the social and the political order from its internal and external enemies for many decades, and the practice of the chiefs of the general staff of communicating directly with their sovereigns without first passing through intermediaries was both a symbol and an instrument of military dominance. Even in the more democratic climate which prevailed west of the Rhine the military had been gaining in importance and independence as international tension mounted, so that Britain and France were not entirely unprepared for military domination by the time that the assassination at Sarajevo precipitated the last in a series of international crises and one which resulted in general war. On 28 October 1913 the French government had published a decree regulating the political control of the army which clearly outlined the respective spheres of influence of politician and soldier:[1]

> The Government indicates the *principal* adversary against whom the greater part of the national forces are to be directed. It divides the forces and supplies of all kinds accordingly, and places them at the *entire disposal* of the generals or admirals to whom the chief command in the several theatres of war has been entrusted.

Inherent in this regulation was the assumption that once war broke out politicians would take a back seat, leaving the direction of the nation's war efforts to their military experts. In England, acting without the benefit of any such clear directive, Sir Henry Wilson effectively gained the same position by virtue of the depth and extent of the co-operation with the French which he achieved. Once war broke out, even democratic regimes were prepared to reinforce the authority possessed by the military experts by virtue of their capacity to win the contest of arms — a capacity they did not in fact possess — and hand over governmental power. In all cases such attitudes were predicated upon the belief that such an abnormal state of affairs would be merely temporary, since the war would be short.

This widespread assumption that war would be brief, indeed must be so, since intricate economic systems and complex societies could not long withstand the likelihood of disintegration under pressure, partially explains the ready acceptance of war by the masses of all the major belligerents before their governments had put before them any precise statements detailing the aims for which the war was to be fought. Italy alone stood as an exception; before agreeing to enter the war in April 1915 she had evolved a clear set of territorial objectives. Otherwise men fought because their governments told them they must and should fight. The socialist international collapsed in the summer of 1914 as its members shifted their hostility from the ruling classes to their own particular national enemy, part of a wave of patriotism and jingoism which swept Europe and which was itself the product of a deep conviction on the part of each of the main participants that it was the threatened power for whom recourse to arms was the only way to avert submission to an aggressive and rapacious opponent. No power made such claims cynically. The result was that each power succeeded in mobilizing those very reserves of national stamina which it had feared did not exist, and thereby rendered itself capable of prosecuting the war not for weeks, or even for months, but for years. The process of re-education undergone by their populations during the course of the war was to be long, horrible and ultimately of profound importance.

The belligerents responded to the outbreak of war with organizational arrangements which were strikingly similar to one another. On 31 July 1914, after the *Confédération générale de travail* had decided not to call a general strike in support of international solidarity among the workers, the French government decided not to arrest the 2,501 anarchists and dissidents whose names figured on the celebrated 'Carnet B'; the anti-clerical republic, knowing very well the need for national unity at such a moment, also made conciliatory gestures towards the Catholic right, ending the closure of church schools and monasteries. Four days later a similar community of feeling manifested itself in Germany with the proclamation of the *Burgfrieden* ('Truce of the Fortress'), a calculated act which had its basis partly in the fact that the German trade unions were opposed to using the strike weapon in wartime since they thought it was likely to be ineffective. Arrangements had also to be made to secure internal order, and it was here that the extension of military power into the workings of civil society went furthest. In Germany the Prussian Law of Siege of June 1851 was called into force on the day mobilization began, and the empire was divided into twenty-four military districts, each ruled over by a deputy commanding general with virtually dictatorial powers to 'maintain public safety'. As the war continued the area within which the deputy commanding generals could claim overriding authority expanded until eventually there was little of importance in civilian life which was not within their purview, though their control was never full and co-ordinated. In Britain the Defence of the Realm Act (4 August) authorized military courts martial for people breaking security regulations by communicating with the enemy or interfering with the means of communication, docks or harbours. On the same day France enacted a Law of Siege handing over powers to the military which were rapidly extended, so that by 8 September the whole country had come under the jurisdiction of summary courts martial, as at the front: the traditional judicial ritual of the preliminary examination was swept aside and trials took place within twenty-four hours of arrest. In each case the measures taken by the government reflected the fact that society was, to a greater or lesser degree, fundamentally divided. The military monarchies enforced submission upon their citizens, whilst the democracies tacitly agreed within themselves to sink their differences and abstain from partisan political activity for what they thought would be only a few months.

Within a matter of days the distribution of power in each of the warring states came to assume a similar aspect as politicians ceded their place to soldiers. The simple assumption that 'all matters connected with the conduct of war fell within the exclusive domain of the military authorities' applied not merely to Germany but to all the participants in the war.[2] However, such similarities were the product of differing military imperatives: in France the soldiers' path to power was greatly facilitated by the pace at which early German advances ate into the *patrie*, with the result that by mid-September thirty-three departments were in the 'war zone', and by the precipitate haste with which, on 3 September, the government left Paris and scuttled to Bordeaux, whence it did not return to the capital until 11 December 1914. By that time Joffre and the *Grand Quartier Générale* had the reins of executive power firmly in their own hands and it would take the government another two and a half years to prise them loose.

Hopes that, with the aid of mass armies, railways and carefully devised deployment plans, war would be soon over were to crumble rapidly. August 1914 was characterized by just those wide-ranging manoeuvres by means of which the soldiers had calculated upon success and resulted in set-backs in almost every theatre, from which the only clear-cut conclusion to emerge was that it was going to be a costly business.

The Russians lost a quarter of a million men in their northern offensive against East Prussia, from which they were smartly ejected by Ludendorff and Hindenburg, but succeeded in their turn in inflicting a third of a million casualties on the Austrians and turning back their drive into Russia from the south-west. The Austrians were also rapidly ejected from Serbia, suffering another 40,000 casualties in the process. These and subsequent defeats for the Austrian army at the hands of the Russians were of more than simply strategic importance, for they undermined attempts to encourage Rumania to enter the war on the side of Vienna and prompted the emperor, Franz Joseph, to complain 'How on earth can we pursue even a tolerable foreign policy when we fight so badly?'[3] Lack of early military success for both sides rendered the enlistment of neutral powers at the same time more important and less likely.

In the west the French obeyed the dictates of Plan XVII and dashed forward into Alsace and Lorraine, from which they were ejected at a cost of some 250,000 casualties. Decisive success appeared to belong only to the Germans but their plan too proved over-ambitious and their advance was halted at the so-called battle of the Marne (6 September 1914) when the Allies chose to advance at just the moment that the Germans withdrew. At the end of the month it was already clear that neither side was going to break through the other's lines and the respective commanders, Joffre and von Falkenhayn, began their 'race for the sea' in an effort to turn one another's flank. By December Germany had failed in her last attempt to break through to Calais and a line of earthworks and trenches snaked its way across western Europe from the Channel to the Swiss border. Europe's armies had begun the war with disastrous offensives and had suffered heavy casualties in the process; now they had to face the prospect of a long war in conditions which were utterly novel to them. They were under strong pressures to win victory, but what did victory mean?

Once the war had begun politicians seemed to have little to do in the day-to-day life of the state. The British government became, for a year, little more than quartermaster to Lord Kitchener, seeing its task as being no more than providing him with the material means by which to conjure up victory; France was in the powerful grip of Joffre; Germany, Austria and Russia were military monarchies anyway. Civilians, no longer concerned with the issue of whether to fight and given no say in when or how to fight, were left to concern themselves with the subsidiary question of what the fighting was for. War aims began to bulk large in the calculations of some of the powers. Germany was at the forefront in terms both of the size and scope of her demands. Pan-German nationalists, the liberal Centre Party, industrialists such as Thyssen and Rathenau, soldiers and sailors amassed between them a composite list of German objectives which comprised Belgium, the French coast as far as the mouth of the Somme, the ore-bearing region of Longwy-Briey in north-west France, Poland, the Ukraine and various extensions of Germany's African empire. All these demands had been voiced prior to the battle of the Marne, at a time when it still seemed possible that the war would be over in a matter of weeks; after that battle it became apparent that victory was not so close at hand and Bethmann Hollweg, the German chancellor, incorporated them all into his 'September Programme', designed to meet the demands of all the major elements within German society and thereby unify the country behind the war. Bethmann Hollweg was wise enough, however, not to publish this programme, for he realized that the best way to keep the German populace united behind its leaders was by not opening up an issue over which they would inevitably squabble.

Other participants proved less clear and more cautious in their aims at the start of the war, although their ambitions were to grow — and on occasions, when the war was going badly, to recede. France fought a war which was primarily defensive, her objective being to regain the lost departments of Alsace and Lorraine and to gain safeguards against another German attack. Publicly the government couched its aims in the general terms of justice, which appealed to the political left, and security, which won over the right. Farther than that it was not then willing to go; when, on 13 October 1914, the Russian ambassador Isvolsky enquired of the French foreign minister Delcassé how he saw war aims, he received the brusque response that it was 'too early to sell the skin of the bear'. Britain fought to recover Belgian independence, but also for a larger and more amorphous goal which was every bit as far-reaching as Germany's aims — the destruction of 'Prussian militarism'. Quite simply, this required a victory of such completeness as to enable her to tinker at will with Germany's social and political structure — rather more than the Germans wished to do in return. Behind these specific objectives, and common to all powers, was a stimulus to amass substantial gains which resulted from the very fact of the fighting itself; to assuage their civilian populations as the course of the war laid ever heavier burdens upon them, the politicians soon began to demand a peace befitting the appalling sacrifices being made at the front. This was a factor of growing momentum which added to the ferocity of the war, just as it added to the problems of the soldiers who were called upon to achieve a result which, sooner or later, most recognized to be beyond their capabilities.

To encourage the home fronts to greater sacrifice a new contestant entered the lists of war — racial hatred. The enemy was to be beaten not merely because he was menacing the peace, but because he was German, or British, or French — because he was, in sum, who he was. Vigorously stoked up by the press on each side, aided by government control over information which was established everywhere in the earliest stages of the war, it rendered an old-fashioned peace, restoring the balance of power, ever more difficult and unlikely. Nations comprising distinct sub-national groups or subordinated peoples were also vulnerable to disruption behind their front lines, and so the provocation of internal unrest became one of the strategies by which victory was to be achieved. Britain encouraged Czech refugees, foremost amongst them Jan Masaryk, to foment trouble within the Austro-Hungarian empire with offers of independence — a tactic which incidentally ruled out the possibility of detaching Austria-Hungary from Germany and making a separate peace with her — and at a further remove encouraged Arab independence in an attempt to weaken Turkey, with results which were not entirely foreseen. Germany forged links with the Irish, Finns, Poles, Flamands and even the Senussi, and also aided the cause of the exiled Russian revolutionaries with gold, eventually transporting Lenin and a group of his closest supporters from Switzerland to Russia in a closed railway carriage in April 1917. This last was undoubtedly the most successful move made by any power in this contest; farther away from Europe, however, the 'war of the white tribes' served chiefly to encourage and foster anti-colonialism. None the less each side did what it could to undermine the political system of its opponent, largely unaware that they might also unbalance the delicately poised social system. In the long run it was to be those states farthest removed from democracy when the war broke out which were to be most at risk; as Tirpitz presciently remarked early in the war 'victory or defeat, we shall get democracy.'[4] However the point at which society became vulnerable to pressures such as these lay at some distance in the future as the second year of the war opened.

By the spring of 1915 a major imbalance faced the two camps as they confronted one another. Each contained a weak partner — Austria, and Russia. At the end of 1914 Paléologue described France's eastern ally as a 'paralysed giant'. In reality she was not as short of *matériel* as she made out — shells were being manufactured, for example, but instead of being delivered they were hoarded. Supply was inefficient and the use of railroads was imperfect, while the Russians were over-ready to depend upon unreliable British and American contractors rather than design simple and unsophisticated munitions which could be easily produced at home. The disparity between Austria and Russia lay not so much in the degree to which the former was the more up-to-date of the two as in the fact that Germany could get at her partner and prop her up, whilst Britain and France were unable to get at theirs. In an effort to resolve this dilemma Churchill, Lloyd George and Sir Maurice Hankey between them fathered the Dardanelles strategy — ill-conceived and worse executed, but none the less an attempt to evade the deadlock which already seemed certain to develop in western Europe. Other factors were also at work in determining this strategy, and were spelled out by Lloyd George on New Year's Day 1915:[5]

A clear definite victory which has visibly materialised in guns
and prisoners captured, in unmistakeable retreats of the enemy's
armies, and in large sections of enemy territory occupied, will
alone satisfy the public that tangible results are being achieved
by the great sacrifices they are making, and decide neutrals
that it is at last safe for them to throw in their lot with us.

The Dardanelles campaign, which absorbed a large part of
Britain's military energies in 1915, was thus an attempt to
reach Russia by way of Constantinople and the Black Sea and
thereby simultaneously release Russian wheat to the west,
open up a channel by which to ship out munitions, knock
Turkey out of the war and encourage Balkan neutrals to join
in on the side of the Allies. This ambitious venture was
probably doomed to failure from a fairly early stage, and fail
it did, although the final bridgehead at Gallipoli was not
abandoned until 8 January 1916. Meanwhile, and in addition
to military force, Britain resorted to a more traditional
weapon in her attempts to conquer the Balkans. In March
1915 moves were made to induce Turkey to change sides in
return for £4 million, and two months later the Bulgarians in
their turn were offered £2½ million to enter the war against
the Central Powers. Neither country found the lure of specie
irresistible.

Where Russia's weakness lay primarily in the realm of
economics, Austria's was to be found in the polyglot armies
she fielded to support Vienna and Berlin. Of every 1,000
men in the Austrian army at the start of the war 267 were
German, 235 Magyar, 135 Czech, 85 Poles, 81 Ruthenes,
67 Croats and Serbs, 64 Rumanians, 38 Slovaks, 26 Slovenes
and 14 Italians. By the end of 1915 the Austrian army had
lost three-quarters of a million men and the old pre-war
professional force had quite literally died. In seeking after
the end of the war to explain what seemed to be the failure
of the Austro-Hungarian armies to achieve success the role
of divisive nationalism was strongly stressed:[6]

Troops of different nationalities did not trust each other.
Hungarian regiments reproached a Czech artillery brigade who,
they claimed, had fired into them. Some Poles argued similarly
against a Honved battery. The Croats were embittered because

the Honveds were occupying their homeland whilst they
themselves had to fight on the front.

In fact the army seems to have been unified by the war
against Italy and to have refurbished itself during and after
1915 so that it was at least as strong as before. It was not
alone in suffering desertions but, despite the heavy strains
upon it, it never mutinied as did the armies of France and
Russia, but broke up only when an imperial manifesto of
16 October 1918 released officers from their oath of allegiance and permitted them to join the national armies of the
new states that were being created from the debris of the
empire. The emotions generated by the war welded the army
together to make of it a more reliable instrument than was
its Russian opponent, and the attack launched on the role of
national elements should be viewed as special pleading after
the war had ended and the empire had gone. 'Within the
regiments, there were never conflicts due to nationality, and
never great difficulties in leading the army due to the varied
languages used by the troops.'[7]

As the war widened both in scope, extending as it did
beyond the armies in the front line to the economic and
social systems behind it, and in terms of probable duration,
it became increasingly desirable to regulate the economic life
of the state in order to permit the least possible domestic
division and to provide the enormous quantities of munitions
of war which the front consumed. Here German forethought
was conspicuously greater than that of any one of the Allies.
From the start of the war Walther Rathenau, head of the
industrial giant AEG, had recognized Germany's weakness in
a war of any duration; self-sufficient in food only with the
aid of imported nitrates and fertilizers (and indeed some
foodstuffs), she lacked oil, cotton, rubber, hemp and phos-
phates. On 9 August 1914 Rathenau had accordingly persuaded Falkenhayn, then minister of war, to create the
Kriegsrohstoffabteilung (War Raw Materials Section) in order
to take an inventory of stocks and distribute them according
to a clear system of priorities. This was one part of a three-
pronged strategy to overcome Germany's obvious deficiencies
in raw materials of which the other elements were a Central

Purchasing Commission, set up to handle German trade with neutrals and ensure that separate German firms did not compete with one another, and a search for synthetic substitutes in the course of which German industry reached very high levels of technical attainment. Rathenau also suggested the introduction of parallel controls for foodstuffs, but these worked less well due to counter-pressures exerted by the powerful agrarian interests who did not wish to risk the losses in profit which such a policy might entail and due also to the inertia of the state secretary for the interior, Clemens von Delbrück, who gave such projects no assistance at all. Rising prices forced the government to take under its control the production first of wheat and subsequently of potatoes during 1915 and then in May of the following year, in response to a marked increase in the incidence of food riots, to establish a War Food Office by which to control food prices. Lacking a military head, this last was destined to remain a weak institution. Falkenhayn also wished to introduce a military or legal compulsion to work in order to strengthen the hand of industry, but was resisted by civil servants in the War Ministry on the very good grounds that such a step would endanger the confidence in the military authorities currently felt by a class which was making a decisive contribution to the war effort.

While Germany had signalled her intention to introduce the *Zwangswirtschaft*, or compulsory economy, should circumstances dictate such a step, the French proved rather slower at coming to grips with the problems of managing their natural resources. Pre-war beliefs in the mass army, the offensive and the short war had meant that the evolution of the nation-in-arms had been retarded in one vital respect, for it had taken no account of the long-term problems of manpower, production and supply. Not until 6 July 1916 was a Central Food Supply Committee established to draw up a general statement of resources and needs, and a further sixteen months elapsed before a Central Foodstuffs Office was created in order to carry out the executive tasks necessary to preserve as much equity as possible in the distribution and pricing of food. France used price controls to try to direct economic activity during the first years of the war, but the solution to the problem of controlling the purchase and allocation of raw materials did not emerge until 1916, and when it did it came in the somewhat unsatisfactory form of the 'consortium' whereby manufacturers of similar products centralized demand, purchased raw materials abroad and sold imports to members under state supervision. In contrast to the German model, the French government contributed to its own backwardness in these areas by its unwillingness to create new administrative institutions to deal with these problems; it was far more ready to add to the responsibilities of existing government departments — thereby increasing the strain on them and lowering their efficiency — or to create *ad hoc* bodies, of which 291 were established to deal with various aspects of the war. This system played straight into the hands of the *Grand Quartier Générale* and greatly enhanced the army's autonomy. It was not until the war minister's functions were split and Albert Thomas became undersecretary for munitions that anything like the much-needed reconstruction of the government with regard to production took place.

In Britain, Lloyd George's Munitions of War Bill (June 1915) forecast expanding government controls by prohibiting strikes and lock-outs, but controls on German lines were a long time in coming. It was a measure of the reluctance of Asquith's government to institute restraints upon the free play of industrial enterprise that it approached the problem from the opposite end to Germany and, like France, first made use of price controls; some of these, however, were disastrous, controlling the price of milk at a low level simply resulting in the farmer putting more of it into butter and cheese. Partial rationing failed to halt price rises or to overcome the problem of shortage of certain foodstuffs, and a Ministry of Food was at last established in December 1916. State intervention along German lines did not begin to appear until 1917 when the Inter-Allied Council of War Purchase and Finance was formed to buy foodstuffs for Britain and her allies. The slow but remorseless growth of state intervention in key strategic industries was exemplified in the case of coal: closely controlled in price from an early stage, the industry was by the end of the war completely state-run.

Probably the worst arrangements in the crucial area of production and supply were to be found in Russia. There War Industries Committees were established in 1915, but enjoyed only a superficial success since the big industrial cartels totally ignored them. Enormous profits were made in the process of supplying an incompetent Tsarist government with the necessary munitions of war, and by 1916 gross industrial profits were running at five times the rate for 1913. In the absence of a Russian ministry of supply all was confusion and disorder, a state to which both British and American industrialists contributed by eagerly settling contracts for munitions they were quite unable to deliver. In the light of her disarray in this respect it is less surprising that Russia collapsed in 1917 than that she managed to keep going more or less efficiently for two and a half years before succumbing to the pressures of war.

In 1915, before the combatants had realized the need to bend all their resources to the quest for success, there was a widespread belief that victory was still possible — a victory, that is to say, sufficiently definite and incontestable as to achieve all the war aims for which the governments were manoeuvring. Two major problems intervened. The first lay in the question of where to apply the strengths of the nation. Both sides had their 'Westerners' who believed that the central confrontation was between Germany on the one hand and Britain and France on the other, that defeating lesser partners would only postpone the day when the major enemy had to be broken and might in the process weaken one's own capacity and resolve, and that too great a diversion of strength from the western front would create just the conditions in which an opponent might break through. To counterbalance such views, each side had its 'Easterners' who held that the power of the defence was such that neither side could hope to break through, that attacks directed towards weaker flanks could undermine an enemy's resistance and that the defeat of the lesser partner in an alliance would of itself defeat the enemy's general will to resist. During 1915 neither side measured its full strength against the other for, curiously, whilst the views of the 'Easterners' dominated in France and Britain, those of the 'Westerners' prevailed in

Germany. However, neither side was able completely to implement its desires. Falkenhayn's hands were tied by the need to provide support for the weakened Austrian army and by the pressures exerted from the eastern front by Hindenburg and Ludendorff for more resources with which to follow up their striking success, which had driven the Russians out of Galicia and Poland and back behind the Vistula. Kitchener was frustrated by Joffre's perfectly reasonable insistence upon continuing attacks in the west in order to drive the Germans from French territory; the Germans now held part or all of ten French departments, and unless the French could get back all their national soil they had lost their war. In pursuit of this objective they launched a series of non-stop offensives throughout 1915 in which the British were forced to take part, culminating in the battle of Loos. Neither side succeeded in concentrating force where it wished during that year.

A second major impediment to victory began to emerge during the course of the same year, and one which was not to be overcome for a further two years. By December 1915 the sheer technical difficulties which had to be resolved before a clear military decision could be obtained were apparent. The only hope of achieving a breakthrough against the enemy lines in trench warfare lay in a heavy preliminary bombardment which would 'soften up' the opposition before the infantry assault was carried out, but such preliminary barrages meant the loss of any hopes of surprising an opponent; building up the necessary munitions dumps to furnish the field guns took time and afforded the enemy the opportunity to ascertain not just the location but also the probable strength of an impending attack and even, within limits, its timing. The weight of the preliminary bombardment also broke up the ground which the infantry had to traverse to such a degree that movement across it became extremely difficult regardless of what the enemy was doing, and advance in depth impossible. The most which could be hoped for was a forward movement of a few hundred metres before the attack ground to a halt. This physical problem was one of the factors which caused the Germans in 1916 and the British in 1917 to adopt a new form of warfare — attrition.

While full military victory was still held to be possible, and before the cruel weight of casualties necessary to achieve it had caused men to pause and question that assumption, the power of the soldier in government remained undiminished. Kitchener, Joffre and, after Italy entered the war in April 1915, Cadorna were all virtually unassailable. Where the omnipotence of a general did prove to be at risk the threat always came not from a civilian but from another soldier with an alternative strategy for victory; thus Kitchener was replaced by Sir William Robertson as military director of Britain's war in December 1915, Falkenhayn by Hindenburg and Ludendorff in Germany in August 1916, and Cadorna by Diaz in Italy in 1917. Meanwhile few politicians were told anything of significance about the war and its prosecution. Kitchener was temperamentally incapable of discussing such matters with cabinet ministers he did not know personally, though in any case behind his mask of military omniscience he had little to offer by way of enlightenment to the curious, while Joffre wrote curtly to Gallieni when the latter became minister of war requesting that he send the government no information concerning operations, since he in his own reports never made known either the object of current action or his intentions. Nivelle, Joffre's successor, summed up the situation which prevailed in France between August 1914 and December 1916 with accuracy: 'Joffre was the director of the war, and the influence of the government made itself felt but little.'[8] Civilians seem never to have entirely freed themselves from the attitude that soldiers should reign unfettered in wartime; in later contests over control they presented alternative military leaders rather than the suggestion of civilian domination. This was largely the result of the commonly shared delusion that force could attain the aims which were being sought after, aims which in any case allied politicians rarely if ever explained to soldiers or to civilians in terms which were anything other than enormous generalities.

The year 1916 was to prove in many respects the turning point of the war. As it opened the failure of the Dardanelles expedition had resulted in Robertson's promotion to the position of chief of the imperial general staff, with direct access to the War Cabinet and the authority to issue all orders. Robertson saw the task of the Allied armies as being to administer upon Germany a defeat of sufficient severity to bring home to her the lesson that she could not play fast and loose with international politics as she had done before August 1914 and hope to get away with it. This was what he understood Britain's chief war aim to be, and since it meant defeating the German army, that in its turn dictated that the decisive action must be on the western front. There were to be no more sideshows; concentration of force was to take place at the 'decisive point' — which meant in effect the only point where a direct lesson in arms could be inflicted upon Germany. In this broad strategy the French concurred, adding the rider that they had been attacking more or less non-stop for a year and a half and in consequence had manpower enough for only one more major offensive and that therefore that offensive must be big.

In Germany Falkenhayn had reached a similar decision. German armies had driven back the Russians, had overrun the Balkans and Serbia and now had little to fear from the entry of Rumania or Greece into the war against them. However, the chief of the German general staff realized that what counted most in the long run was Britain's capacity to apply to the war not just her own resources but those of her empire and, indirectly, the globe. He reasoned that Britain was in fact using France as her sword and that once deprived of her ally she herself was an inconsiderable force and might well sue for peace. France therefore had to be attacked at a point which she would feel compelled to defend, and then eviscerated. 'Within our reach behind the French sector of the Western Front,' he wrote,[9]

> there are objectives for the retention of which the French General Staff would be compelled to throw in every man they have. If they do so the forces of France will bleed to death — as there can be no question of a voluntary withdrawal — whether we reach our goal or not.

The place Falkenhayn selected was Verdun. Early in the war Joffre had stripped the fortress of its heavy artillery for the battles in the north and had allowed the partial demolition of its fortifications. Unable now to admit his short-sightedness and classify the fortress as expendable, Joffre chose instead to declare it impregnable. 'I ask only one thing', he thundered, 'that the Germans attack at Verdun.' This the Germans obligingly did on 21 February 1916. The appalling slaughter which ensued lasted months; de Gaulle, Maginot, von Manstein, von Paulus, Guderian, von Brauchitsch, Keitel and Rommel were among those who experienced it, and upon whom it left its mark. When it closed the statistical record — in as far as one could be drawn up — seemed to indicate a draw: the French had lost 377,000 men, the Germans 337,000. However the over-all effects of the battle probably bore more heavily on France, for Pétain's policy of moving units out of the battle after only short periods in action meant that no less than 259 battalions of infantry experienced the holocaust. This was to have its full effect some six months later.

The struggle at Verdun dislocated British plans for a major attack on the Somme, chiefly by dictating that the proportion of French troops taking part be reduced. The battle was to blood Kitchener's 'New Armies', raised during the course of the previous year from the volunteers who had joined the colours, and viewed with acute suspicion and mistrust by the regulars who officered them because they lacked extensive training and tended to display an alarming degree of independence and initiative. Accordingly when the attack was launched on 1 July 1916 the troops rose from their trenches, crossed the parapets and then, in broad daylight and under continuous enemy fire, dressed by the right into long, neat lines before advancing at walking pace towards the enemy. When the first day of the battle ended they had suffered 60,000 casualties. Since this was to be a decisive battle no one contemplated breaking it off and it therefore continued until November. When it finally ended the Allies had won a strip of land some forty kilometres long and ten kilometres deep at a cost of 600,000 casualties. German losses ran at a comparable rate. At its initiation the Somme had been a battle to achieve a breakthrough; by its close it had signalled the onset of the strategy of attrition, whereby the enemy's human, material and moral resources were to be worn away in the assumption that his side would crack first. The fighting front was thus no more than an extension of the home front, at which military efforts were now directed.

For Germany the internal tensions which marked 1916 as the year of crisis began on 13 January when the kaiser, persuaded by Bethmann Hollweg, indicated that there would be changes in Prussian suffrage after the war which would render it more democratic. Shortages of raw materials and skilled labour were beginning to emerge when the battle of the Somme revealed all too clearly that Germany was engaged in a *Materielschlacht* and that measures must be taken to boost productivity and apply all her resources effectively to winning the war. This would require the concurrence of labour, yet a partnership to win the war was becoming increasingly difficult to achieve; the three-day strike called by 55,000 Berlin metal workers in June as a protest against the prison sentence imposed upon Karl Liebknecht for leading a May-day demonstration against the war signalled the ease with which radicals might turn economic grievances into political strikes.

In this climate Falkenhayn came under increasing attack from several quarters. Industry complained about his disorganized munitions policy, army commanders on the western front attacked him for failing to foresee the magnitude of the Somme offensive, and from Austria-Hungary came indications that he was regarded with disfavour by Germany's principal ally. Attacks on Falkenhayn's direction of the war mounted and political support shifted away from him, even Bethmann Hollweg looking elsewhere. Then on 27 August the final blow fell when, as a result of Brussilov's Russian offensive in the east, Rumania entered the war on her side and against the Central Powers. Falkenhayn, who had by now ceased to believe that a decisive battle was possible, resigned the next day and was replaced by Hindenburg as chief of the German general staff, with Ludendorff as his first quartermaster general. The change-over was greeted with universal relief: Bethmann Hollweg saw a better cover behind which to launch his peace note; right-wing annexationists got a successful general; social democrats welcomed Hindenburg as a general who did not use up lives. While there were those within the higher reaches of the German army who recognized that, in order to win the war, compromises were essential between labour and the authoritarian mandarins of the state who had earlier forged the alliance of rye and steel, the new directors of Germany's war effort set about achieving the 'Hindenburg victory' which was designed to make democratic and socialist reforms unnecessary and unite the people behind the Emperor. The paradox that to win the war Hindenburg and Ludendorff would have to grant in the short term what they were fighting the war in order to avoid conceding in the long term, namely social and political reform, lies at the heart of Germany's efforts during the last two years of the war.

The effects of military set-backs were also visible on the home fronts in Britain and France in 1916. Britain had been forced to recognize that she could not hope to fight the war and maintain intact her peace-time sensibilities and on 5 January the first step towards full conscription — applying as yet to unmarried men only — was taken in order to supply the generals with the men which volunteering and attesting had failed to produce. The pressure to expand output in munitions and to accumulate larger stocks of military supplies produced an important change in ministerial office in June, when Lloyd George took over as war minister; however the limitations of his new post made it temperamentally impossible for the mercurial Welshman to remain contented with such a position for very long. In November he entered a coalition with the conservative leader Andrew Bonar Law and in the following month Asquith was manoeuvred out of office, a change effected chiefly as a result of his undistinguished performance as a wartime premier. Lloyd George took over the job and at once signalled the advent of a more rigorous civilian control over the war by setting up a small War Cabinet consisting of only five members — himself, Bonar Law and lords Milner and Curzon (conservative) and Arthur Henderson (labour). It soon became clear that Robertson was no longer to act as sole military adviser to the government, and Lloyd George began to cast about for alternatives.

After Verdun a considerable volume of criticism was directed at Joffre on the grounds that he was attempting to do too much and carried too much responsibility, and the French Chamber of Deputies moved to regain some of the authority they had abandoned at the outbreak of the war some twenty-three months earlier. On 16 June the deputies held their first secret session of the war, a move which emphasized their intention to assert their independence and which resulted in a vote of confidence which the government managed to carry. Pressure mounted for direct parliamentary supervision of France's armies, in order to avoid another similar débâcle, and in July parliamentary committees on the army and the budget established their right to carry out inspections, something which, in an era of success, the military had denied them. The events on the Somme and the defeat of Rumania brought about a second secret session on 28 November, and Briand moved to take advantage of the impetus created by strategic setbacks to increase the power of ministers. He sacked the minister of war, Roques, on the grounds that he was too compliant with the wishes of the soldiers, and rid himself of Joffre by creating the new, and totally hollow, post of 'technical adviser to the government' and raising the newly-created marshal above the level on which he could take any executive decisions. Finally in December 1916 Briand set up a war committee containing five key ministers which, though it had no powers of decision, signalled the civilians' intention to get back a measure of the executive control they had earlier lost.

Though the measures taken by England and France represented considerable advances on the somewhat casual direction of the war which had preceded them, they did not match up to the demands Hindenburg and Ludendorff were making on their home front in order to win victory. On 31 August they presented the 'Hindenburg Programme', by the terms of which the output of munitions was to double and that of . machine-guns and artillery to triple by the following spring in readiness for a German onslaught on the west. Though impressive at face value, this programme was in reality founded on an unsteady basis, since it had been drawn up with no other considerations in view than strategic ones and its authors had neglected to carry out any serious investigations as to its feasibility. They had however indicated their wish to introduce compulsory civilian mobilization in order to provide the labour — female as well as male — which was necessary to complete the programme. Control of all questions relating to the war economy was taken out of the hands of the war minister and passed over to the newly created Supreme War Office, to which general Wilhelm Groener was appointed head on 26 October. Two days later Groener presented Ludendorff with the draft of a 'Patriotic Auxiliary Service Law' by which to implement Ludendorff's industrial objectives.

As finally passed, the Auxiliary Service Law rendered all adults between the ages of seventeen and sixty who were not already in the armed forces liable for the war economy. Heavy industry at once opposed it, and similar 'social experiments', since it meant the introduction of arbitration committees, recognition of trade unions and workers' committees in factories, whilst progressives registered great interest in the opportunities it presented to control employers and raise the status of organized labour. Groener's own objectives were less straightforward; there were signs that he already foresaw the possibility that Germany might lose the war and believed that the monarchy could best survive such a disaster if by then the unions had the workers under control. All parties saw something to be gained from the law, and on 5 December it was signed by the emperor. Whether it represented a turning point in German social history due to its enshrining government recognition of the unions' right to equality with the employers, or whether it better represented the repressive 'Bonapartism' of the dictatorship of Hindenburg and Ludendorff remains a matter of dispute.

The other plank of the strategy by means of which Hindenburg and Ludendorff intended to win the war was the reintroduction of unrestricted submarine warfare. The first submarine campaign had been launched in 1915 with the objective of preventing merchantmen from putting to sea, and so depriving Britain of vital supplies of foodstuffs and raw materials; however, the spectacular breaches of maritime law which it entailed, notably the sinking of the *Lusitania* in

May of that year, caused such an outcry in America that the government overrode the admiralty in the summer and stopped the campaign. There were in any case not yet enough U-boats capable of keeping the sea at any one time to have an overwhelming effect. Meanwhile the surface fleet had achieved little. After some success with a series of cruiser raids during which it had bombarded Yarmouth, Hartlepool, Scarborough and Whitby between November 1914 and January 1915, it had been bottled up until 31 May 1916, when it had fought the apparently indecisive action at Jutland. Thereafter the prospect of meeting the might of the British Grand Fleet a second time kept it in port. Its ineffectiveness began increasingly to irritate the German high command: colonel Bauer, one of Ludendorff's closest aides, complained to his wife in April 1916, 'Our Navy!!! In peacetime it took money and men away from the army, in war it has achieved nothing — for basically the successes of the submarine are just pin-pricks for England. And for that to make an enemy of the whole world!'[10] Ludendorff regarded unrestricted submarine warfare as an essential complement to his military programme, but one which should only be introduced when the military situation was more favourable. For the time being he supported Bethmann Hollweg, who was very reluctant to return to it. However, he took the collapse of Rumania on 6 December 1916 to be the change necessary, and he at once announced that unless the campaign was restarted by the end of January he and Hindenburg would resign. It duly began on 1 February 1917.

The land campaigns of 1917 were played out against a background of determination on the part of both British and French politicians to ride their soldiers on a much tighter rein but though they had lost faith in the soldiers as a result of the events of 1916, neither the public nor the press had done likewise, a factor which considerably hindered their attempts to regain full control over the war. Moreover a new general had appeared with the claim that he had the key which could unlock the door to military success. General Robert Nivelle argued that the tactics of *rupture* which he had developed during the battle at Verdun, and which entailed the maximum possible concentration of men and guns on the narrowest front, could be applied as a doctrine to entire army groups. Lloyd George, scenting a chance to be rid of Robertson and Haig, supported Nivelle's candidacy as commander-in-chief of both British and French armies, a move only thwarted when Haig appealed directly to George V, after which the British prime minister climbed down and had to agree to the subordination of the British army to the French as being only temporary and limited.

The friction created between the two armies over this incident did not augur well for the Nivelle offensive, and further reservations about it flowed from the turns of French domestic politics. In March 1917 Briand was replaced as premier by Ribot, a change which brought in its train a new minister of war — Paul Painlévé — who was sceptical of Nivelle's claims about the likelihood of success of his doctrine and who had in Nivelle's superior at Verdun, Pétain, his own candidate for command. Painlévé was however frustrated in his designs by domestic political considerations: Pétain was a clerical anti-Dreyfusard who associated with Jesuit groups, while Nivelle was a Huguenot and as such the more reliable of the two men in the eyes of many republican politicians. So Nivelle stayed and the plans for his offensive began to take shape despite the fact — which Painlévé forcefully pointed out — that the over-all situation of the war had been transformed to such an extent that it was now scarcely necessary at all. Tsarist Russia had fallen victim to the first revolution of the war, and though it was not yet obvious that she would leave the Allied coalition, her future looked extremely uncertain. America had entered the war on 4 April 1917 as a direct result of Germany's recommencement of unrestricted submarine warfare, so that her immense strength might now slowly be brought to bear upon Germany without there being any need for France and Britain to expend their last reserves. And in any case Germany, lacking any sentimental attachments to the front line she had won from her enemies, had now retreated to the almost unassailable fortifications of the Hindenburg line.

Despite all these considerations Nivelle launched his Aisne offensive on 16 April 1917. Committed to the assault in appalling climatic conditions and against a skilful foe, it had totally collapsed after eight hours. Nivelle had sworn that if his efforts were not rewarded with early success he would break off the attack, but instead he succumbed to the temptation which had gripped his predecessors and fed more men into the battle in the hope of turning set-backs into success. As a consequence of his failure the French army had lost 120,000 men after ten days. He was immediately replaced as commander-in-chief by Pétain, and within a few days the French army signalled to its leaders that it had had enough of futile slaughter at the hands of its own generals by mutinying. The theory current during the previous year that France could mount only one last attack had proved correct.

Many members of the government and the majority of the senior officers believed that the mutinies were the result of a conspiracy of secret organizations within the ranks, and it was suggested that the recent revolution in Russia had played its part by adding to the heat of the situation and by presenting a seductive example. Subsequent research has revealed what Pétain seems to have believed at the time, namely that the mutinies were not general but were regionally distributed and reflected not radical political or social aspirations but rejection of a method of fighting — Nivelle's method — by those who had been its chief victims. The mutineers numbered approximately 40,000, of whom 554 were condemned to death and forty-nine were actually shot. Pétain, meanwhile, at once set about improving the army's conditions and raising its morale. The French would take part in no more spendthrift assaults; instead they would dig in and wait for the war to be won by a combination of tanks, aeroplanes and Americans. In adopting this policy Pétain gave rise to a new image of the republican soldier as cautious, defensive and sparing of lives which was quite at odds with the pre-1914 image, typified in the person of marshal Foch and his theories of the efficacy of the offensive. This new military image was to be a potent one in inter-war France and would ultimately deposit Pétain at the head of the Vichy regime, the first soldier-president since MacMahon left office in 1877.

Whilst the French were prepared to sit back and await the arrival of the military forces of the New World, the British were not. They felt a certain desire to win the war before the Americans got to Europe — perhaps in part a matter of professional pride — and there was also the real need to initiate some action which would draw German pressure off the weakened Russians and French. There existed also the alarming prospect that, despite what was happening on land, Britain might yet lose the war to the German submarines. This generated a strong pressure from the Admiralty to seize the Belgian ports and thereby restrict the activities of U-boat commanders before they succeeded in winning the war at sea. Finally, Haig was convinced that Germany was near cracking point; local intelligence reports were talking of the possibility that the breaking point might be reached in June. This combination of pressures led Haig to undertake the Passchendaele offensive, which lasted from July to November 1917. It began with a ten-day preliminary bombardment which broke down the elaborate drainage system in the area but had little effect upon the sophisticated German defences. A number of set-piece attacks were launched; some were successful, some were not. There was never at any stage any question of a breakthrough; 300,000 British casualties were accepted because it was thought that the Germans were suffering more grievously than their opponents.

By the beginning of autumn even the most optimistic generals were beginning to have their doubts about the efficacy of attrition. Charteris, Haig's over-confident intelligence officer, admitted to himself that 'the temptation to stop is so great', and at home Lloyd George was now determined to wrest control of the war out of the hands of the western front generals before they cost him the victory he wanted. Strategically the prime minister supported a 'Neo-Eastern' school which had revived the idea of defeating Germany by knocking the props away from beneath her, and was now concentrating on the relatively distant theatres of Italy and Palestine. Lloyd George's espousal of this strategy, which had the added bonus for him of tearing the Allied armies from the grasp of Haig and Robertson, was aided by the German transference of troops to Italy in November and the defeat which they then helped to inflict on the Italians at Caporetto. Politically the prime minister succeeded in splitting apart the Haig-Robertson axis, forcing Robertson's resignation and replacing him as his chief of the imperial general staff with the supple person of Sir Henry Wilson, thereby determining that strategic decisions were now taken in London. To make sure that no more men were squandered, Lloyd George retained some 300,000 troops in England and thereby placed the whole Allied front in some jeopardy the following spring.

Within Germany the effects of attrition were beginning to manifest themselves during the year 1917 as she faced the central problem of how to squeeze greater results from her economy when its structural weaknesses were beginning to become gravely acute, and without at the same time succumbing to the need to strike bargains with labour which would undercut the social objectives for which the conservative establishment was fighting. A transport crisis and a coal crisis together rocked the economy in the winter of 1916-17 and were only resolved by some drastic rationalization of production by Groener. In the first three months of the new year there were strikes in the Ruhr and at Berlin. On 7 April the kaiser announced that Prussia's three-tier suffrage would come to an end once the war was over, a gesture Ludendorff dismissed contemptuously as kotowing to the Russian Revolution. The need to admit that times had changed and that some form of partnership was essential between labour and employers, governors and governed, was underlined by major strikes which occurred nine days later in Berlin and Leipzig, strikes which started from economic grievances and ended with promises to cut the working week and raise wages, but which, in the course of their existence, rapidly picked up political objectives.

Ludendorff appreciated neither how far and how fast the state had moved since 1914 under the pressure to win its preventive war nor how much potential power he had in his hands to strengthen Germany's war effort if he were only prepared to make concessions. In fact his cast of mind was so rigidly conservative that he wished not only to halt the advance of the new social and economic forces within the state but to reverse it; in May 1917 he was looking forward to control of the economy by the army in peace-time, at least as far as preparations for economic mobilization went.

His answer to the problem of how to get more out of the mass of Germany's workers without giving them in return a real place in the running of affairs was to lay before them the prospect of spectacular territorial gains, by which Germany's future greatness would be assured. Fortunately a victim from whom such prizes might be torn lay to hand in the east. Accordingly at Kreuznach on 23 April 1917 the German high command formulated its war aims: Lithuania, parts of Livonia and Estonia, the Gulf of Riga, Poland, Rumania, Belgium as a vassal state, the Flanders coast, Briey-Longwy and a string of naval bases in the Atlantic and East Indian oceans and the Mediterranean and China Seas. The chancellor, Bethmann Hollweg, accepted these terms provided that Germany was in a position to dictate them when the time came, a somewhat lame reservation which failed to achieve any tactical objectives it may have had, but simply resulted in victory for the high command.

The last obstacle between Hindenburg and Ludendorff and complete control of Germany lay in the person of the chancellor, and on 13 July growing opposition to him from the Centre Party and others was mobilized to have him replaced as a result of a Reichstag vote by Dr Georg Michaelis, whose candidacy was put to Hindenburg for approval even before it was mentioned to the emperor himself. The dismissal of Groener on 16 August and the repossession of the Supreme War Office by the high command seemed to end any prospects of a rival springing up in the political field. In reality, however, although Hindenburg and Ludendorff were running the country, they exercised little real control over workers, government, press or Reichstag — in fact, by mobilizing the Reichstag majority against Bethmann Hollweg, they had strengthened it and not themselves. When, in October 1917, Michaelis committed political suicide by accusing the independent socialists of fomenting revolutionary activity in the navy he was pulled down by the Reichstag and replaced on 1 November by count von Hertling, the aged minister-president of Bavaria, without the army's being consulted. Parliamentary control was being exerted much more slowly in Germany than in France or Britain, but it was clearly apparent by the winter of 1917-18. Where Groener had bargained, Ludendorff, faced with the threat of a general strike in August and with trouble in the High Seas Fleet, could resort only to giving more power to the deputy commanding generals in order to repress dissent.

At this moment, when it was patently apparent that Ludendorff did not understand how a civilian and political machine worked, an avenue opened up by which to gain a peace so dazzling that it might dissolve political and social discontent. The day after their November revolution, the bolsheviks opened peace negotiations with Germany. The military situation improved dramatically with the Russian armistice, signed on 15 December, which offered the chance to transfer enough German manpower to the west to achieve victory there too, and the attitude of the high command grew tougher as they stuck to their Kreuznach programme. The German Foreign Office wanted to exploit bolshevik dominance to win a peace quickly, which meant moderating some of those demands, since they believed that such dominance might be only short-lived. The army however held resolutely to its goals and defeated the combined forces of emperor and Foreign Office, as well as the papacy which at this moment also suggested a peace formula, since Hindenburg and Ludendorff simply threatened to resign if they did not get their way. It looked as though they could now win the war, and as though any alternative leadership would probably lose it, and so they won their way. The peace of Brest-Litovsk (3 March 1918) gave Germany all that she had wanted in the east. It remained to see if she could achieve the same result in the west.

For France, too, 1917 was a year of great domestic strain, as the greatly increased number of strikes bore witness. She confronted two problems: the need to keep herself going and prevent her Russian ally from falling out of the war, when the position on the western front would become dangerous in the extreme. Under Ribot's premiership (20 March-7 September 1917) the central strategy adopted to maintain unity among the disparate elements of French political society and to contain pressures for France's withdrawal from the war was one of the public profession of limited war aims and the repudiation of any notion that a spirit of

conquest prevailed in official circles. Thus Ribot loudly
declaimed the government's intentions of establishing 'une
paix durable fondée sur le respect des droits et de la liberté
des peuples'.[11] To keep Russia in the fight Ribot abandoned
France's claims to the Saar and the right bank of the Rhine —
in line with the principle of 'peace without annexations'
which was now abroad — and stuck only to Alsace-Lorraine.
The question of guarantees for France against future
aggression was left open.

On 13 November 1917, after a brief reign by Painlevé,
Georges Clemenceau took over the office of premier. Both
his policies and his person exemplified France's intention of
winning the war first and then clearing up the political and
social problems which might emerge. The new prime minister
rapidly abandoned the war aims of the powerful French
colonial party, apparently without prior consultation with
them, and signalled in unmistakable terms that his twin
objectives were to win the war and to avoid getting committed by the Allies to a plebiscite over the return of Alsace-
Lorraine. One of Clemenceau's central concerns was to
achieve greater efficiency in waging war by raising the level of
inter-Allied co-operation: what he really wanted was a unified Allied command under marshal Foch, but he wanted
someone else to ask for it. Ludendorff resolved the problem
for him: when his great offensive was launched in March
1918, Lloyd George suggested exactly what Clemenceau
sought. A second major problem related to the apparent
laxity of political life and the absence of leadership by
example at home. In the aftermath of the mutinies Painlevé
had charged that they were the result of military errors and
Pétain had answered that the central explanation was the
laxity of control over the home front. In this respect too, the
winter of 1917-18 saw great improvements as Clemenceau
imparted a drive and a clear sense of purpose to France's
war effort; the symbol of this change was the appearance in
dock in November of the former minister of the interior,
Malvy, on a charge of treason arising from the accusation that
he had been giving information to the enemy. Behind this
front of public toughness, however, the president showed
private political suppleness; thus in his dealings with the

syndicalists he was harsh in parliament but conciliatory in private.

For Britain the central experience which conditioned the reactions of the home front to the war during 1917 was the campaign of unrestricted submarine warfare which had begun on 1 February. A number of factors which had not existed during the brief campaign of 1915 now augured well for Germany's second attempt to strangle the British war effort. There were now 111 submarines available for active operations, far more than previously, and there seemed at the same time to be no answer to them; an assortment of destroyers, armed merchantmen, Q-boats (gunships disguised as commercial vessels) and others had sunk a total of only nineteen submarines during the course of the previous year. Furthermore the vagaries of climate and agriculture combined to enhance the Central Powers' chances of success. In 1916 both America and Canada had experienced poor grain harvests, which meant that in the coming year more wheat would have to be imported along the exposed sea-lanes from Australia. The economic solution was to grow more cereals at home, a policy introduced by Lloyd George in February 1917 and embodied in the Corn Production Act the following April. The only strategic solution which Jellicoe, the new first sea lord, could offer in this dismal situation was to increase the number of craft hunting the submarines, a move which had little effect.

By April the food shortage was so severe that the government was forced to ration supplies of meat, bacon, butter, margarine, lard and sugar partially in order to conceal the inroads that German U-boats were making on British stocks of food and partially as a psychological act to restore confidence in itself. It did not, of course, increase the amount of food available at all. Two months earlier the eminent author Arnold Bennett had determined upon his response to the widespread conditions of shortage and had taken to asking guests he had invited to dinner to bring their own food with them. By the summer widespread strikes were signalling the reactions of the workforce to the prospect of a fourth year of war, and one which promised to be much harsher than those preceding it. Miners, cotton spinners, railwaymen and the metropolitan police all struck, and a general strike of midlands engineers was only averted by a government threat to conscript them all. By now, however, the response to the submarine had already been devised — or rather, re-discovered, in what in Tudor times had been termed 'wafting'. Lloyd George claimed in his memoirs to have instituted the system of convoying on 30 April 1917; in fact the convoy had been resuscitated by the energetic Sir Maurice Hankey nine days earlier and the Admiralty had formally approved an experimental convoy three days before the prime minister's 'decisive' intervention. It sailed from Gibraltar on 10 May, lost no ships *en route*, and proved what professional sailors had persistently doubted, that merchantmen could keep in station and not wander away from the convoy.

In August convoying was applied to outward as well as homeward runs and the number of sinkings began to fall. U-boat losses were still lower than the volume of new submarines being launched, but Germany was losing one element she could not replace — experienced crews and commanders. However, the war at sea proved long and costly and the technical turning point, when the tonnage of new shipping launched for the first time exceeded the amount sunk, came as late as July 1918. At that point, when the war had only four months more to run, its conclusion was still a distant vision for many in the Allied camp; on 19 July 1918 Hankey recorded in his diary 'So long as we can maintain our general command of the sea; so long as we can build ships as fast as we lose them, I for one will remain confident of ultimate victory.'[12] Even at that late stage in the war, however, it seemed as though Britain had only succeeded in staving off defeat and that she yet had to find a means of converting survival into victory.

At the beginning of 1918 the Allies still had no clear idea of how to win the war. The Germans were in what appeared a more favourable position: although they had failed to inflict an overwhelming defeat upon their opponents they did have a plan to force a peace on favourable terms. No longer fully engaged on two fronts, the high command calculated that it could transfer enough manpower to the western front to achieve a 10 per cent superiority there, win a victory, and shock the British and French into accepting terms. The *Friedenstoss* ('rush to peace') of March 1918 was designed to finish off French resistance and to persuade the Allies that Germany had sufficient material and moral resources to continue the struggle for years if necessary. Ludendorff's offensive scored a brilliant tactical success and rapidly brought about the total collapse of one British army, thanks to a well-developed technique of deep penetration and inferior staff work and defensive tactics on the part of his opponents. Victories followed against the French in April and May but, despite first appearances, they were essentially inconclusive. After her last reserves had been thrown in and her tactics discovered, Germany was powerless to resist determined counter-pressure. Paradoxically her very success told against her, for she succeeded in bringing about what four years of war had failed to impose: a supreme command was forced on the Allies, and vested in Foch.

Greater co-ordination, superior resources, the entry into the fray of fresh American troops and the weakness of the opponent all counted in favour of the Allies now, and in July British tanks began to open up the front. The following month they took the offensive, meeting with considerable initial success and demonstrating that, once freed from the cloying embrace of the trenches and able to conduct the type of war for which they had prepared before 1914, Allied generals were no worse than any others. However, it was still far from clear that the war would end with the total collapse of the Central Powers; the only thing which could be said with confidence was that it would not now end with the total collapse of the Allies.

Germany had committed everything to her March offensive, for many believed that anything less than complete victory would spell the end of the imperial system. As early as May 1916 Wolfgang Kapp of the Pan-German league had first begun to speak of 'the democratic swamp into which we should be drawn undoubtedly after a luke-warm peace', and events on the home front during the following year seemed to bear that out.[13] Ludendorff added another face to the prism through which the German conservatives viewed the outcome of the war: he believed that a peace which did no more than guarantee the *status quo* would mean that Germany had lost since she would be in a less advantageous military position after such a war than she had been before it. For Germany, the alternative to victory could scarcely be contemplated.

Enormous gains in the east buoyed up hopes that the western front too would be the scene of success. Two days after the signing of Brest-Litovsk Rumania followed Russia's example and capitulated to Germany by signing the Treaty of Bucharest. Finland came under German control, the Ukraine followed soon after and by the summer moves were being made to acquire Georgia too. In this atmosphere of success a conference at Spa on 26 June concluded that military victory was within Germany's grasp and, as if to assuage the fears of Kapp and others, the Prussian Franchise Bill passed into law on 4 July in such an attenuated form as to defeat the notion of equal suffrage it was supposed to enshrine. Eleven days later, amid high hopes, Germany launched her Rheims offensive.

Less sanguine members of the German high command were already preparing their justifications for failure. There was some concern in July about Ludendorff's mental condition, which created alarm lest he lose his grip on the situation, and his aide colonel Bauer was now beginning to talk about the likelihood of success 'if the homeland no longer stabs the army in the back'. There was only the slenderest of foundations for such a contention, and morale on the home front had remained good until the end of the previous month and declined only as a result of military set-backs at a time when food supplies were improving. Those set-backs commenced with a major Allied breakthrough on 8 August, after which Ludendorff suffered some kind of nervous collapse. Even at this hour, however, all was not regarded as lost — although it must be said that from this moment German calculations took on an air of unreality. At a second conference at Spa on 14 August no change or modification in Germany's war aims was proposed, and Ludendorff suggested basing future German strategy on paralysing the enemy's will to fight by conducting a strategic defensive.

By mid-September Germany's slender hopes had

disintegrated: Bulgaria had collapsed, as had Turkey under the pressure of Allenby's brilliant campaign, and on the fifteenth the proverbial bolt from the blue came with the news of the Austrian peace note. Germany was now alone. By the twenty-eighth both Hindenburg and Ludendorff had been brought to accept the necessity for an immediate armistice, though they intended to use it not as a vehicle for peace but as a respite during which they could gather Germany's strength for a resumption of the war. To get this temporary respite Ludendorff was prepared to admit the Social Democrats into the government and thus have the odium of a peace fall upon them as well as upon the parties of the right. He and Hindenburg also appear to have believed that even if Germany could not win the war in any military sense she could still hold out against the *entente* and avoid losing it. The invitation to the left was a shrewd move which would avoid revolution from below and democratic reform from above, and which might later permit the army to swing once again into the political saddle.

On 29 September Hindenburg and Ludendorff approached the kaiser with their request for an armistice and an early peace. Wilhelm II responded somewhat pathetically. 'The war has ended,' he remarked, 'quite differently, indeed, from how we expected', but he hurriedly made it clear that he laid the blame at the door not of the soldiers but of the civilians: 'our politicians have failed us miserably'.[14] All did not go according to Ludendorff's design however. The new liberal chancellor, prince Max of Baden, and his deputy stood firm against any continuation of the war and headed off the attempts of the paladins of the high command to block peace negotiations by such means as refusing to end the submarine blockade — an essential prerequisite for negotiations. Ludendorff, prophesying bitterly that within a few weeks the army would succumb to bolshevism in its ranks, offered his resignation and it was accepted. Hindenburg's was not, and the massive partnership was at last broken. The army made one last sacrifice: it refused to follow the kaiser in a final glorious crusade against bolshevism, and instead general Groener was sent to inform the war-lord that his departure too was felt necessary if peace was to be attained. The terms devised by Foch to ensure that Germany, once having agreed to cease fighting, could not again restore herself to such an extent as to be capable of renewing the struggle were accepted, and the war ended on 11 November 1918.

The First World War cut down a grievously large number of Europe's young men, and many who were not so young. Six million Britons served in the armed forces, of whom one in eight were killed, a rate of loss slightly higher than those of Germany and Austria, comparable with Italy and less than France, where one in six Frenchmen who served died. In the east the figures were harsher still: Rumania lost one in three of her soldiers, Serbia two in five. But though the absolute losses were great, the effects of the proportional losses suffered by the different classes in each society were probably of more long-term significance. In Britain the social elite suffered proportionately heavier losses than any other group — through the pattern of officer recruitment and mortality — while the industrial working classes suffered less directly because, with the exception of the miners, they were physically less fit for combat than men in commercial or clerical employment. Similar patterns of disequilibrium seem to have occurred elsewhere: the figures for one French department indicate sharp class differentiation, with the upper classes suffering 5 per cent of the losses, artisans 16 per cent, salary earners 20 per cent and peasants 33 per cent. In Italy the active army absorbed three-fourths of all the soldiers but less than half the available officers; at the front there was one officer for every twenty-six soldiers whilst behind the lines there was one officer for every seven men. Whether the Italian peasant paid a heavier price than the Italian worker is still the subject of some debate, although the most recent authority is in no doubt:[15]

> the sacrifice of blood imposed upon the workers was even more heavy in percentage terms than that — already harsh — of the peasants, above all because the other social groups succeeded in finding a way of spilling very much less blood for the war which they had wanted and from which they would have derived all merit and advantage.

The war swept away the empires of Germany, Austria-Hungary and Russia, replacing them with two republics and the first communist state. The absolute cost of it helped to change patterns of diplomacy, replacing secret treaties and alliances with 'open diplomacy' and the League of Nations, and deeply affected men's attitudes to the place of war in international life and towards the measures which the state might legitimately take for its own defence, now that the price demanded by Mars was seen to be so great. It produced such profound changes in every aspect of European society that the last word upon it is perhaps best left to Thucydides: 'if one looks at the facts themselves, one will see that this was the greatest war of all.'

7
Expanded horizons

---◀◀◀◀◀◀◀◆▶▶▶▶▶▶▶---

Before 1914 states had ordered their military arrangements chiefly by legislation which conformed to the general and fundamental proposition that mass armies were of considerable military utility, and which also aimed at engineering patriotic nationalism and thereby fending off the challenge of socialism. Democracies and autocracies alike found that mass conscription served their sometimes different purposes, and served them well. This situation did not survive the First World War. The autocracies disappeared, whilst the democracies themselves were profoundly altered as a result of their exposure to the hideous realities of mass warfare waged with all the support which modern industrial systems could provide. A general reaction against the gross waste of life and of resources which had characterized the war was both echoed in and stimulated by much of post-war European literature and led to an emotional revulsion against war and a common inability to perceive a future combat. In the Europe that emerged from the war, military organization and defence policy had to be reconciled with the domestic situations and political priorities of states whose ideologies now differed widely, which allotted different amounts of significance to different factors in designing policy, and which differed even over the fundamental question of what was to be learned from the experience each had so recently undergone.

EXPANDED HORIZONS

A central problem for all Europe's soldiers was that no one could agree on what had caused Germany to collapse in 1918, thereby ending the war. One school of thought attributed allied success to the effects of a combination of attrition and blockade, and as a result Britain and France especially came to conceive of economic strength as being the crucial factor in modern war, ordering their military policies on the basis of the belief that victory would be the product of the effective mobilization of the nation's material resources, a process which would require time above all else. Others deemed the collapse of Germany's allies to have been the decisive factor, whilst yet a third group pointed to the technical developments which had begun to exercise a real influence on the battlefield during 1918 and which would, they believed, transform war by breaking the deadlock imposed by the power of defensive weapons. The aeroplane and the tank were to exercise a strong influence over the minds of civilians and military alike during the next two decades, and a variety of considerations – not always simply technical – were to shape each country's response to them, but experience could not serve as a guide for there was little to go on; Britain's independent air force had dropped less than 600 tons of bombs by the time that the war ended, providing no proof either way of the effectiveness of strategic air power. Faced with this new technology, the potential and the limitations of which remained alike problematical, the general reaction of Europe's soldiers to the prospect of another war was one of acute caution. As general Hans von Seeckt remarked in his memoirs, 'The experienced and knowing soldier fears war far more than the fantasizer can who, not knowing war, speaks only of peace.'[1]

Out of the debates which ensued on purely technical considerations there emerged two schools of thought. One held that modern war was a conflict of economic strength, that defence was the safest strategy, and that offensives should be contemplated only with gigantic numbers of men and after considerable preparation. The other school asserted that the deadlock on the battlefield could and must be broken, and that imaginative use of the new weapons could achieve this. The two doctrines were not simply the product

182

of military considerations, however, but reflected also the social and political environments in which each was propounded. Thus although its leading theoretical exponents were to be found in the western democracies, the school of the offensive gained a firmer hold in Germany and in Russia, states which were prepared to allow political imperatives to play a much greater role in determining their attitudes to war than the more prosaic considerations of orthodox economics and the pursuit of political and social stability which governed the actions of Britain and France. The elite theories of war organization, propounded by men such as Fuller, de Gaulle and Culmann, which laid heavy emphasis upon the tank and the aeroplane, and which rejected the doctrine of mass that had ruled Europe since Sedan on the grounds that it led only to wasteful defensive warfare, were attractive to the totalitarian regimes of inter-war Europe not only because they appeared to meet the diplomatic situations in which they found themselves but also because they conformed with many of the tenets which lay at the heart of the totalitarian vision of the ordering of society and state. The democracies too resolved the problems of military organization and defence policy within the limits imposed by their own liberal-democratic ideologies. Thus where attitudes towards war had been broadly similar in Europe before 1914, they were in the years between the two world wars profoundly different.

The problem of reconciling ideology and military organization first appeared in Russia after the bolshevik revolution in October 1917, and was to remain one of the most awkward problems facing the Soviet regime for the next two decades. The problem at this stage was brutally simple. The European left had always disclaimed and mistrusted professional standing armies as both reactionary and potentially counter-revolutionary, and had preferred to advocate a militia system incorporating a minimal period of military training for the mass of the people and a small, and therefore politically insignificant, core of regular troops. However, the advances made in weapon technology during the second decade of the twentieth century had been such that the exercise of force was now clearly a specialist function, a concept which bore the endorsement of theory since Engels himself had pointed out that, to be defended, the revolution must have an army. Thus in 1917 Lenin and Trotsky were faced with the dilemma of sticking to the old ideas on military organization and probably being destroyed by their White Russian opponents, or setting up a more professional army which was at the same time potentially counter-revolutionary. The problem was resolved when, on 29 January 1918, Lenin brought into existence the Workers and Peasants Red Army, a force which had as its nucleus the 'Red Guards', units raised from among the workers as spearheads of the Revolution and designed to seize and hold the factories, and which also gathered to itself local peasant guerrilla forces which were rapidly repelled by the conservatism and incompetence of the White Russians. However, the core of the army which Leon Trotsky welded together as first commissar for war was to be found in the ex-Tsarist officers, or *voenspets*, whose military expertise was essential if the Revolution was to survive at all. By a mixture of appeals to their patriotism and sheer blackmail Trotsky recruited a large number of such officers, among whom perhaps the best known was Svechin, who provided the leadership without which the conscripts also being raised would have been of small value.

Though undoubtedly justified in military terms, Trotsky's decision to compromise with left-wing ideology to the extent of using the *voenspets* aroused considerable hostility in some sections of the bolshevik party and by March 1919 a 'military opposition' had emerged, centred around the person of Chicherin, which charged Trotsky with creating a 'Red Army of state capitalism'. With the war against the Whites not yet won Lenin was not prepared to allow an open-day for ideological struggles; he therefore denied the charges of the Chicherin group, and the Red Army was formally deemed 'transitional'. The pressure to conform to the dictates of ideology and convert the army into a militia continued however, and Trotsky bowed before it in April 1920 to the extent of proposing a 'Worker-Peasant Red Militia' which was designed to create a mass of worker-soldiers who would be diverted only briefly from productive labour and who would serve to spread party control on their return from the army.

The outbreak of the Russo-Polish war in August 1920 revealed the dangers which might confront Soviet Russia if she chose to rely on a militia army which would not be capable of responding rapidly to external threats, and in any case the bolsheviks' hold over the Russian countryside was still so tenuous as to make the creation of such a militia unwise, if not impossible.

By the end of 1920 the Poles had been repelled and the Russians in their turn checked at the very gates of Warsaw by a determined Polish effort which owed its success to the military capacity of Pilsudski and the organizational feats of Sosnkowski, and the immediate threats to the continued existence of the communist regime in Russia, both internal and external, had been checked. By now the army had swollen to some 5,500,000 men, a burden the state could support no longer than was strictly necessary, and there was now a pressing need to demobilize the bulk of it in order to begin the considerable tasks of economic and social reconstruction facing Russia after six years of world and civil war. There was also the same central problem to be faced all over again; what sort of military structure could Soviet Russia adopt which would best meet both her security needs and the dictates of ideology? Here a fundamental contradiction already existed in Soviet military policy, for a centralized machine, comprising especially the All Russian Supreme Staff and the Revolutionary Military Committee, had already been set up; thus 'while the machinery most vitally needed for the operation of a powerful standing army was strengthened and amplified ... the very idea of a standing army, or even an orthodox military force, was still an open question and one liable to be opened still wider.'[2]

There were by 1920 a number of seemingly irreconcileable positions occupied by the leading political and military figures in the matter of Russia's military structure. They ranged from Trotsky's support for a territorial militia, by way of Voroshilov and Budenny who wanted a short-service mass army best capable of aiding revolution wherever it broke out, to Tukhachevsky, who termed the militia 'the crucifixion of Soviet Russia' and who wanted a strong, long-service regular army which could create a revolutionary situation by attacking capitalist powers. To complicate the matter even further, a major theoretical contribution to the debate was made by Frunze in July 1921 when he put forward the concept of the 'Unified Military Doctrine'. This was founded on the belief that military doctrine could not be invented but was the product of material conditions before all else, and that the class structure of the state and the level of development of its productive forces were the vital factors which determined how a state resolved its military problems. Funze was in effect saying that there was a specifically marxist military science, and a form of war which was both proletarian and revolutionary. In support of this contention he could call upon no lesser person than Engels, who had remarked that 'the emancipation of the proletariat . . . will have its special expression in military affairs and will create its special, new military methods.'[3] What this meant to Frunze in practice was a part-regular, part-territorial army committed to offensive warfare and a strategy of manoeuvre.

Frunze's ideas attracted the full measure of Trotsky's scorn at the XIth Party Congress in 1922, when he ridiculed the notion of inevitable clashes between the proletarian state and the capitalist world as both wrong and dangerous and suggested that founding an offensive strategy on the supposed lessons of the civil war was absurd. Lenin remarked consolingly to Frunze that he thought that in any case communism was as yet too immature to sustain such a doctrine, and he also had to reconcile future Soviet military organization with the New Economic Policy which was one of introspection and retrenchment. So the reforms of 1924 created a compromise force which was to last a decade and which comprised a large territorial army of forty-two divisions in which the conscript served for two years, alongside a twenty-nine division regular army in which service was for five years. Either could dominate, but events were to determine that it would be the militia group and the 'political' view, not the regular 'professional' one. The lack of any pressing international threat to the survival of the USSR after 1924, together with the need to use the army to indoctrinate the mass of the people in order to ensure the survival of the revolution

within Russia, helped to bring this result about. The dominance of political considerations was clearly in evidence in the
decision taken by the XIIIth Party Congress in 1924 that
commissars were to be attached to all officers save commanders of outstanding military merit, such as Timoshenko,
to watch the officers and also to ensure that their orders
were obeyed by the troops. The emerging political group
captured the military machine under the guise of reform,
reinforced by the findings of a personnel commission that in
its present form the Red Army was unfit for combat, and
dominated it for the next five years. Though Voroshilov as
commissar for military and naval affairs personified this
period his short-lived predecessor, Frunze, coined the phrase
which was to be the watchword of military organization and
policy until rising military dangers in both the east and the
west dictated a revaluation of priorities: 'make way for the
Red Commanders'.

Russia was by no means alone in permitting her military
affairs to become subject to the dictates of a prevalent ideology in the decade after the end of the First World War.
Both Britain and France reacted to political considerations
which, though less immediately obvious, were none the less
profound. Scarcely had the war ended than Britain reverted
from being a power with primarily European interests, which
she had been for four years, to being once again an imperial
power. There was every reason for her to do so. With her
empire now at its largest extent, and with the troops garrisoning India, Persia, Palestine, Mesopotamia, Egypt, European
Turkey and Ireland as well as making up the army of occupation in Germany, imperial considerations impinged upon
Britain at every turn. Moreover, the problems with which
Britain had to deal in her empire were different from those
of the pre-war era in one critical respect: they were now
predominantly internal threats within different parts of the
empire, and as such not receptive to the action of the traditional British palliative, the Royal Navy. What the empire
required in the 1920s was policing, not protecting; this was
to prove a powerful consideration in determining Britain's
choice of military organization during the first decade after
the war.

The imperial orientation in British policy was reinforced by the attitude of the dominions themselves, for they soon signalled in unmistakable terms that the notions of dominion co-operation which had underlain British defence policy immediately prior to the world war no longer held good. Dominion reluctance to become involved in European affairs was made quite plain at the Imperial Conference in 1921, and Canadian hostility to the notion of renewing the Anglo-Japanese alliance that same year forced Whitehall to reverse one of its fundamental defence policies and allow the treaty, and the relationship, to lapse.

If imperialism was one of the dominant strains in British policy, economy was the other. Defence expenditure for the year 1919-20 amounted to the enormous figure of £604,000,000, and a large proportion of that unsustainable figure was taken up with paying the cost of ground troops in the empire, Iraq alone requiring £18,350,000. In the depression which quickly followed the end of the war, the economic theory of the day could offer no other alternative but to reduce costs in line with shrinking revenue. Thus the burden of the Geddes report of December 1921 was that there must be swingeing cuts in all branches of public expenditure, of which the services must bear their share: the army was called upon to prune £20,000,000 off its estimates, the navy to effect a £21,000,000 reduction. Looking beyond the immediate future, a much reduced defence budget was to be a feature of British expenditure for some time to come.

On the face of it the two essential components of Britain's position — imperialism and economy — seemed irrevocably at odds. No British politician seriously considered extending conscription into peace-time, though it was assumed that compulsory service would be introduced if a future major war broke out, so that cheap manpower did not offer a way out of the dilemma. As it happened, an instrument was fortuitously to hand which would enable Britain to conform to both parts of her ideology at the same time, and thereby save money whilst not being forced to relinquish one metre of her imperial possessions. The instrument by means of which this apparently impossible feat was achieved was the aeroplane. Attractive because it was cheap, air-power soon demonstrated that it was also effective when, in February 1921, it put paid to the perambulations of the Mad Mullah of Somaliland. Striving to maintain its independent existence, the Royal Air Force pressed its claim on the basis of cost and won the tender. By 1930 it had reduced the charge of policing Iraq to only £650,000 a year, and in the first thirteen years of imperial policing it suffered a total of only twenty-six casualties. Cheap in every way, the aeroplane allowed Britain to play the role of a great imperial power for another two decades.

In the mind of the British public engagement in Europe, mass conscript armies and the bloodletting of the Somme and Passchendaele were inextricably linked, so that an attitude grew up which was best encapsulated in the phrase of the times — 'never again'. However, the British public had in truth little reason to fear that their leaders would force upon them the direct demands which a military organization geared to a 'Europe First' policy would dictate, and shift from planes and ships to conscripts, for defence considerations played no great role in Britain's European policies. In so far as a threat seemed to exist in Europe, it lay in the French air force, which by 1923 had some 3,000 planes, but here the answer was to be found in building a bomber force which offered a (relatively) cheap deterrent. The one act which did dictate the need for a land-orientated military organization capable of operating in Europe was the guarantee Britain gave to France's frontier with Germany by the Treaty of Locarno in 1925. In proposing the Locarno pact Austen Chamberlain, the foreign secretary, totally ignored all military conditions and though as a consequence of the pact Britain's frontier effectively became the Rhine, she possessed then and for some time thereafter neither plans and instructions upon which to act in the event of a violation of the pact nor the forces with which to oppose such a violation.

Throughout the 1920s, and for most of the subsequent decade, the army was Britain's 'Cinderella service'. Within the context of a world view composed in equal measure of imperialism and economy, this was necessarily so. Ships and planes together could provide all the force which imperial diplomacy might require, as the Imperial Defence Review of

189

1928 demonstrated when it listed the army's priorities as the defence of ports abroad, Indian garrisons, local security in the Empire and areas of special interest such as the Sudan and China, anti-aircraft defence, garrisoning UK ports, internal security and, finally, the provision of an overseas expeditionary force. The direction being imparted to British military organization and policy by economy and by imperialism, and the retreat from Europe, was perfectly reflected in Liddell Hart's *The Decisive Wars of History* (1929), all of which he proved to have been determined by the 'Indirect Approach' and not by the meeting of major land forces in decisive combat. Britain shrank from mobilizing more than the smallest amount of her human and material resources, and took comfort in assurances proffered by Liddell Hart that her way in warfare was the best way.

A power such as France which nursed vital interests in Europe at the same time as she guarded a widespread overseas empire might seem on the face of things to have little in common with England in the ordering of her military affairs, and yet similar forces were at work to determine her policies, forces which were generated by her own special brand of liberal ideology and which were frequently in evidence. Conscription could never be removed from French public life, but social pressures wrought very considerable changes upon it, while financial pressures and imperial considerations also played their part in the balance which Frenchmen sought to achieve between the need to guarantee French security and the need to conform to pressing political and social imperatives. For a variety of reasons France's European posture soon became a defensive one, and her military organization followed suit — an arrangement which was all the more acceptable since it seemed to conform perfectly with the lessons France had learned since the First World War.

The French nation-in-arms had gone to war in 1914 in the grip of the doctrine of the offensive. By 1916 she was confronted with the complete failure of that doctrine, and Verdun became the symbol of the efficacy of a carefully-controlled and well-handled defensive engagement. Nivelle's offensive on the Aisne, and the mutinies which followed, contributed to the growing conviction in the mind of France that the 'French way in warfare' must change so that dogma accommodated itself to the facts of technology. In reaching this view the inescapable facts of French demography played a part; the immense casualties sustained during the war, the population pyramid which had long ceased to be a pyramid, and an obsession with the birth-rate during the years of low adult population in the 1920s and 1930s were all instrumental in helping to create the collective mentality on military organization. Thus France emerged from the First World War with a new image of the republican soldier — Pétain, not Foch, conformed best to what Frenchmen wanted of their future military leaders — and a new model of 'republican war': cautious, defensive, costive as regards manpower. Sarrail, the general whose political credentials left-wing republicans found most satisfying, emerged from the war a firm believer in the powers of the defence and a disbeliever in the efficacy of tanks and aeroplanes, while Pétain, who symbolized the conversion of republican military ideals, continued to exercise a very strong influence in military affairs until 1936. By his handling of the Riff War in 1924, Pétain showed that his principles were apparently universal in their applicability; abandoning the flying columns begun by Bugeaud almost a century earlier, he joined with the Spanish to encircle the Riffs and defeat them by means of advances which were slower but more effective, and which halved the casualty rates among French troops.

From the end of the First World War until 1935 the stock ideas of the left dominated the French Chamber of Deputies with regard to military organization, and with them the desire to reduce the term of service for French conscripts. In December 1921 it was reduced from three years to two, and in April 1923 reduced again to a period of only eighteen months. This reduction was justified by a number of considerations which had priority in French society during the inter-war years, not the least of which was the financial question. The franc had begun its steady slide in value as early as 1919, and the French pinned their hopes on extorting a full measure of reparations from defeated Germany in order to shore up what was a deteriorating financial situation. As long as she was committed to the notion that reparations must be enforced at all costs, and as long as she felt that her wartime allies would support her in this stance, France was prepared to maintain a form of military organization which would allow her to act in a coercive role if necessary. But by 1923 it was becoming apparent that neither of these two articles of faith now held good, and the eighteen-month law reflected a decline in France's commitment to enforcing reparations at all costs. The enactment of the Dawes Plan, which provided Germany with a measure of international financial support, in the following year demonstrated that France's political leaders had calculated correctly and that the international community did not regard reparations as inviolable. There was, therefore, no need for a military force capable of safeguarding them — and therefore no need for anything other than a short-term army. 'You tell us on the one hand: an army is necessary', remarked the communist deputy Renaud Jean during the course of the debate. 'On the other hand, you say you are renouncing offensive war-fare. Thus you don't want any more victories. Consequently you are building your army to prevent defeat.'[4]

The curtailing of the term of military service reflected also the growing power of the political left in the life of the Third Republic, a growth which produced their electoral victory in 1924 and increasing pressure from the radicals and socialists led by Daladier and Renaudel to reduce conscription to a one year term. In part this was dictated by the political ideology of the left and their determination to signal in unmistakable terms that France was no longer in the grip of imperialist, aggressive aims by creating what was patently only a defensive force; in part it was a response to a further collapse of the franc and to the need for financial retrench-ment. It also corresponded to the left's answer to another of the republic's problems — how best to ensure and maintain her diplomatic position in Europe. Whereas the right pre-ferred to base its diplomacy on a measure of demonstrable military force, the left was prepared to rely to a large extent on the League of Nations and international organization to preserve France inviolate: the symbol and instrument of this reliance was her signing of the Treaty of Locarno in October 1925, by the terms of which she, Belgium and Germany accepted their frontiers and the demilitarization of the Rhineland as inviolable, and Britain and Italy guaranteed military assistance in the event of armed aggression across this frontier. Treaties between France on the one hand and Poland and Czechoslovakia on the other promising mutual military assistance in the event of attack — the so-called 'Little Entente' — completed France's exchange of military for diplomatic defence.

Such moves would not have been possible without a considerable degree of unanimity on France's military posture, and most people, no matter what their political complexion, believed that the Great War had demonstrated that the nation-in-arms 'avait fait ses preuves'. Men and *matériel* were the instruments of victory, but the latter would take some considerable time to provide — there was a delay of twelve to eighteen months between the ordering and delivery of war goods — so that France's first requirement was to provide herself with the means to resist attack during the early stages of a war while she was equipping herself for decisive action later on. As early as 1921 both Pétain and Joffre proposed that the *couverture* which this policy rendered necessary should be provided by permanent fortifications, although they differed over the question of whether those fortifications should be constructed in the form of a single continuous front or a series of fortified regions. In 1925 a Commission for Frontier Defence was established to determine the question, and by this time the value of fortifications was so strongly embedded in French military thought that the young De Gaulle even wrote a study favouring them. The commission produced its recommendations in 1927, and directives were issued the following year to begin construction of what was to become known as the Maginot Line.

The Maginot Line was the physical expression of France's defence requirements at the end of the first post-war decade. It signalled a return to the traditions of Vauban. It expressed France's abandonment of the doctrine of offensive war for the new, defensive form of republican war which would be less prodigal of French lives. It confirmed France's diplomatic posture in Europe. And it provided the means by which France could convert the short-term army which political and social considerations demanded into the highly trained force which modern war would require: behind her impregnable barrier France would spend the early months of any future war amassing heavy equipment and training her conscripts for the business of war, and when these twin processes were completed she would sally forth to victory. That, at any rate, was the theory. Its existence permitted the army, in January 1928, to accept a further reduction in the term of conscription to twelve months, in conformity with the political pressure of the left, although now it had learned enough to insist on terms of its own – an annual intake of 240,000 and a regular core of 106,000, neither of which could be legally varied in size.

Although France's organization for war in the 1920s perfectly met her domestic political and social requirements and conformed to her diplomatic posture, this was only cause for brief satisfaction, for the next decade would bring changes in almost every element which had determined the system of the post-war years. Calculations about the efficacy of defensive weapons were about to be challenged, at the same time as France's international position weakened with the break-up of the system of interdependence which had characterized the conduct of European diplomacy in the 1920s. The very army itself, which had taken on a distinctly lower middle-class tone after 1920 when most of the nobility remaining in it had resigned, was composed of precisely those groups which felt most keenly the rising taxation and falling rents that marked the progress of the domestic economy for most Frenchmen. The wives, and even some of the officers themselves, were forced to take a second job to make ends meet. Poorly paid, so top-heavy that there was little chance of promotion and suffering from too many foreign tours, the officer corps showed all the symptoms of a growing crisis of morale. Painlévé complained querulously in 1926 'The army is at present the prey of a deep uneasiness. Its cadres are dispirited and look for an opportunity to leave the service. The young turn away from our military schools.'[5] Doubts about the army's capacity extended beyond such subjective impressions; after the 1928 law, France relied for her defence at any time upon half the regular contingent and half the annual class of conscripts — a total of some 150,000 men, the better part of whom had had only six months' military training. In order to mobilize the whole annual contingent, Pétain counted on being given diplomatic warning of an impending crisis — an example of the degree to which French military organization depended upon, rather than supported, French diplomacy. The withdrawal of her occupation troops from Germany in 1929 emphasized the difficulties France was beginning to find herself in; to function properly, her military organization depended upon advance warning and yet now, with the Maginot Line barely begun, she faced what she saw as a mounting likelihood of attack, with no warning and no real barrier, from what appeared to be one of the most modern and proficient of European armies — the *Reichswehr*.

The army which in 1929 appeared to pose such a grave threat to France had only eleven years earlier been close enough to revolution for its leaders to determine that politics should be removed from its field of consciousness and that professionalism should become its central and abiding concern. At the war's end there were fears that the military would follow the sailors into revolution, and the Hamburg Points of December 1918 — which called for the abolition of saluting, the election of officers and the institution of soldiers' councils — were an alarming echo of the Provisional Government's Order Number 1 in Russia the previous year. Retention of the power of command was the central priority of the army leadership, a requirement which was all the more necessary now that the kaiser, traditional source of authority and focus of obedience for the army, was no longer the ruler of Germany. General Wilhelm Groener layed down the bases for the immediate rebuilding of the army on 22 March 1919: 'The High Command is of the following opinion: 1. Politics do not exist in the army. 2. Soldiers' councils which do not toe the line have to be eliminated.'[6] The die was soon cast, its two faces 'obedience' and 'efficiency' and its objective corporate self-preservation.

The task of remaking the German army under the rule of the Weimar Republic fell in 1920 to general Hans von Seeckt as a result of the Kapp *putsch* that same year. The *putsch*, caused by general Luttwitz's refusal to follow von Seeckt's recommendation and dissolve the Ehrhardt brigade — one of the best known of the notorious 'Free Corps' whose presence in Germany in the years immediately following the end of the First World War had contributed to the lack of a strong central authority — threatened to break the new army almost before it had come into existence, should the soldiers who supported the new government be called on to fire on those who did not. Declining either to fight for the government or to take orders from the Kapp regime, von Seeckt shrewdly took leave of absence. Only Noske, the minister of war, and Reinhardt, the chief of the army command, were prepared to fight the putschists. On 17 March what amounted to a plebiscite of the officer corps chose Seeckt to replace Luttwitz as head of the army; Noske resigned, to be replaced by the more pliant figure of Dr Otto Gessler, and von Seeckt was appointed to replace Reinhardt as *de facto* head of the army. The civilian government, dependent upon a bargain with the army to support its political authority, had allowed what in retrospect appears a fatal latitude to the military; it had permitted them to establish the principle that they obeyed the legitimate government only within limits determined by themselves, and by doing so to take the first of what was to be a series of political steps. From this time onwards the leaders of the *Reichswehr* applied to their subordinates the principle that the army did not engage in politics, whilst always excepting themselves from it.

Under the terms of the treaty of Versailles, Germany's army was limited to a maximum size of 100,000 men. To accommodate this shrinkage three-quarters of the old imperial officer corps had to be dismissed, and von Seeckt took the opportunity to create from the remainder a social and intellectual elite. Educational requirements for officers were raised to the levels they had been under Scharnhorst a century before, and those required of rankers were correspondingly high. At the same time von Seeckt took care to ensure that no democratization of the officer corps took place: the bulk of the officers were from the old regular or reserve armies, and throughout the Weimar period 95 per cent of officer candidates were drawn from the same social areas as before 1914. The social profile which resulted — during the 1920s some 20 per cent of the officer corps was of noble origin, at a time when the nobility comprised 0.14 per cent of the population — was somewhat out of alignment with that of society at large, but preserved the army from the incursions of groups less likely to accept unquestioningly the shibboleths of obedience and efficiency. The troops themselves were composed of twelve-year volunteers whose training emphasized co-ordination, communication and mobility, and were designed to form a pool of potential officers upon which the army could draw when the time came to free itself from the restrictions upon its size imposed by the Versailles treaty. This was the explanation for the somewhat Ruritanian appearance of the ranks in 1922, when a mere 20,000 privates came under the orders of 75,644 non-commissioned officers.

Von Seeckt's basic principles in creating the *Reichswehr* were to form an army which was well-disciplined, faithful to the Prussian tradition and loyal to himself. He embodied his philosophy in a decree published on 30 December 1920 in which he demanded that 'the army and every soldier must be filled with a burning love of the fatherland, willing to sacrifice his life, loyal to his oath and in the fulfilment of his duty. The army is the first instrument of the power of the Reich.'[7] (There was, of course, no Reich in 1920, only a republic.) Hitler was in the next decade to make skilful use of the success with which von Seeckt had implanted these principles in the German army. But Seeckt had other objectives besides that of gratifying his desire to become a substitute monarch. His belief was that Germany could not begin to adopt an active foreign policy until she had regained her military and political power — exactly the opposite of what the great civilian politician Stresemann believed — and it was to this end that he worked on the *Reichswehr* and fostered the links with the Red Army which were formalized at Rapallo in 1922. This was not done without a concrete objective in view. The enemy against whom von Seeckt's military-political activities were directed was Poland; a few years after his retirement he explained that there 'cannot be any reconciliation between equal and equal; there remains only the subjugation of Germany. But if a reconciliation is impossible and a subjugation excluded, only struggle remains.'[8] In seeing themselves as the immediate object of German intentions after 1924 the French were suffering from a pardonable delusion.

Von Seeckt also nurtured ambitions in the field of domestic politics, for which he probably intended to use his control over the army as a springboard. His attitude during the Bavarian *putsch* by Lossow and Kahr in 1923 was somewhat ambiguous, perhaps the result of the fact that he was preparing his bid for power at the same time as Hitler sought to use the Bavarian revolt to establish the National Socialist revolution. The purposes for which he sought that power were the final defeat of socialist influence, especially in Prussia, and the full support of the state apparatus for secret rearmament.[9] Hitler's abortive Beer Hall *putsch* resolved the situation: the rebellious Bavarian division moved to suppress it, thus allowing von Seeckt to bring them back within the fold, whilst president Ebert declared a state of emergency on 9 November 1923 and handed over executive power to von Seeckt, thereby adroitly heading off the possibility that von Seeckt might move to sieze that power for himself.

The state of emergency ended on 1 March 1925, and Ebert's sudden death later in the same year took von Seeckt by surprise, aiming at the presidency but not sufficiently prepared to announce his candidature. Nor could he have hoped to defeat the successful successor to Ebert's place, field marshal Paul von Hindenburg, who became for the army the king-substitute that von Seeckt sought to be. In September of the following year von Seeckt was dismissed on the pretext of having countenanced the participation of the elder son of the crown prince of Prussia at army manoeuvres, and in uniform. When his wife suggested that the officers of the army might form a *fronde* to resist his removal, von Seeckt's reply demonstrated how well aware he was of the traditions he had imparted to the new army — 'I have not educated them in that spirit.'

With the appointment of general von Heye as chief of the army command many recognized that a turning point had been reached in relations between the army and the state,

and a number of younger generals were prepared to lead the
Reichswehr out of its French-style isolation and towards
closer co-operation with the republic. Of no one was this
more true than general Kurt von Schleicher, for whom
almost a decade of increasingly tortuous political mani-
pulating was now ushered in. 'The question is not republic
or monarchy', wrote the general in December 1926,[10]

> but what should this republic look like? And it is quite obvious
> that it can develop according to our wishes only if we co-operate
> in its constitution cheerfully and tirelessly. Once we have
> acknowledged this idea, then we shall no longer evade the word
> 'republic' so nervously or look around timidly [to see] whether
> anyone had heard it.

This was a signal that Schleicher intended to move the army
more directly into the political arena than von Seeckt had
done.

Certain parts of the Seeckt tradition remained firmly
embedded in the *Reichswehr* however, not least that part
which laid down the unspoken rule that politicking was for
senior officers only. The recruiting pattern established by von
Seeckt did not change, with the result that the social profile
of the officer corps remained imperial in style — the proportion of noble officers had in fact risen by 1932 from 20 to
almost 24 per cent. German military activities in Russia,
which now came under the guiding hand of the foreign
minister, Stresemann, increased in volume, enabling the
German army to profit by experiments in the use of tanks
and air-power in combination, and at the same time giving a
number of future high-ranking Nazi officers a close acquaint-
ance with the powers and capacities of the Red Army. The
Reichswehr was still not as strong as outsiders — particularly
the French — calculated it to be: in 1929 it was estimated, as
a result of a war-game played the previous year, that it might
be capable of resisting a French *advance* by 1933. However,
Germany's very lack of defences had forced her to think in
more adventurous terms of mobile defence rather than of
positional warfare, and the secret testing facilities in Russia
enabled her to begin to perfect equipment and techniques
which would be seized upon by the Nazis in the next decade.

New lessons were being learned about warfare, but the political climate was vital to their future: in 1929 Guderian tried out the first armoured division in field exercises only in the face of continual discouragement from his superiors.

The most marked change in Germany was the shift in power within the army after 1926 from its military to its civil leadership, a phenomenon which owed something to the fact that Heye was much less politically aggressive than his predecessor and a lot to the arrival as minister of defence in January 1928 of general Groener, accompanied by his protégé von Schleicher. Schleicher's manipulation of promotion in the high command began to earn him the enmity of a growing number of influential officers, headed by Blomberg and Fritsch, while at the same time his intervention in 1930 in favour of Brüning and a more right-wing government demonstrated that the army was prepared to move into a fluctuating political world in a way in which its French counterpart was not. While the French army became increasingly irritated in the decade which followed at the lack of a strong civil power, its German counterpart was to take a hand in making just such a government.

After a period of some confusion over its peace-time role and character, the Italian army fell into the French pattern in 1923, when regulations devised by Diaz introduced a period of eighteen months' conscription as being the minimum possible term bearing in mind the need for frontier defence and for the employment of an effective military force in war. Mussolini himself took over the portfolio of minister of war in 1925 and brought in what was termed the *organizzazione della Nazione per la guerra*, which amounted to cutting the term of military service to the minimum, developing a system of physical education alongside conscription and attempting to couple this with safeguards for the industrial and agricultural districts of the north, all at a time of economic stringency and persistent reductions in military expenditure. A law of 11 March 1926 retained the term of eighteen months' service but offered alongside it a much-reduced period of six months for those with family commitments or where one son was already serving in the army. This system remained in force for most of the inter-war period.

Mussolini's military organization of Italy was based on a memorandum drawn up by Badoglio, newly installed as chief of the general staff, which was founded on an acceptance of the existing military structure and an attempt to improve it rather than on the idea of complete innovation. His system, which meant strengthening existing units rather than creating new, weak ones when war broke out, was based upon a calculation of the worst possible strategic situation which Italy might face — simultaneous attacks by France and Yugoslavia. Italy's military structure was based on the defensive, and since her terrain offered little opportunity for the effective use of tanks, not much account was taken of their capacities until the eve of the Second World War. 'The work of Badoglio and Cavallero was substantially positive', writes the most recent authority, '. . . inspired by a moderate and realistic conservatism which set definite and possible objectives in a vision of Italy's military role which was Euro-centric and defensive.'[11] During a brief period from 1929 to 1933, when Mussolini relinquished the war ministry to general Pietro Gazzara, the army managed to complete plans to increase its military power in the light of this basic posture, but then the *Duce* took up the reins again and at once faced it with overseas tasks and international complications in Europe, neither of which it was properly organized to face.

The twin themes which had preoccupied most of Europe's armies during the 1920s had been their professional response to the technology which was being developed and their recognition of the need for strong political leadership. In the 1930s, the governing factor determining the responses of those same powers to the problem of military organization was to be the threat of war. The differences between the experiences of the powers are to be explained chiefly by the distinctions drawn between the ideologies of communism, fascism and liberalism in their readiness to contemplate extending heavy demands upon their inhabitants after a decade during which those demands had for the most part been low. Yet as the international system broke down during the latter part of the decade and the powers prepared to contemplate not just measures of defence but the act of war itself, they all shared a single powerful stimulus. The deciding factor in the decision to resort to war was for all parties the result not of calculations of present strength so much as of fears of future weakness.

The first force to feel the effects of the increased importance placed upon military efficiency in the conduct of international affairs was the Red Army. After 1928, with the inauguration of the first five year plan, heavy equipment began to flow on a scale sufficient to enable it to begin to compare itself with the much better equipped western armies. The means for this military renaissance were provided because Stalin was well aware of the need to defend the communist state and, more specifically, because of the mounting threats present in the international situation. In 1929 China drew up large forces on the Manchurian border and seized the jointly run Chinese Eastern Railway, to which Stalin's response was to create the Special Army of the Far East. In 1932 the Japanese, who had invaded southern Manchuria the previous year, extended their operations into northern Manchuria despite the promise they had given to the Russians not to do so. The following year Hitler's seizure of power made Russia aware of the growing threat to her western border as well as that already existing in the east. By 1934 the threat of war was readily apparent, and Stalin realized that his commissars and secret police could not fight it alone; the power of the professionals had to be increased — and with it, as a by-product, their status — if Russia were to stand any chance of surviving such a war. Accordingly a number of important changes were made in the ordering of Russian military affairs. The principle whereby military authority and command was shared between commissar and commander, which had been established ten years earlier, was abolished in the latter's favour as party dogma was forced to bow to the dictates of efficiency. Two years later, article 132 of the new Soviet Constitution of 1936 extended liability for call-up to all regardless of their social origins, whereas previously educated members of Russian society had been excluded by the 'workers and peasants' formula, which had been rigorously applied since 1928. As an inevitable by-product of a process which raised the army in importance, Stalin was now being confronted with a number of brilliant, semi-independent military commanders such as Tukhachevsky and Blyukher — the former chief of staff, the latter commander of the Special Army of the Far East — whose very professional status would in time make them appear to Stalin as a likely political threat.

With the increase in manpower, the acquisition of more modern weapons, the strengthening of aviation, further progress in heavy industry and the attempt to increase efficiency in the transport system, the Soviet armed forces were by the middle of the decade a formidable opponent for any power contemplating hostilities. They were also becoming ever more aware that military efficiency dictated certain responses on the part of government which were not necessarily in line with the crude application of party dogma then in favour. This was especially the case with regard to collectivization. The task of the army was no longer simply one of indoctrinating the mass of the populace with bolshevik ideals but of preparing for war, which meant raising the military efficiency of the army. Collectivization, which lay at the heart of Stalin's domestic policies, was a direct obstacle to what the new Red commanders were seeking to achieve; recruits were arriving in the army at best lukewarm and at worst mutinous, and there was widespread bloody-mindedness. Accordingly, taking what for many was to prove a fatal step, the army moved into the arena of domestic politics in 1936 and called for drastic modifications in the policy of collectivization in the interests of military efficiency.

Hitherto, although the civil section of the party had since Kirov's death in 1934 been undergoing a purge of mounting ferocity, the armed forces had been left out of the maelstrom. Now Stalin's suspicions were aroused by their growing independence, and he began to look for evidence of questionable activity on their part. It was soon forthcoming. In 1935-6 the German army had cautiously re-opened its old contacts with the Red Army in an attempt to reawaken the spirit of Rapallo, but was treated with considerable reserve and circumspection. Stalin may have got wind of these abortive dealings; he may have been fed evidence of them by Heydrich, head of the SS Intelligence Service, as part of a contest between the SS and the German army for supremacy in intelligence matters; or Stalin may have primed the NKVD with forged material which was deliberately fed to Heydrich in the knowledge that it would soon resurface in Moscow. The only certain fact in the whole tortuous episode is that the NKVD paid the Germans for their assistance in forged currency. They had provided Stalin with the only lever by means of which to attack an opponent who, unlike those undergoing the civil trials, was too strong merely to be broken at will.

At once the Russian high command was broken up and dispersed, and with the dossier complete by April 1937 the arrests were made. The charges were treasonable contact with powers unfriendly to Russia, espionage on behalf of those powers, sabotage of Soviet defence measures and of the Red army, and planning a restoration of capitalism. Tukhachevsky himself was tried and shot in May. He was followed by, in all, some 35,000 officers or roughly half the total officer corps. Three of Stalin's 5 marshals perished, along with all 11 vice-commissars of war, 75 of the 80 members of the Supreme Military Council, 13 out of 15 army commanders, 51 out of 85 corps commanders and 110 out of 195 divisional commanders. In all, 90 per cent of all Russian generals and 80 per cent of all colonels disappeared. Stalin had done to the Red Army what no opponent could ever have done.

In acting in what would appear, in the light of the threatening international situation, to have been a rather short-sighted manner, Stalin was probably motivated first by the need to rid himself of a potential source of leadership which might one day rival his own. He was also making a tacit admission that, after the havoc which he had wrought upon it, the political-bureaucratic machine was probably too weak to control the army. And he was recognizing the degree to which the course pursued by Tukhachevsky in the interests of military efficiency was leading the army out from under strict political control, so that it might one day become identified with the nation first and with the party only second. For a totalitarian state, even when contemplating war, political docility was a higher priority than intelligence and the exercise of independent professional judgment — as Hitler was also to demonstrate.

The result of the decapitation of his army was, for Stalin, to bring on a younger generation of promising communist officers, untainted by an imperialist background and — unlike their predecessors — owing everything to him. In terms of the military efficiency of the army, it is perhaps all too easy to assume that the results of the purge can only have been harmful. In fact, promotion of such figures as Shaposhnikov and his protégé Zhukov seems to have facilitated the development of new military doctrines which included provision for a more imaginative use of armour. Nor was the Soviet Union rendered an easy prey as a result of these moves: the opinion of foreign observers on the capacity of the Red army to undertake offensive action after the purges varied greatly, but the French military attaché, colonel Palasse, reported a year after they had started that 'the Russian army seems to me capable at the present time of assuring the defence of the country in good conditions, and even of carrying out a sharp and limited offensive', an opinion later shared by the American military attaché, general Raymond Faymonville.[12] Having thus put political considerations — and the exercise of strong government — before purely efficient organization for war, Stalin resolved the dilemma of confronting an ever more hostile Germany by means of the Russo-German pact of 22 August 1939, thereby postponing Russia's entry into war for another twenty-two months.

Strong political direction was conspicuously lacking in Germany at the start of the decade, and was something which the army fervently sought. The army now occupied a powerful political role, but not out of choice, for it was ready to relinquish it to a regime which enjoyed a good measure of popular backing and promised to defend an independent presidential cabinet. Besides these broad political conditions, however, they were also concerned to obtain guarantees that the army would continue to exist in its independent form and not become subordinated to a political militia as had happened in Italy. Thus the trial of three junior officers for publishing a pamphlet calling for a national revolution which opened in Leipzig on 23 September 1930 became in effect a trial of Hitler's intentions. Whilst the young officers favoured the Nazis, many of their seniors feared that Hitler intended to destroy the independence of the *Reichswehr* and reduce it to a party army. Others, Groener chief amongst them, looked with abhorrence on the socialism of National Socialism, which they regarded as being little different from communism.

Nothing in Hitler's progress to power was of more importance than the need to convince the army that, in military organization as well as in the broader fields of policy, he was a conservative nationalist. A legal ascent to power and the adherence of the army in that ascent were essential to his success, as he afterwards admitted:[13]

> If I had seized power illegally, the Wehrmacht would have constituted a dangerous breeding place for a *coup d'état* ...; by acting constitutionally, on the other hand, I was in a position to restrict the activities of the Wehrmacht to its legal and strictly limited function.

Hitler's concern for the support of the army was dictated not simply by the fact that it alone possessed the physical capacity to unseat him, but also by the realization that its approval would carry a political as well as a professional undertone. Accordingly he reassured the generals that he did not aim at the disintegration of the army and that he opposed revolution. Von Hammerstein, the commander-in-chief, was won over on this basis and von Blomberg and Hindenburg too swung behind Hitler as he became ever more convincing in the posture of a right-minded and malleable patriot. The final factor tipping the scales in Hitler's favour was the outcome of a war-game played by the German high command in November 1932 which envisaged a joint insurrection by the communists and the Nazis — not altogether an unlikely prospect, since the two parties had combined during the Berlin transport strike that summer — at a time when there appeared to be a real possibility of a Polish incursion across the border. This was a scenario which the army felt itself incapable of mastering, although the results of its theoretical explorations may have been fudged in a deliberate effort to avoid being called out on the streets and compromising its apolitical status as a result.

Hitler came to power in January 1933, and in that same month it was announced that as of 1 April Germany would be once again sending military attachés to her embassies abroad. This was apparently a signal that the status of the army was about to rise again, just as its role seemed to be secure, and indeed there was much cause for military satisfaction with Hitler's early pronouncements and actions. After 1933 the return to a vigorous patriotic policy, the announcement of German rearmament and the reintroduction of universal military service all seemed to indicate to the soldiers a return to the old traditions. Theirs was to be a tragic miscalculation. But for the immediate future the army could announce its loyalty to a government which was both patriotic and popular — two attributes the Weimar regime had never seemed to possess — and begin to plan for expansion.

The immediate issue confronting Germany in matters of military organization on Hitler's accession to power was whether the army was to fall victim to the party or vice versa. Hitler gave repeated public assurances that there existed no real competition between the two sides of the state; on 1 July he announced that 'the army of the political soldiers of the German revolution [i.e. the SA, or storm-troopers] has no wish to take the place of our army or to enter into competition with it.'[14] However, no sooner did the army begin serious planning for conscription the following year than it clashed headlong with the SA, who wanted it reduced to a training branch within their own organization. Shrewdly Hitler chose to announce his intention not to support Röhm's militia army at a dinner held on 28 February 1934 to celebrate the anniversary of Schlieffen's birthday, and at the same time announced the probability of an economic recession in eight years time and the need for military action to the west and the east in order to secure much-needed living space. The most accurate pointer to the future of the army lay in the fact that the hosts for the banquet were the SS.

The threat posed by Röhm's SA was removed by the SS in the 'Night of the Long Knives' on 30 June 1934 when most of its leaders were massacred, together with Schleicher and others. Then on 2 August the aged president Hindenburg, focus of the army's loyalties, died. Hitler moved quickly to combine in his own person the two offices of chancellor and president and with the enthusiastic support of his *Reichswehr* minister, von Blomberg, the army was persuaded to swear an extraordinary personal oath to their new president:[15]

> I swear by God this holy oath, that I will render to Adolf Hitler, Leader of the German nation and people, Supreme Commander of the Armed Forces, unconditional obedience, and I am ready as a brave soldier to risk my life at any time for this oath.

The army seems to have regarded this as a legitimate repayment for Hitler's support against the SA and his apparent rejection of the notion of a party army, but it was really an example of Hitler's uncanny sense of vulnerabilities, for by taking such an oath the army had trapped itself by the standards of loyalty and honour which it still retained into a personal servility to an individual rather than to the state. The oath made it difficult for many officers to contemplate replacing Hitler, even when the war was at its worst.

On 16 March 1935 Hitler announced his intention to reintroduce conscription and two months later the details of rearmament were published in the *Wehrgesetz*. Conscription was to be for a term of one year, subsequently raised to two years on 24 August 1936. The army at once became heavily occupied in coping with the intakes of recruits and devising and carrying out training procedures, as well as receiving quantities of new weapons and equipment. This it did with something approaching enthusiasm, for this was its job. Hossbach was perhaps typical of many in his outlook at this time. 'We are soldiers,' he remarked. 'We do not want to have anything to do with and understand nothing about politics. We occupy ourselves only with military affairs.'[16] The question of what the new army was to be for was, however, a political one with which the soldiers would have to concern themselves in due course. At first Hitler was at pains to reassure them that the new mass army was not being formed to wage wars of aggression but to guard and protect the German people so that they might never again suffer the fate they had had to endure after 1918. Hitler's generals, already alarmed at the prospect of the re-militarization of the Rhineland in March 1936, could not have been reassured by the Führer's announcement five months later that he required the German army to be ready for use and the German economy to be ready for war within four years.

It was at the Hossbach conference on 5 November 1937 that Hitler revealed in detail his intentions to use war within the next few years and before the stockpile of modern arms which Germany was building up had grown obsolescent, in order to carve for Germany the 'living space' which he felt convinced the impending population crisis would demand. The military, in the persons of Blomberg and Fritsch (the latter commander-in-chief of the army), and the Foreign Office in the person of von Neurath expressed severe doubts in the face of the revelation that Hitler proposed to begin his programme by exerting pressure upon Czechoslovakia up to the level, if necessary, of active military operations. Within a matter of a few months the dissidents were removed, and Hitler had ensured himself of a politically pliant high command much as Stalin had done earlier. Neurath was permitted to resign, as he had repeatedly endeavoured to do. Hitler was presented with unmistakeable evidence that Blomberg's second wife had posed for obscene photographs and Blomberg himself, deceived by Goering into believing that as a result of this revelation the generals were against him, proved more than ready to cast himself upon the Führer's mercy and retire quietly. Fritsch was framed on an old and blatantly trumped-up charge of homosexuality but, despite the herculean efforts of the Gestapo, was acquitted by a court of enquiry. None the less he refused to allow himself to be used as a focus for political opposition to Hitler, or even to defend his honour by challenging Himmler to a duel (which he could have done, since duelling had been made legal once again on 22 February 1937), but feeling that his honour had been irreparably stained he preferred to resign.

Like Stalin, Hitler brought in new men distinguished more for their subservience than for their brains. Brauchitsch, the new commander-in-chief, was bought by Hitler for the sum of 80,000 marks, the amount necessary to buy him a divorce from his wife and permit him to formalize his liaison with a widow. Keitel, head of the newly created Armed Forces High Command (OKW), was nicknamed *Lakeitel* ('lackey') and perfectly suited Hitler because he had, according to the Führer, the brains of a cinema commissionaire. A number of highly able senior officers, among them von Leeb, von Kleist and von Manstein, were retired for 'non-political sympathies' and replaced by pliant party soldiers or men whose loyalty was only to Hitler. The last focus of opposition within the army to the course along which Hitler was leading it towards war with the major European powers in pursuit of expansion was the chief of the general staff, Beck. Learning on 29 May 1938 that Hitler intended to go ahead with the Czech venture, he stated categorically that Germany and Italy together could not hope to challenge either Britain or France militarily. Brauchitsch put these views to a conference of army commanders in August, but though they agreed with them Reichenau warned of Hitler's violent reaction to a group expression of such views, and von dem Bussche spoke of the duty of soldierly obedience. Beck resigned on 27 August, and Hitler's control over the army was complete.

The Fritsch *prozess* had in fact been far more than a personal injustice. Hitler had skilfully used the soldier's concepts of honour and loyalty against the army to render it his accomplice in his adventuristic plans; honour was the means of ridding himself of the dominant figures in the military opposition and loyalty would ensure that the remainder of the army stayed obedient to him. The non-political training which many senior officers had received during the Seeckt era had made his task that much simpler. From this time onwards Hitler lacked support among only a few of the senior officers; younger men, bitter about Versailles and anxious to show their efficiency, saw National Socialism as at best the only hope for Germany's future and at worst a mechanism for quicker promotion. The largest group, typified by Guderian, passed up neither professional advancement nor the direction in which that advancement would lead them. The Russo-German pact quietened their main strategic fear — that of having to fight a two-front war — and they followed Hitler into Poland confident of their expertise and their weapons.

Military efficiency and strong political direction were the twin themes which dominated the French military machine, too, during the second inter-war decade. The dilemma which faced France's generals was that of assuring national defence at a time when the threat from Germany was mounting, while the size of their conscript force was diminishing due to the decline in birth-rate and the consequent fall in the numbers of men arriving for training each year. The conscript's value was in any case lessened by the twelve-month term of service, during which time it was very doubtful whether soldiers could be adequately trained and fitted into good fighting formations. At the same time they had to deal with a series of civilian governments which appeared to put economy and political conviction before the disinterested calculation of the nation's requirements. In 1933 the government slashed over 1,000,000,000 francs from the military budget, with the immediate result that manoeuvres had to be suspended that year, and general Weygand, commander-in-chief of the French army, announced bitterly that his troops would not be able to defend the country as a result. Such considerations apparently had little sway in the minds of French socialists: in February 1933 Daladier moved to retire 5,000 officers — one-sixth of the entire complement — from the army in the interests of economy (a measure which was ultimately cancelled), and in December Leon Blum apparently cut off the avenue of longer periods of conscription with his announcement in parliament that 'We shall always be against the prolongation of military service .... It is a mistake to rest the security of a nation in its military strength.'[17] However, the advent of more pressing crises during the next two years was to force the socialists — reluctantly — to compromise with their principles to a modest and insufficient degree.

The rioting which occurred in Paris on 4 February 1934, in which members of various right-wing and fascist organizations and not a few military men took part, added further to the army's difficulties since its loyalty to the republic now came under scrutiny. The distance preserved by the army from the rest of France had already given the socialists pause for thought and when Weygand was appointed commander-in-chief in 1930 he was required to deliver to parliament a statement of his loyalty to the republic. Now it seemed that the army, or elements within it, were about to show their true colours. The politicians became alarmed about the officer corps to an extent which rivalled the alarms in 1887 and during the aftermath of the Dreyfus affair, and the commission of enquiry into the events of 4 February was about to establish the political opinions of all the officers in the Paris garrison when it abruptly ended that part of its work. At this juncture, with the question of the army's political reliability added to all the other concerns about the efficiency and effectiveness of France's organization for war, a revolutionary new proposal was made which amounted to a reversal of all the republic's newly found principles about military organization and about how the next war would be fought.

Challenging the intellectual passivity of the high command, colonel de Gaulle published in 1934 his study *Vers l'armée de métier*, in which he proposed that France entrust her defence to an all-regular, long-service, 100,000 man army which would be mechanized and motorized and would rely upon co-operation between tanks, artillery and aeroplanes for its effect. Although not entirely new — they had been voiced in 1927 — these ideas challenged the very basis of the Third Republic's military policies. The notion of offensive war which was inherent in de Gaulle's ideas was greeted by the left as inherently immoral and as a betrayal of the citizen-soldier, whose virtues provided a central part of France's rationale in matters of military organization. The belief that an *armée de métier*, carefully recruited, would ensure internal order in the case of grave social conflicts proved as repugnant to the left as it was attractive to the right. De Gaulle's book had a number of flaws, as well as being politically unsound, and was more a visionary discourse than a rigorously logical discussion; however the future of his ideas was decided by the fact that they affronted not merely the social and political precepts of the left, but also the strategic conservatism of most regular soldiers.

The strategic basis of de Gaulle's ideas was the belief that future wars would not be — or need not be — total wars; this flew in the face of all orthodox ideas, which indicated that they would be so. Thus the *armée de métier* was challenged first on the basis that a small force such as de Gaulle proposed might achieve a quick local success on a narrow front but would have no chance of exploiting that advantage: as the war minister's *chef du cabinet* remarked,[18]

> It is . . . an elementary truth that no fruitful offensive operation is possible without first having assembled the necessary means to ensure, at the decisive point, a superiority which is both indisputable and lasting.

Then it was held that in any case direct assistance to an ally was not necessary, since support could be afforded by a variety of indirect pressures and, if necessary, by the use of overseas expeditionary forces. Tanks were attacked as offensive weapons for which a defensive army had no use, and it was pointed out that the Rhineland — which was after all the most likely theatre in which they would be acting — was unsuitable for their operation. Professional scepticism over the role of independent armoured divisions mounted: general Brécart made an impassioned plea for the retention of horsed cavalry and in 1938 general Chauvineau, the high priest of defensive warfare, announced that the war of movement had had its day. De Gaulle's theories conflicted with so much in French thought about war and about military organization — both for professionals and for civilians — that they had no chance of adoption. In the long run, his adversaries were to be proved correct, although the Third Republic did not survive to witness that triumph.

Though reluctant to make any move to increase the burden of military preparation on French society — in 1934 radical socialists tied funds for the Maginot Line to a guarantee not to increase the length of military service — the left was forced to recognize that even the defensive force they favoured was being gravely affected by the decline in numbers of each annual class of conscripts, and on 15 March 1935 they took advantage of a provision made in the 1928 law to extend service from one year to two, a move of which Hitler took advantage the following day, declaring Germany's reintroduction of conscription. The weaknesses of the French system were cruelly revealed shortly afterwards when, on 7 March 1936, Germany reoccupied the Rhineland. Gamelin informed the politicians that no coercive action against Germany was possible without a full mobilization of the army, an act which in itself might lead immediately to war. The government, he added, could count upon him to be prudent, though they would never find him cowardly. The French military machine, devised to meet only the worst possible occurrence, that of total war, proved quite incapable of dealing with Hitler's adventurous policy backed by the threat of lightning action. An exasperated Pietri, minister of the navy, pointed out on one occasion that many people were avoiding the fundamental truth that the only way to coerce a strong power was war. France was quite unprepared for this on Hitler's terms, mostly through sheer lack of will. The left was opposed to war in general; the right had ceased to be anti-German, while remaining anti-British.

Between the Rhineland and Poland little changed in the essentials of French military organization. Her position grew weaker after October 1936 when Belgium backed out of the military convention established 16 years earlier and left the north-western end of the Maginot Line hanging in mid-air. The response of the politicians during the next two years was to heap more powers on Gamelin who was both chief of the general staff and, after 1935, commander-in-chief of the army, to which in 1938 he added the role of chief of staff for national defence. Debonair in style, Gamelin was more acceptable to the left than his predecessor had been. He was Joffre's protégé, and his political reliability carried the seal of his marriage to the sister of general Picquart, hero of the Dreyfus case. However Gamelin was restricted in his freedom of action both by France's refusal to alter the essentials of her philosophy about military organization and the likely shape of the next war, and by his conviction that it was not part of his function to recommend policy in a situation of crisis. Thus at the time of Munich, two years later, the army again demonstrated excessive caution, pointing out that what looked like an overwhelming French military advantage (twenty-three French divisions to ten German divisions on a war footing in the west) was at best parity since Germany could mobilize more divisions in all and do so faster than France. In truth neither France nor her army were prepared for anything other than an all-out war against Germany with the support of allies and over a period of years. Against such a system as Hitler's, which presented a series of limited but cumulative demands, each seemingly backed by the threat of pulverization before she could even get started, France not unnaturally took every possible step to avoid plunging herself into disaster. Essentially her actions were controlled by her perception of the nation-in-arms as the form of military organization which best suited her social and political situation, and by the technological conservatism of her generals. Gamelin alone appeared to bridge the gap between the ideals of the socialists and the conservatism of the generals, and that was both his and his country's misfortune. When France was eventually forced to follow Britain into war, the same man commanded her armies, was his own chief of the general staff, and had overall command of all three armed forces. France sought to make her system work by heaping all authority on the shoulders of one man. The result, not surprisingly, was total confusion.

Paradoxically, the threat of war which was to be one of the most marked features of the 1930s was felt first in a severe form by none of the major continental powers for whom it was to assume mounting importance but by Britain, who had distanced herself from direct participation in European affairs. By dint of her position as a great, if not a strong, imperial power she was presented with her first likely opponent when Japan invaded Manchuria in 1931 and then captured Shanghai the following year. The mounting threat in the far east prompted the chiefs of staff to abandon the ten-year rule — an administrative maxim established in 1919 which ordered British defence policy on the basis that there would be no engagement in a major war within the next ten years — on 22 March 1932. However a second threat to Britain's position was also becoming apparent in the rise of

Germany. By the end of the year a division was forming between navalists who saw Japan as the major enemy Britain
must face and a group of civilians (including Vansittart and
Neville Chamberlain), soldiers and airmen who saw in
Germany the greatest menace to Britain's well-being. The
former group proposed that Britain's meagre defence budget
would be spent to best effect in building ships, especially
battleships, whilst the latter saw the best hope of salvation
in building bombers, with which to deter Germany.

The force which figured least in such computations was
the army. This was no less a product of circumstances than it
was of tradition, for not only had the army reverted to its
nineteenth-century role as imperial policeman, but it was
being presented with serious domestic problems at various
points in the middle east. Its leaders thus opposed an organization geared to a big war in Europe and saw their primary
responsibility as being the policing of the empire. In 1934
the Defence Requirements Committee issued its first pro-
nouncement on how to resolve the dilemma of facing in two
directions at once and building a navy to defeat Japan and
an air force to deter Germany: Japan was to be appeased and
Germany to be accounted the major danger. The army
remained in its customary third place, briefly countenancing
the prospect of mounting an expeditionary force to the
continent in order to deny the Low Countries as a base for
German bombers; however the chief of the imperial general
staff, Montgomery Massingberd, was quite unwilling to state
even the size of army he wanted to produce such a force, so
there was little danger of military pressure reversing the
traditional British attitude to direct miliary involvement on
the continent. Instead it was agreed that in order to meet
and counter the German threat Britain was to build a bomber
force, which would enable her to maintain her independence
in Europe whilst at the same time spending much less than a
capital ship programme would require. The degree to which
the air had been Baldwin's obsession during the Geneva
disarmament conference (1932-4) may have helped bias
rearmament towards the most feared of the new weapons of
war. Politically such a solution was eminently acceptable
since it evaded the need to call on British manpower via

conscription, and banished the spectre of another British expeditionary force committed to the killing grounds of Europe.

To Britain's two prospective enemies was added a third when, on 3 October 1935, Italy invaded Abyssinia and the traditional British hold on the Mediterranean was thrown into disarray. Again land forces were discarded as the best means to meet the new crisis; the Defence Requirements Committee called for the expenditure of £417,500,000 over the next five years on bombers and ships, a conclusion which conformed absolutely with Neville Chamberlain's complete rejection of any proposals for a land force for intervention on the continent. The Royal Navy calculated that although it could beat Italy single-handed (a debatable proposition in view of its lack of anti-aircraft ammunition), it would then be too weak to confront the Japanese in the Far East. The revival of the German threat in March of the following year, when Hitler remilitarized the Rhineland, determined the outcome of this dilemma. Italy must at all costs be appeased. The pattern of British diplomacy in the latter part of the decade was being set in conformity with the inescapable realities of defence.

Many factors were acting to constrict Britain's freedom of action at this time, not least the manifest opposition of all the dominions save New Zealand to any departure from the policy of appeasement in Europe, a position made brutally plain at the Imperial Conference held in May 1937, and one which resulted in pressure being put on Britain to make peace with Germany in October 1939 and again in August 1940. Among the forces which operated on policy-makers at this time, social pressures had no small role to play. No British politician of any significance was prepared to consider a large land commitment in Europe and risk a repetition of the Somme and Passchendaele. The cabinet had recognized the power of public opinion in the matter during the Mediterranean crisis in August 1935 when it had refused to mobilize the naval reserves on the grounds of the resounding effect such a step would have on public opinion at home as well as abroad. Baldwin made further obeisance to the shrine of public opinion on 1 April 1936, announcing that the government would never introduce conscription in peace-time. (It did.) In view of the confusion prevalent in most military minds about whether it would be possible to win a future war at all, his caution was doubly justified.

It is easy to assume that, in conforming so precisely to what all available indicators suggested public opinion on the matter was, the government viewed the prospect of a major effort like that of 1914 simply as likely to reproduce the slaughter of the Great War. However, more subtle social considerations were also at work, the medium through which they were being expressed being the Treasury. Simply put, its attitude was that the cost of defending Britain against her enemies might be greater than she could bear without irreparable damage to her economic and financial stability. Such a view helped determine Chamberlain, during his time as chancellor of the exchequer, to put brakes on the process of rearmament in order to avoid the distortion of the economy which might result from concentration on defence-related industries, a loss of exports, and an artificial boom induced by rising wages which would be followed by a slump. Economics meant, however, not just prices and trade but the relationship between demand and supply and the place of capital in the economy. Here too there was reason to retard what looked in the light of diplomatic calculations an obvious need to maximize Britain's defences; by 1937 it was the view of the Treasury that 'the rearmament programme was a far more profound threat to the social and political order than Germany was to the national security.'[19] The threat arose due to the government's having adopted the role of consumer of the products of industry whilst at the same time retaining its responsibility, as custodian of the tax-payer's money, of ensuring that the country was not paying an excessive price for its defence requirements and thereby contributing to the well-being of the barons of industry and of the City. The spectre of state intervention was appearing, initially at the level of the placing of defence contracts, and none of the financial interests cared much for that. They had reason for alarm. Hawker Siddeley, the aviation company — which was heavily involved in rearmament — announced its 1938 shareholders' dividend at 32.5 per cent, plus a 10 per cent bonus. The following May a secret government report, which was kept from the cabinet, demonstrated beyond doubt that the profits being made in the aircraft sector were excessive — profits being made at the public's expense. Perhaps if Hawker were making profits out of Hurricanes, then no profit was excessive. Certainly a country not prepared to pay for its defence in manpower was being made to pay in money.

Britain's defence posture was radically transformed only nineteen months before the Second World War broke out as a result of a memorandum produced in December 1937 by Sir Thomas Inskip, minister for the co-ordination of defence, in which he argued that the German menace might best be met by using the air force not to threaten Germany with a knock-out blow should hostilities commence, but in order to confront her with the prospect of a long war which Britain would be able to win by mobilizing greater economic pressure than her opponent and by using her superior striking power — the Royal Navy — when and where she wished. The role of the air force was now no longer to carry an irresistible offensive to the enemy but to proffer instead the prospect of a successful air defence which would secure the home country as the base for a subsequent attack. Radar and the eight-gun monoplane fighter were to be Britain's equivalent of the Maginot Line. Both were designed around the same end: to offer Germany the prospect of the one type of war she could not hope to win — a long war in which the relative strength of economic power would decide the victor. The command economy of Nazi Germany required much less time than the market economies of Britain and France to gear itself up for war, but, given protective cover behind which to mobilize, they stood a better chance in the long run.

Inskip's proposals did recast the basis of Britain's defence programme but they did not result in any increase in the status of the military in relation to the other two arms. A very narrow interpretation of limited continental liability was accepted, and in the new plans a small expeditionary force was prepared, to be equipped for operations not in Europe but in an eastern theatre. In the spring of 1938 the army viewed co-operation with allies in the defence of their territory as bottom of its list of priorities, with home defence and internal security at the top. The chiefs of staff supported appeasement in order to reduce the number of potential enemies Britain had to face and to give the new phase of rearmament a chance to get under way. There was thus nothing Britain could realistically hope to do when the Munich crisis arose; the secretary of state for war bluntly informed his colleagues on 30 August 1938 that 'We cannot at present put an army into the field large enough to have any decisive effect.'[20] The Munich agreement was thus a mute recognition of the sheer incapacity of Britain's defence structure to act against Germany at that time, though the sudden appearance of 10,000 Italian troops in Libya helped determine her apparently passive stance.

After Munich the place of the land forces in Britain's defence policy changed radically as she moved towards a *de facto* alliance with France against Hitler. France looked to her to make up the thirty-five divisions lost with the dismemberment of Czechoslovakia, and the chiefs of staff came to support the notion of a positive land role in Europe in the belief that buttressing France was the best way to guarantee Britain's security. The army at once took on two vital attributes which it had hitherto lacked, and which together made up for the lack of a military tradition such as was common among the continental powers. For, in an alliance, a land commitment had a symbolic force which neither ships nor bombers could ever have: the army's physical presence on the continent was a guage of the firmness of British intentions to resist Germany, and as a result it had great influence in reassuring France about the steadiness of her partner. It also had a powerful practical value as the means best calculated to support a major land power in what looked increasingly like a lengthy engagement on the continent rather than a brief spasm during which one side's bombers destroyed the will-power and resistance of the other. Britain was facing the hard reality that European commitments meant first and foremost a military presence.

France's move to her side somewhat eased Britain's parlous strategic situation since it meant that the French navy could take the strain against Italy in the Mediterranean and relieve her of one of her three strategic burdens. There remained Japan, but here too help miraculously appeared in the person of President Roosevelt who agreed in mid-April to move the American Pacific Fleet back to its stations on the west coast and thereby exercise a restraining influence on the Japanese. Britain was now free to face up to Germany, and did so by guaranteeing the neutrality of Poland and introducing conscription. Yet as well as being at last free to face a single opponent — and the one she had deemed the most dangerous for the past six years, at that — Britain was also under some compulsion to resolve matters in the near future. In May 1939, the treasury sombrely pointed out that Britain could afford to go on financing rearmament for only another six to nine months; thereafter her efforts must rapidly dwindle, since there would exist no more financial resources on which to draw, and she would again become vulnerable to a threat such as that posed by Germany, a power with a high degree of armament readiness. Then in July it was disclosed that the 'war chest' contained only £500 million in gold and £200 million in foreign securities. Without American aid the prospects were grim, yet the Johnson Act had expressly ruled out any such aid. Britain's decision to honour her guarantee to Poland thus seems both honourable and somewhat foolhardy. Economic decline may have hastened her into the war before it was too late to have any hope of victory at all.

Prior to the outbreak of the First World War, all the major European powers had possessed armies which resembled one another both in structure and in purpose — excepting always Great Britain — and all shared common beliefs about the military efficiency of such forces, based on the assumption that it would be possible to fight a short, victorious war in which the mobilization and concentration of as large a proportion of the nation's human resources as was possible would play the major role in determining the outcome. By contrast, the existence of conscript armies among all the belligerents in 1939 marked only a superficial similarity behind which lay deep divisions. In a military sense, these amounted to very different calculations about the capacity of societies to bear the burden of war: in Britain and France conscripts were to help take the strain in what no one thought would be a short war, symbolizing an intention to muster every scrap of the nation's resources necessary to win victory; in Germany and in Italy, however, conscription represented an intention to gamble on winning a war before it became necessary to call on the greater part of the nation's resources. To a large extent the decisions for war were those of the politicians, for common to most of Europe's military was doubt whether it was possible to win a war at all in conditions of such technical complexity. The challenge of war tested the different military institutions which all the participants had devised under unique and separate pressures. To meet it the notion of military organization would expand far beyond any bounds it had known hitherto as the war pitted the world's leading economies against one another.

8
The Second World War

Social considerations played an important part in Hitler's decision to launch a European war in 1939 and were also to play a large part in his direction of the German war machine. In conformity with his belief that the goal of foreign policy was the preservation of a people's means of subsistence and that the path to this goal would always, in the last analysis, be war, he demanded in 1934 that the German army and the German economy both be ready for war within four years. Three years later he was convinced that the inevitable population crisis was a matter of half-a-dozen years away at most, and in 1938 he began a series of moves in Europe designed to resolve that crisis by providing the extra territory and foodstuffs which Germany's population would need if the regime were to survive. To support his diplomacy Hitler had built up an imposing military force, apparently heavily armed with the most modern weapons. Nor did his gamble on being faced with a European war look entirely preposterous in the light of the indexes of world production. In 1939 the United States accounted for some 42 per cent of the total world production of capital goods, Germany for 15 per cent, Great Britain for 14 per cent and France for approximately 5 per cent. Provided that America kept out of the war, Germany's slight inferiority might perhaps be compensated for by more imaginative and skilful use of a better integrated fighting force.

The front that Germany convincingly presented to Europe was one of a power armed to the teeth, whose people had cheerfully sacrificed butter for guns in order to achieve a massive military superiority over all potential rivals. This was a deception in which plain trickery had played a part; general Vuillemin, chief of the French air force, had returned from Germany convinced of her massive aerial supremacy after a trip during which almost the entire stock of aeroplanes had been paraded before him at each aerodrome and then flown swiftly to his next destination whilst he was conveyed along more circuitous routes. On a larger scale, Germany had perpetrated this illusion before all the major powers in Europe and had convinced them all. Yet in reality her economic position made it hopeless for her to comtemplate fighting another war of the 1914-18 type, for she depended upon the outside world for one-fifth of her foodstuffs, two-thirds of her oil, one-quarter of her zinc, half her lead and amounts between 70 and 99 per cent of her copper, rubber, tin, nickel and bauxite. Moreover her Italian ally had no raw materials at all and was dependent upon imports which came by way of Gibraltar or the Suez canal and were thus at the mercy of the British fleet. In the long run she was to prove as much of a liability to Germany in the Second World War as had Austria-Hungary in the First.

Hitler's solution to this dilemma was to prepare a military machine which acted as an effective tool of diplomatic blackmail and could if needs be threaten a particular type of war — *Blitzkrieg*. After 1933 Germany had armed in width not in depth, creating a 'shop-window' force which might hope to overcome any opposition immediately fielded against it, but which could not hope to overcome the product of a stronger economy which had been allowed the luxury of time to mobilize its full capacity for war-making. It was a system prepared for short wars, but one which fostered the illusion of depth by reason of Hitler's own apparent readiness to risk war and which, because of the speed with which it could be put into operation, was a particularly effective support to diplomacy. Its central weakness was that it could not cope with a long campaign against an opponent who had failed to collapse swiftly and totally under the weight of a lightning strike. 'The Blitzkrieg', it has been well said, 'allowed Germany to play the part of a great power, which she no longer was.'[1]

The course of the war which Hitler was to initiate revealed the most significant deficiency in Germany's organization for war to be the fact that, as the servant of short-term policies, it completely lacked provision for long-term planning. This 'short run' mentality obstructed the development of a long-range heavy bomber and resulted in violent switches of priority in the section of the German economy devoted to arms production. Only on 7 September 1939 could Hitler be brought to agree to a programme of economic priorities, and then it was drawn in terms so broad as to be valueless, amounting to no more than a vague command to the economy to supply the fighting troops with the necessary munitions and with those articles of equipment of which losses had been heaviest. The basic miscalculation as to Germany's capacity to wage modern war — wherein inferiority of resources was to be compensated for by speed, skill and ingenuity — had not, however, passed by unremarked within the German war machine. General Georg Thomas, armaments chief of the OKW (Armed Forces High Command), had warned as early as 1928 that 'modern war is no longer a clash of armies, but a struggle for the existence of the peoples involved. All the resources of the nation must be made to serve the war: above all, besides men, industry and the economy.'[2] In May 1939 Thomas warned representatives of the German Foreign Office that war with the west would not be a matter of *Blitzkrieg* and seven months later Keitel, chief of the OKW, admitted to Thomas that Hitler saw a long war as impossible for Germany. All the Führer's efforts were to be bent towards avoiding that prospect, and for two years they met with little but success.

For Britain and France, the concept of organization for war was built upon premises that were quite opposite to those operating within Germany. For them another war would entail all the wearisome effort and organization which had been a feature of the grapple with Germany from 1914 to 1918 — a view of war which went a long way towards explaining their unwillingness to back their own diplomacy with the threat of force until rather late in the day. However, once embarked upon hostilities both Britain and France depended upon a long war in order to bring to bear their superior weight and crush their opponent. France required at least a year in which to train her short-service recruits up to the levels required by modern combat and to convert her industries to the manufacture of war *matériel*; Britain, needing to raise large military forces almost from scratch, train them for action on the continent and convert her industrial base to full war production, needed if anything a longer period. National organization for war was now responding to more overt economic considerations, which were in turn a recognition of the disparities between the peace-time military policies of the combatants. Reluctant to start a shooting war and also convinced that the key to victory in the First World War had lain in the collapse of the home front, the western allies made enemy morale the target of their first efforts; the initial moves in what was to become the complex propaganda war were made, whilst in the air Bomber Command pounded Germany with leaflets, fearful that more direct attacks on civilian morale might stimulate damaging reprisals.

Table 1 *Military expenditure as a proportion of Gross National Product*

	Germany	Great Britain	Japan
1932	—	—	6.8% average
1933	3%	—	
1935	8%	—	
1936	13%	—	
1937	13%	—	13.2%
1938	22%	8%	17.4%
1939	23%	22%	
1940	38%	53%	
1941	47%	60%	
1942	55%	64%	

When Hitler launched his forces against Poland on 3 September 1939 he was taking a considerable gamble; only seventy German divisions were fit for active service, whereas the Poles disposed of fifty divisions and the combined Franco-British forces of 104. Aided by massive aerial supremacy, fifty-nine divisions of the *Wehrmacht* were deployed against the Poles and within two weeks had crushed all enemy resistance. Though large, the Polish forces had few aircraft and even fewer tanks, depending on large bodies of cavalry to prod lurking attackers. They were also in an impossible strategic position, since the salient of East Prussia lay behind their forward positions and provided a magnificent jumping-off point for a German attack. Logic dictated that the Poles withdraw from this bulge, but since it contained the vital Poznan industrial region such a move was impossible. By a combination of outflanking attacks and deep penetration using strategic air strikes, the *Wehrmacht* had crushed Polish resistance by 17 September; the following day Russian troops moved into Poland from the west, seizing territory which had formerly belonged to the Russian empire and at the same time establishing a protective shield between Russia and Germany. 694,000 Polish prisoners had been taken at a cost of 44,000 German casualties and the loss of half of Germany's stock of motor vehicles.

For Britain, concentrating upon the eventual defeat of Germany, there was no question of any immediate defence of the country on whose behalf she had ostensibly gone to war. The legacy of pre-war military organization meant that for Britain and France only two options existed: light air attacks on Germany, or a land attack by France against the Siegfried Line. The fear that a second strike by Germany would obliterate the United Kingdom meant that the first course was out of the question, whilst the second faced the obstacle that the French armed forces were not organized for an attack even if they had wanted to launch one. General Gamelin talked of sixteen days as being the period necessary to position the requisite heavy artillery, and France fulfilled her undertaking to attack Germany by slowly closing up to and halting at the German defensive front. Two days before the earliest date on which France could hope to mount an offensive the Polish campaign was over and German forces were transferred back to the west. Germany's military organization had apparently proved its worth, and Hitler's diplomatic gamble had come off, a result which Hitler attributed to the successful combination of all arms and to himself: 'As the last factor, I must in all modesty name my own person: irreplaceable.'[3]

The Allies were now reduced to waiting for Hitler to take the initiative, as their entire organization for war determined they must, whilst he waited for them to make peace and buy security. But the expected approaches never materialized, and by the end of the first week in October Hitler had decided to attack the west at once, believing that the relationship of forces could never be more propitious, and proposed an immediate offensive to acquire Holland, Belgium and northern France and knock out the French army quickly. Hitler's generals, conscious of the weak base of the German war machine, objected that an attack on France was a very different proposition from one on Poland and that the *Blitzkrieg* technique could not work; von Leeb recorded in his diary 'The French have some 60 divisions available. Surprise impossible. Our losses will be enormous .... An attack against France cannot be conducted like an attack on Poland; it will be longer and much more murderous.'[4] Germany, the generals pointed out, lacked the necessary raw materials, armaments and even ammunition for such a conflict. Hitler was not to be swayed by such arguments, though other factors were to delay the start of the operation until 10 May 1940, its twenty-ninth deadline.

The so-called 'Phoney War' of 1939-40, to which the Allies soon acclimatized themselves, suited their organizational situation and suited also their concept of strategic blockade. But blockade failed to work, despite the pre-emption of raw materials in neutral countries, largely because Germany's open European frontiers enabled her to import oil from Rumania and Russia, corn from the Ukraine and iron ore from Sweden. Britain in any case grossly overestimated the importance to the German economy of supplies of Swedish iron ore, perhaps smarting from the manner in which the trade was being conducted by way of Narvik and the North

Sea under the very noses of the Royal Navy, and determined to try to interrupt it. A useful pretext behind which to deploy Allied troops in neutral Sweden, crossing to it by way of neutral Norway, lay coveniently to hand in the shape of the war being waged by the Finns against the Russians.

Russia had been concerned about the likelihood of a German attack on Finland from 1938 but the Finns had repeatedly rejected the active military co-operation she sought and Finnish politicians had calculated, wrongly, that Russia would not press her demands to the point of conflict. Talks between the two powers broke down at the beginning of November 1939, and on the last day of the month war broke out. Aided by the onset of winter the small, poorly equipped Finnish army managed to hold the Russians at bay on their eastern front. They achieved brilliant early tactical successes in cutting off and then breaking up the Russian *mottis* (columns), but mistakenly took this for strategic success. In January 1940 revitalized Russian forces under the command of Timoshenko attacked the Mannerheim Line again, and on 17 February they broke through it.

As news arrived in the west that the Finns were preparing to negotiate with Russia, the Allies grew frantic. France promised 50,000 men in a month, an offer which quickly shrank to 12,000 in two months, while Britain prepared a 100,000 strong expedition to go to the aid of the Finns, travelling by way of Narvik and the Swedish iron ore fields. The unwilling hosts for this excursion objected to it, but on 12 March, after agonized discussion, the expedition was none the less confirmed. Providentially the Finns sued for peace that same night. Had they not done so Britain might well have found herself at war with Russia and Germany at the same time, as well as having ruptured her relations with the Scandinavian neutrals, and committed to a campaign the outcome of which would have been highly problematical. As it was, Britain was forced to revert to an earlier proposal to mine Norwegian territorial waters.

Once again Hitler moved too quickly for the more ponderous allies. On 9 April, the day after the mining operation had commenced, he launched Operation WESER — planned only a month before — and within a short space of time

German troops were in possession of Denmark, Oslo, Trondheim, Stavanger and Narvik. The failure of allied attempts to intervene, which were frustrated by bad weather, imparted some hard lessons about the need for more effective co-ordination of land and sea forces in any combined operation and for command of the air, without which any amphibious operation lay vulnerable to easy interruption. These lessons were well learned and would be applied later, so that in the long run the Norwegian campaign was not disastrous for the Allies. But in the short run it was. Hitler's boldness had once again brought complete success, paralysing his opponents before they could move to counter him and providing another demonstration of the effectiveness both of the *Blitzkrieg* system and of the Führer's own strategic judgment.

When Hitler launched his long-postponed attack on France on 10 May 1940, his forces again faced an opponent whose material superiority was, if not overwhelming, at least marked. A German force of 114 divisions, of which ten were Panzer divisions, confronted a total of 135 British, French, Belgian and Dutch divisions. German numerical inferiority even extended to the very area where the *Wehrmacht* was held to be strongest, its armoured troops; France disposed in total of more tanks than did Germany (4,688 to 3,862), and though both armies possessed approximately the same numbers of the newest heavy tank-killing tanks, the French used 25 per cent more of their tanks during the attack than did the Germans, and did not disperse them in penny-packets — one of the explanations proffered afterwards to explain the French defeat.[5] The Germans did, however, have ten Panzer divisions against only four French armoured divisions, and a slight numerical superiority in numbers of aircraft. They also enjoyed the advantage of a single army with a single command; the Allied troops differed in equipment and training, and the Belgians and the Dutch did not have even the vestiges of joint command possessed by Britain and France.

A further advantage did accrue to the Allies, however, when, on 10 January 1940, a plane carrying a German staff officer crashed at Mechelen in Belgium and the original

German plans of attack fell into Allied hands. This remarkable windfall failed to divert Gamelin from his original
intention of marching the French armies into Belgium at the
moment of a German attack, but it did provide the necessary
impetus for the German commanders — under some pressure
from Hitler — to drop their earlier plans in favour of a more
imaginative and daring advance through the Ardennes,
hitherto believed by most soldiers to be impenetrable, a
scheme proposed by von Manstein and his subordinate
Guderian. Hitler now switched the weight of the attack from
the Northern to the Centre army group and at the same
time imparted a more aggressive tone to the proceedings:[6]

> The objective of Offensive Yellow [the attack on France] is to
> deny Holland and Belgium to the English by swiftly occupying
> them; to defeat, by an attack through Belgian and Luxembourg
> territory, the largest possible forces of the French army; and
> thereby to pave the way for the destruction of the military
> strength of the enemy.

When the attack was launched, the mass of the French
army moved north into Belgium to meet the Dutch and block
the advance of von Bock's Northern army group. Meanwhile
von Rundstedt's troops forced a path through the Ardennes
and three days later crossed the Meuse near Sedan, covered
by heavy dive-bombing. According to one of the German
participants, there was at this stage considerable disorganiza-
tion among the German troops; spearheads got confused and
support did not arrive quickly enough at the front. Victory
in battle usually goes to the participant who is best able to
overcome the inevitable dislocations and frustrations which
attend the movement of troops in the 'fog of war', and in
this instance the French were psychologically defeated
almost before they had lost the battle in material terms.
Caught off-balance by the speed and pressure of the combined land-air offensive, they were never able to overcome
the defects in the organization of their defence. Divisions
allocated to counter-attacks moved too slowly and arrived
too late; air interdiction failed to arrest the progress of the
armoured spearheads by destroying bridges and communications; and over-all co-ordination from headquarters, designed

for a war of an altogether more leisurely pace, failed to respond to the demands for speed made upon it. The fact that Gamelin's Allied Headquarters, based at Vincennes, lacked even a radio by which to keep in touch with events, was both a symptom and a cause of this failure. For their part the Germans took advantage of the situation they created, if necessary by upsetting previously agreed schedules: Guderian twice challenged orders to stop the advance, and by 20 May had reached Abbéville and the sea, cutting the Allied armies in two.

The effects of the *Blitzkrieg* meant that the Allies quickly found themselves unable to squeeze out what should have been no more than a local breakthrough. Bombing destroyed their own communications as much as those of the enemy; refugees clogged the roads; orders and commands were routed by circuitous paths at a moment when speedy reactions were of critical importance; rumour spread feelings of nervousness and alarm and helped to turn setbacks into defeats. The substitution of Weygand for Gamelin at the height of the battle, and the unfortunate death of general Bilotte, who had been entrusted with the plans for a counter-attack, helped paralyse the French response. However the effects of uncertainty and fatigue did not make themselves felt on the Allies alone: the need to recuperate and re-supply caused von Rundstedt to call a halt for twenty-four hours with German armour only sixteen miles from Dunkirk, and the prospect of having to turn south after defeating the British and face the rest of France's forces prompted Hitler to prolong it for a further twenty-four hours, secure in Goering's confident assertion that the Allied troops at Dunkirk could safely be left to the *Luftwaffe* to finish off. When the port finally fell on 4 June, 338,000 Allied troops had been evacuated despite the claims of the *Luftwaffe* to be able to destroy such an operation, but at the cost of all its heavy equipment — in August 1940 the British army possessed only 500 guns and 200 tanks. Twelve days after the fall of Dunkirk the French asked for terms, and the campaign was over. At a cost of half a million casualties the Germans had taken 2,000,000 prisoners and defeated the armies of Britain, France, Holland and Belgium. Once again the *Blitzkrieg* system had proved its effectiveness, but this time it had vanquished a power whose military organization and industrial base were at a level not incomparable with Germany's own. Only Britain remained to be subdued before Germany could turn east.

The attempt to subdue Britain was to reveal one of the most critical weaknesses of the military machine built up in the Third Reich. The *Luftwaffe* had been developed chiefly in order to operate in a tactical role, but was now required to act in a strategic one and reduce Britain by a bombing campaign for which it possessed neither the equipment nor the doctrine. The essential preliminary to an invasion of England was the moral and physical reduction of the RAF to a level where it would be unable to offer any significant opposition to a German channel crossing. Attempting to seize command of the air in this way, Goering launched Operation ADLER ('Eagle') on 13 August 1940, and directed it against every part of the machine which put the RAF into the air. Although it had the advantages of superior equipment and early warning, by August the RAF was losing pilots at a rate of 460 a month and was on the point of exhaustion when, early in September, the *Luftwaffe* switched its attentions to cities and docks as well as air stations in an attempt to destroy civilian morale and produce panic by area bombing. This dispersal of effort weakened the impact of the German offensive and, together with the damage sustained by the invasion barges assembled at Dutch ports, forced Hitler to postpone the invasion of England until the following summer.

By this time the effects of the war were being felt in Germany almost as much as in England, and the prospect of another winter of war was causing the German authorities some concern as morale began to decline. With the abandonment of Operation SEALION, complaints mounted at home and the authorities responded by instituting a downward shift in war production, especially that of aircraft, and by imposing a wage freeze which was designed to conceal from the working population the shortage of perishable goods. At the same time the quality of the goods was adulterated, as being preferable to rationing, and finally in February 1941 the government ceased to publish cost-of-living indexes.

For Britain the next moves in the war against the Axis were fairly obvious. The hasty entry of Italy into the war on 10 June 1940 and Spain's flirtation with the Axis powers combined to focus her attentions upon the Mediterranean theatre, her lifeline to the raw materials of the far east and to the oil of the Persian Gulf. In the event Britain's fears about the vulnerability of this area proved to be without foundation: Spain did not enter the war on either side; Vichy France proved, at least as far as its North African possessions were concerned, to be less in Germany's pocket than had been feared; and Italy's decision to enter a war towards which the majority of her population felt little but apathy proved to be a great error. None the less fear of German activity in the area resulted in 1941 in first a campaign in Iraq in May, when an army revolt under Rashid Ali was crushed, and then in the following month the capture of Vichy-controlled Syria in order to forestall any possible German leap from Greece and Crete into the middle east — a move which the Germans seem never to have seriously contemplated making.

North Africa was to be the focus of Britain's major land action against the Axis for the next two years of war, and in both 1941 and 1942 witnessed a see-saw action in which Axis troops under the command of general Erwin Rommel — a general whom the British found charismatic but whom his superiors deemed 'that lout'[7] — surged twice into Egypt itself and on each occasion were pushed back. This thrilling combat, which gave Britain her first and much needed land victory at El Alamein in November 1942, was determined less by the generalship or fighting capacity of the British forces than by the logistical truth that the further Rommel got from Tripoli the more impossible his supply situation became as a thin filament of motorized transport was strung out behind him. It did, however, provide the British with useful experience in fighting major land battles, which they manifestly needed.

Russia had always been Hitler's ultimate objective, and yet when the attack against it was launched in June 1941 it had a marked hand-to-mouth character which accorded ill with the widespread view of an efficient and deadly Nazi war machine. Detailed planning for the campaign was long delayed; whilst the German navy had been basing its war-games on a war with Russia since 1936, the army only began to study such a campaign in 1940. When Hitler came to set down his objectives in a war directive on 21 July 1940, they were vague and confusing: the setting up of states in western Russia which would be politically dependent upon Germany, and the defeat of the Russian army — or at least the occupation of as much Russian soil as was necessary to protect Berlin and the Silesian industrial area from air attack and enable the *Luftwaffe* to destroy the most important areas of Russia. Defining objectives which would simultaneously defeat the Russian armies, seize the Baltic states and put Germany in possession of the raw materials of the Black Sea area resulted in a three-pronged axis of advance: Moscow, Leningrad and Kiev. Hitler was confident that after early defeats the USSR would simply disintegrate — by mid-March 1941 he declared that the capture of Moscow was 'completely irrelevant' — and his confidence was at last being shared by his generals, who believed that the war would be over in three to four weeks and therefore gave little thought to secondary targets or to the subsequent course of the campaign in the event of a rapid collapse not taking place. In fact, as Guderian later ruefully admitted, the Germans were completely wrong in their assessment of their enemy, underestimating the productive capacity of Russian industry and the stability of the social system.

The need to clear his southern flank by securing Greece and Yugoslavia occupied Hitler during April, although it did not cause the delays to the offensive against Russia, which were due to the lack of equipment for the assault troops. When Hitler finally launched Operation BARBAROSSA on 22 June 1941, thirty-three armoured and motorized divisions and 112 marching infantry divisions were put into the field against what German intelligence estimated as being 225 Russian divisions but turned out to be 360. Supporting the ground forces were 2,770 aircraft — only 170 more than had been massed against England a year earlier — and all of types not less than five years old. The deficiencies of the *Blitzkrieg* system were beginning to show. In order to permit the mechanized and motorized units to have their maximum disruptive effect in a country whose distances dwarfed those of France, road transport was to shuttle between the advanced motorized units and the infantry, making the former independent of base supply, whilst in the no-man's land between the two echelons railway troops were to convert Russian lines and rolling stock so as to provide the necessary bulk transport over distances at which lorries could not operate efficiently.

The attack achieved immediate and overwhelming success, and to western observers the question rapidly became not whether success would attend Hitler's initiative but when it would do so; as the vice-chief of the British imperial general staff recorded in his diary on 29 June, 'It is impossible to say how long Russian resistance will last — three weeks or three months.'[8] By 5 August the advancing armies had taken 590,000 prisoners, and then the centre thrust opened outwards to aid the northern and southern wings of the advance. Kiev was taken and with it a further 665,000 prisoners, but at the cost of great wear and tear on machines, and then at the end of September the impetus of the central attack on Moscow was renewed. On 7 October the first snow fell, and six days later German pincers closed around the last of the great 'pockets', at Vyazma, taking another 650,000 prisoners. Shortly afterwards the autumn rains began and the *rasputitsa* — the infamous Russian mud — brought the German army to a halt.

The Russians had responded slowly to the initial German advance and in the first weeks of the war betrayed some of the same symptoms as had afflicted the French a year earlier. However in mid-July dual command was again re-imposed as an earnest of the party's intentions to control military operations, a state committee of defence (GKO) was set up, and the high command was reorganized and weeded of incompetents such as Budenny. This thorough reoganization of the command structure was accompanied by a series of firm and clear decisions on priorities, the foremost of which were the defence of Moscow and Leningrad, and by a truly remarkable feat of industrial relocation as Russia's factories were literally uprooted and replanted behind the Ural mountains where they would be safe from the German advance. In Moscow alone 80,000 trains transported 498 factories east whilst the German armies were advancing to the very gates of the capital. The Russian political and military machine had survived the shock of the initial German assault as much by virtue of the success of its leadership in regaining its psychological balance after early hesitancy as through the possession of vast physical spaces into which to retreat. Once it had achieved this feat of recovery a lightning war against Russia was no longer possible and Germany's military organization faced its greatest test in eight years of existence.

The German armies halted before Moscow in December in temperatures of -30° centigrade, but even before the full force of the winter made itself felt the *Wehrmacht* had had to face severe transport problems: railway conversion from the broad Russian gauge proved troublesome, and the troops had become increasingly dependent upon air supply. Moreover, not just the means of transporting war *matériel* but the very material itself was becoming a source of concern; at the end of November general Wagner, quartermaster general of the German armies, recorded in his diary 'We have come to the end of our resources in both men and material.'[9] It was plain that defeating Russia now meant mobilizing more of Germany's material resources behind the war and putting more physical effort into it than had hitherto been the case, and on 3 December Hitler recognized this by issuing his first *Führerbefehl* ('Führer Command') calling in general terms for the introduction of modern methods of mass production on a greater scale than before and using simpler designs. Production was to be concentrated in plants with the best and most economical working methods, and there was to be further construction of floorspace.

This was a rational response to the demands made by the new phase of war, yet shortly afterwards Hitler manifested the unreasonable side of his nature by accepting the resignations of all three army group commanders in Russia (von Leeb, von Bock and von Rundstedt) sooner than allow them to retreat to better positions from which to sit out the winter. Their successors were grudgingly allowed to make the very step-by-step retreats which they had been denied at the same moment that Stalin, perhaps doubting the capacity of the Red Army to stand in a firm and disciplined defensive, threw his armies into a counter-attack despite their chronic shortage of equipment and ammunition. By the end of March 1942 both sides were near exhaustion as Stalin drove the Red commanders forwards and when on 17 April the spring thaw put an end to all movement — much to the relief of both sides — the Germans had lost 900,000 casualties in ten months, whilst the Russians had lost 3,461,000 in prisoners alone.

The failure of the first campaign against Russian began a process by which Germany gradually and reluctantly adopted a mode of organization more akin to that of her rivals in its emphasis upon long-term planning and the maximizing of economic potential, though it was never to be fully realized. In their efforts to win the war, and in their incursions ever deeper into civil society, all the combatant powers had to confront the central and exacting task of managing their economies and controlling the raw materials at their command in order to make the best use of what resources they possessed or to which they could gain access. On this plane a difference of great significance existed between Germany on the one hand and the western Allies on the other, for whereas Britain and America could use all the resources of capitalism — not least among them the profit incentive — in order to maximize output, Germany sought for far too long to accommodate powerful ideological considerations which militated against getting optimal benefit out of her possessions.

At its most simple, the Nazi notion of managing the European economy which had by 1940 largely fallen under its control amounted to little more than regarding all natural resources as booty which should be carried off to Germany. A more sophisticated version of Germany's *Grossraumpolitik*, or policy of large economic areas, envisaged Europe as a giant cartel, at the centre of which Germany would carry out all the necessary scientific and technological research and the more advanced industrial production, whilst her satellites provided labour and raw materials or were allowed limited manufacturing rights under licence. However, the fortunes of war soon acted to destroy this ideal, a process accelerated by the demands the Russian campaign made on the economy of the Reich. Prior to that campaign, France had been regarded as a state which should be carefully incorporated into the New Order rather than simply being pillaged; however, once the first months of BARBAROSSA had passed without the expected collapse of the communist system, the French economy could no longer be viewed as a whole but rather as a series of constituent elements, some of which could be used to reinforce areas of German weakness. To meet specific demands, German controls were extended initially into raw materials such as bauxite, iron ore and phosphate, but by 1942-3 had come to encompass also the manufacture of aircraft and finished armaments.

The organized exploitation of the French economy hinged upon two fundamental requirements: the reversal of that part of party dogma which required that France remain a non-manufacturing state, and the presence of a level of co-operation within France sufficient to make use of French industry and manpower worth while. Collaboration, often fuelled by exaggerated visions of the benefits of the New Order in Europe, secured the second of these prerequisites; thus Laval saw a reorganization of the continent upon new principles as the justification for aiding the German war effort:[10]

> On the material plane, the countries must help one another and harmonize their economic interests so that the needs of each can be satisfied without recourse to the competition and violence which have too often been the rule in the past . . . On the moral, cultural, and political plane, the individuality of the peoples must be respected.

Party dogma proved altogether more obstructive.

As the level of German exploitation of Europe mounted, labour became a crucial issue. This was a reflection of the general fact that as the war went on the addition of labour was of more importance than the addition of manufacturing capital in increasing wartime output. The critical issue was where foreign labour was best employed. Under both Todt and Speer, the ministry of armaments always preferred to use

French labour in France whereas the party line, put forward with some vehemence by Fritz Sauckel, Reich plenipotentiary for labour, was to import all foreign workers into Germany. In the event Hitler backed Sauckel — certainly a mistake, since foreign labour seems to have been less productive away from home, deportations caused domestic hostility within France (and of course elsewhere), and such labour was frequently employed in Germany in small and unproductive concerns. The needs of the war demanded that the Nazis compromise with their ideological view of the economic ordering of Europe, but Hitler found calculations of relative economic benefit less convincing than Sauckel's vision of Europe, which fitted better with the ideas of national revolution that he had never entirely discarded. Thus ideological considerations greatly hampered Germany in her prosecution of the war.

The eastern nations which fell under German domination assumed different relations with the parent economy. Austria and western Czechoslovakia became virtually organic parts of the Reich, and here complete integration and German ownership brought prosperity, wiping out unemployment which prior to the war had been running at levels of between 20 and 30 per cent. By 1944 200 Austrian firms, or some two-thirds of the country's entire joint stock capital, had gone into German ownership. The results were broadly beneficial to Germany as industrial production increased markedly up to the autumn of 1943, when for the first time the Bohemian industrial area came within range of allied bombers based on the newly captured airfields in Italy. The population was generally well treated, and as a result production in these areas rose by some 230 per cent during the war years.

At the start of the war Germany had aimed at preserving the agricultural status of Hungary, Rumania, Bulgaria and Slovakia and permitting them to produce only semi-finished goods. This ideal foundered due to the fact that all four countries lacked manpower, machinery and fertilizers, and in any case they all experienced a rise in domestic consumption during the war years which left no significant surplus for Germany. Their poor performance was exacerbated by a series of droughts and floods; only in 1944 was the harvest good. In 1943 the pressure of military exigencies forced the Reich to end their semi-independence. A year earlier, Germany had been faced with precisely the same choice as confronted her in the case of France: whether to conform to the ideological requirement of semi-agrarianism or to alter her vision of the eastern economy in conformity with her immediate need for greater industrial output. In the east, ideology lost to economics, with the OKW giving heavy backing to demands for more industrialization, and as a consequence of this an aircraft manufacturing industry was established in Hungary. Although this reached its planned output only once – in February 1944 – it did add something to Germany's stock of armaments and could have added more had the decision to reverse party dogma in the eastern lands been taken earlier and carried out more completely.

The fact that Germany applied different principles to the different parts of her economic empire, where the western economies by contrast operated on only one fundamental principle, undoubtedly had an adverse effect on the German war machine. Nowhere was this unwillingness to compromise with ideology in particular instances more harmful to the Nazi effort than in Poland and Russia. Polish capital was destroyed in 1939-40, and Polish labour expropriated; in all some 2,000,000 Poles were shipped to Germany, to work there in conditions of extreme hardship. For Russia, the *Generalplan Ost*, produced in June 1942, proposed a system of rural colonization and the creation of a healthy peasantry by 'appropriate biological selection' – in other words, a system of colonial domination. The doctrine of the *untermenschen* ('sub-humans') which underpinned the bestiality of German occupation policy in Russia further weakened the over-all war effort, for not only did it obstruct any proposals to use Russian nationalism or sub-nationalism against Stalin's regime but it also denied Germany any opportunity of using Russia as a part of the economic machine to fight the war. In the long run the doctrine of racial inferiority also undermined faith in the Nazi regime itself; notions that their Russian opponent was sub-human were soon disproved by the enemy's feats of war organization and by the quality of his weapons design and production, and by August 1942 intelligence reports from within the Reich were remarking on a growing feeling that the people had been deluded about their opponent: 'The main and startling impression is of the vast mass of Soviet weapons, their technical quality and the gigantic Soviet effort of industrialization — all in sharp contrast to the previous picture of the Soviet Union.'[11] Here, as in many other areas of the Nazi war effort, ideology which was unyielding to circumstance proved disastrous in the long run.

Where Germany tried to fight the war without a single unitary economy or economic system, the west had the priceless advantage of first access to and then partnership with the American economy. This was relatively easily geared to the needs of war because there was considerable slack in the economy which could easily and profitably be taken up; there were, for example, 3,000,000 unemployed in December 1941 who could quickly be taken in by the war industries. America had a second advantage in that she was able to determine the guiding principle behind her war economy, which was to outproduce the enemy in volume, at the start and then apply the means to hand to achieve it, rather than switching gradually and hesitantly from partial concentration upon the war as did Germany. The means to this end consisted in operating within the framework of the capitalist system as it had developed in the United States by a strategy of co-operation and consideration rather than by the application of government power. Thus businessmen were recruited to the war effort and industry was wooed away from a reluctance to manufacture arms by means of government underwriting of expansion, whilst the problem of guiding the deployment of crucial raw materials was resolved by a system of autonomous agencies headed by recognized figures from the business world (known as the 'czars') or by a wide allocation of power across a series of boards or commissions. The philosophy behind the American government's approach to the problem of maximizing war production without creating internal stresses was put clearly by the secretary for war, Henry L. Stimson: 'If you are going to try to go to war, or to prepare for war, in a capitalist country, you have got to let business make money out of the process or business won't work.'[12]

For both sides in the partnership, America's ordering of her war economy was a triumphant success. Businessmen were placated as New Deal anti-trust legislation went by the board, innovations like the National Youth Agency were dismantled, and conservatives such as Stimson, Forrestal and Acheson entered the administration in the place of the New Dealers. The businessman began to enjoy a new prestige in America, and with it went the enjoyment of large financial rewards: corporate profits after tax rose from 6.4 billion dollars in 1940 to 10.8 billion dollars in 1944. In return, the government enjoyed the fruits of intense economic effort with which to fight the war. From 1940 to 1944 the physical output of American industry increased by 15 per cent each year, and America's production of Lend-Lease exports alone amounted to a value of 32,500 million dollars. The latent strength of the American economy was effectively tapped for war by a careful conformity to the existing business philosophy with a single overriding objective in view, the achievement of the greatest possible volume of output. The contrast between the simplicity of America's war economy and the complexity of Germany's is stark. Whether the constituent parts of American society made any real advance beyond the freedom to spend larger wage packets as they chose is debatable.

The war economies of the other major combatants, though important, were of a smaller order of magnitude than those of Germany and the United States and sooner or later all revealed fundamental weaknesses which affected their participation in the war. Britain began to manage her war economy on the basis of a severe underestimation of how enormous the costs of war were to be; during the winter of 1939-40 she gave priority to an export drive in the mistaken belief that she could pay for the war as she fought it. From 1940 onwards the principle behind her war effort changed to one of the fullest utilization of resources — America's as well as her own — regardless of cost. This resulted in amassing huge debts both to America and to the countries making up the sterling area, the existence of which was to help reduce

Britain's political freedom of action once the war ended. Shortage of raw materials and a relatively restricted production capacity were exacerbated by a shortage of labour which became by 1942 the decisive factor in planning the war economy. This accounted in part for one of the most striking differences between the gains made by British and American society as a result of fighting the war, for British labour was now increasingly in a strong bargaining position, rather than volunteering its efforts out of patriotic national fervour as it had done in the First World War. The fruits of the political recognition of this fact and of the self-restraint shown by labour in the face of it were to be found in all those innovations which made up the welfare state as it emerged in 1944-6.

The other economies, with one exception, had to find considerable supplementation in order to continue their wars. Italy's weakness in terms of raw materials was to be a constant drain on the resources of the Axis; by the end of 1941 she possessed only enough oil for one month's consumption. Japan's rapid expansion in the far east did not increase her industrial capacity, since she occupied non-industrialized countries; in the whole of the Greater East Asia Co-Prosperity Sphere only Korea had a production amounting to more than 5 per cent of her own. Her small industrial sector and shortage of human and technological resources was eventually to render her especially vulnerable to economic warfare. Russia was forced to fight the war with no significant outside supplementation of her economic resources, a fact which, though allowance must be made for the size of her unexploited resources of minerals and other raw materials, highlights the feats of organization performed by those fighting the war behind the front line. As Alan Milward has pointed out, 'Alone of all the major combatants the Soviet Union had to fight the war out of a diminishing rather than a rapidly increasing national product and from an industrial base much smaller than the pre-war one.'[13]

The war economies were fundamental constituent elements in a conception of military organization which, by the time that the Second World War was being waged, had widened its scope considerably, and they were to be the target of much military effort in an attempt to gain victory. Even before these assaults reached their height, the morale of the labour force and of the domestic population as a whole became an important focus for the activities of governments, whether attempting to prop it up or to undermine it. For the Axis, social cohesion was to become a pressing concern in 1942 as a result of the twisting fortunes of war. At first it seemed that these would favour them by diverting some of the Allied effort to another quarter, for on 7 December 1941 Japan brought America into the war by attacking her fleet at Pearl Harbour. Hitler hastily associated himself with his diplomatic consort by himself declaring war on America.

Limited objectives coupled with the achievement of complete surprise brought the Japanese extensive initial success. After a brief and inglorious campaign in Malaya the British and Commonwealth forces surrendered at Singapore on 14 February 1942. American forces in the Philippines hung on until May, when general Douglas MacArthur was evacuated to Australia after making his celebrated promise to return, and in the same month further Japanese advances enfolded within the boundaries of their Co-Prosperity Sphere the Solomon Islands, Guadalcanal and Papua. The tide of Japan's advance, tempted beyond its originally planned confines by the scale of its success, was eventually turned at the battles of the Coral Sea (3-8 May 1942) and Midway (5-6 June) by American carrier-based aircraft. For Europe the critical fact in these first months of global war was that sweeping setbacks in the Pacific did not divert American attention from Europe, as some feared it would. True to the plan first devised in November 1940 and elaborated during the Anglo-American staff conversations in 1941, the United States remained firmly wedded to the 'Europe First' principle. The Axis would continue to feel the main weight of America's military capability.

As the war began to take on new and longer perspectives, and particularly as the campaign in Russia came to assume the character of a long and gruelling contest rather than a rapid war of conquest, the furtherance of which would require much more in the way of sacrifices than Germany had yet been called upon to make, the Reich began to show a greater concern to indoctrinate the troops with National Socialist ideology in order to fuel their struggle. In this it was reverting to a use for military organization which had a lengthy tradition. On 31 May 1942 Keitel, chief of the OKW, published regulations on the responsibilities of the German officer which stressed the need for educating him so that he became 'capable of educating his soldiers to become convinced representatives of this [i.e. Nazi] Weltanschauung which — stemming from the front experience of 1914-1918 — was brought to singular heights by the Führer.'[14] In an endeavour to make the army more completely National Socialist in its composition all educational qualifications for officer cadets were abolished and the National Socialist Leadership Organization was founded to indoctrinate the officer corps. Coincidentally Hitler's eastern opponent felt the same need to provide a firm ideological basis upon which to support the hard fighting to come, for in the summer of 1942 the Red army followed a deliberate programme of calling up party members in order to strengthen its fibre, and political education was stepped up.

Just as the economy and civilian morale were both of fundamental importance for every belligerent in the search to maximize war effort, so both were legitimate targets for direct military action by means of the twin forms of economic warfare, air action and naval blockade. In the air the bomber was the main instrument by which it was hoped to cause dislocation of the home front, but here a profound difference developed between Britain and the United States over how best to deploy their fleets of bombers. By the end of 1941 the RAF had been forced to abandon daylight bombing raids due to the vulnerability of bombers to the German fighter defences. Operating at night, however, bombers could hit only large and semi-precise targets such as railway marshalling yards, and then only when they could locate them; the Butt report of 1941 revealed that only 8 per cent of the force despatched actually dropped their bombs within five miles of the target at all, so severe were the navigational problems. Strategic bombing could not, however, be abandoned; for one thing, it provided a means by which to assuage Stalin's repeated calls for the establishment of a second front in Europe, and as such was diplomatically invaluable. The choice, therefore, lay between daylight bombing, which would be accurate but suicidal, and night bombing, which was safer but less accurate. In February 1942 the chief of air staff, Sir Charles Portal, opted for the latter course of action, termed area bombing, and for the erosion of civilian morale as the main objective of the bomber offensive.

Area bombing conformed with the theoretical proposition established by the inter-war theorists that civilian morale was vulnerable to the psychological and physical effects of a general bombing offensive to the point at which a collapse of the enemy war effort would occur — which proved in the event to be incorrect — and also conformed to the dictates of operational experience, which seemed to show that the bomber could not effectively do anything else. However the Americans had their own air doctrine which was based on quite different premises. They believed that it was possible to carry out daylight raids, and therefore bomb more accurately, provided that enough heavily armed bombers were massed together to be able to beat off the attacking fighters — which the B 17 'Flying Fortress' was specifically designed to do — and they believed also that bombing would have its greatest effect not on enemy morale but upon specific parts of the German industrial system: ball-bearing factories, oil cracking plant, transport and communications and other utilities or components. The American theory of precision bombing, which was much closer to pure economic warfare than area bombing, thus rested upon the presupposition that there did in fact exist within a modern industrial economy bottlenecks which if closed completely would bring about an economic breakdown.

In the event the German economy, like all modern industrial economies, proved to be very versatile, and was for a considerable time capable of devising alternative sources of supply, power and the means of production and of dispersing industry in order to minimize the likelihood of loss of output. In any case it was not until after 1943, when it was reorganized for total war by Albert Speer, that the German economy was stretched to an extent which made it vulnerable to such a strategy. Until that time it proved possible to make good the losses suffered as a result of bombing by taking up the slack in the system or by devising alternative means of production. Once the economy was fully stretched bottle-necks did make their appearance, perhaps the most critical being oil (for example, lubrication oils could not be manufactured by either of the two common synthetic processes), but the problems then arose first of agreeing what they were, and second of hitting them.

Bomber command launched its policy of area bombing with a raid on Lübeck on 28 March 1942 in which the centre of the city, being medieval and therefore largely constructed of wood, was wiped out. There followed raids on Rostock and then, on 30 May, the first 'Thousand Bomber' raid on Cologne. This venture, for which Sir Arthur Harris scraped the United Kingdom in order to put into the air practically every plane and every crew that could fly, probably had a greater effect upon allied morale than upon that of Germany. But by the end of the year the heavier, four-engined Lancaster and Stirling bombers had come into service, and this, together with improvements in navigation by radar and target location, meant that bombing raids became both heavier and more accurate. By the summer of 1943 huge attacks were being launched — sixteen on Berlin alone. The process reached a pinnacle in July with a week of non-stop raids on Hamburg in the course of which 10,000 tons of bombs were dropped, 40,000 people were killed and the labour force was permanently reduced by ten per cent. Although the city was back to 80 per cent of its output within five months, it now seemed that area bombing was going to have the hoped-for effect. Goebbels wrote in his diary of[15]

a catastrophe the extent of which simply staggers the imagination. A city of a million inhabitants has been destroyed in a manner unparalleled in history. We are faced with problems that are almost impossible of solution. Food must be found for this population of a million. Shelter must be secured. The people must be evacuated as far as possible. They must be given clothing. In short, we are facing problems there of which we had no conception even a few weeks ago.

However, German morale did not break, and although internal security reports spoke in early 1943 of a 'psychotic fear' of air raids, allied bombing seems to have drawn communities closer together. Over-all the area bombing campaign may well have backfired, since resistance to the Nazi regime seemed doubly suicidal in the light of the foreign threat and demands for unconditional surrender.

Although sceptical as to the logic of the American philosophy of air warfare, Britain could not intervene to stop it being put into practice, and after a directive had split the air effort into two distinct parts the USAAF duly began its daylight precision bombing raids. At first the results were much better than had been expected in Britain, chiefly because the appearance of large formations of bombers in German skies in broad daylight took the *Luftwaffe* somewhat by surprise, but by the summer of 1943 the Germans had devised adequate means to counter American penetration and the attacking forces began to suffer heavy casualties. The culmination of this process was the raid on the Schweinfurt ball-bearing plant on 14 October 1943, when 291 American bombers were despatched against a well-defended target. What followed was described by one of the German participants as a 'turkey shoot', and by the time the day was over 198 American planes had been lost or badly damaged. To keep up the air war at this rate of loss would require an entire new bomber force every three months. This was a rate of attrition which rivalled that experienced during the First World War and one which simply could not be sustained. The resolution of the problem was to come with the development of the long-range P 47 'Thunderbolt' and P 51 'Mustang' escort fighters which could win the battle for command of the air and thus allow the bombers the freedom to attack their targets unimpeded by enemy fighters.

In the second form of economic warfare which preoccupied the warring powers, that of naval blockade, the advantage lay more immediately and apparently more decisively with Germany. In 1940 the German navy found itself the possessor of a great and unexpected advantage in the fact of its control of the western coast of Europe from Narvik to Bordeaux. At this moment, when Britain was critically vulnerable to any interruption of her sea-borne supplies and had even forgotten the lesson learned in 1917 about the value of convoys, the *Kriegsmarine* was poorly provided with the one type of vessel best calculated to permit her to take the maximum advantage of her position – the submarine. Since Admiral Raeder's surface ships were too few in number to contest the command of the sea in a major naval engagement with any hope of success, they were split up and used as commerce raiders, a role in which they enjoyed little success and during the performance of which they were gradually hunted down and destroyed. However by April 1942 the German navy had redirected its attentions on the prospects opening up before it and already possessed 125 operational submarines, which Raeder hoped to increase to 400 by the end of the year. As their quality and armament were improved, their efforts assisted by air spotting and their range lengthened by the use of 'tanker' submarines to re-supply them while still at sea, the German U-boats began to wreak increasing havoc on Britain's lifeline to America.

What followed was a war of attrition not dissimilar from that which was to occur in the air. Between September 1939 and December 1941 some 8,000,000 tons of Allied shipping had been sunk and only one third of it replaced. American entry into the war now offered Britain direct access to her ship-building capacity, but also offered the German submarine commanders more targets, obligingly illuminated by the lights of the eastern American seabord. During 1942 a further 8,000,000 tons of Allied shipping was sunk; and at one point – during the month of June – one Allied ship was being sent to the bottom every four hours. The measure of the extent to which Germany was winning the war at sea lay in the fact that the combined capacity of the British, American and Canadian shipyards together amounted to only 7,000,000 tons of shipping per year, whereas the *Kriegsmarine* was able to replace the fifty submarines lost in the course of the year and still have submarine-building capacity to spare. The war at sea thus became a deadly race in which the Germans sought to sink allied merchant shipping faster than it could be replaced whilst the Allies sought to limit their losses and to inflict on the U-boats greater losses than they could sustain.

The year 1943 saw the mounting of a two-pronged strategy by the Allies in their attempt to win this war: losses had to be cut, which they were by the use of convoys, escort vessels and long-range, shore-based aircraft; and submarines had to be sunk, a process in which radar, mobile protection groups and carrier-borne aircraft all played a part. In March 627,000 tons of Allied shipping was sunk; in April losses amounted to 328,000 tons, and sixteen U-boats were destroyed; in May 265,000 tons went to the bottom in exchange for thirty-eight U-boats. The graph had crossed in April, when for the first time the amount of Allied shipping being launched matched that being sunk, whilst the number of German submarines destroyed was greater than that built. There remained much stern action to be survived, but the pendulum had swung ineluctably in favour of the Allies. It was for Britain a stroke of the greatest good fortune that when, in 1940, she had been most vulnerable to this form of economic warfare Germany had had too few submarines to capitalize upon her strategic advantage.

For her part, Germany never proved to be as vulnerable to either naval or air warfare as the west had supposed. Sweden, Switzerland and Turkey, each of which traded highly significant commodities to the Reich, were immune from naval blockade, and Portugal and Spain prepared to engage in a measure of commerce, although less important, so that Germany proved able to survive for a considerable length of time, and expand her economy, on the basis of the resources of the European land mass. Her vulnerability to the bomber also proved less than the more optimistic had expected. In part this was due to the operational deficiencies of the strategic bombing forces, which required unhindered command of the skies before they began to operate at anything like full effect, and to the difficulties of determining priorities among the many possible targets, and in part it reflected the fact that the pundits of strategic bombing underestimated the resilience of a modern economy, which substitution of raw materials, stockpiling and the continuance of international trade all helped to reinforce.

Germany's move towards a total war economy, a transition

which multiplied her capacity to carry on the war to a remarkable degree, was largely the product of the set-backs suffered in Russia during 1942, and especially of the débâcle at Stalingrad. The main industrial centre of southern Russia and one of the prize achievements of Stalin's programme of forced industrialization, Stalingrad was selected by Hitler as one of the twin targets of the 1942 campaign because, like Verdun before it, it was a prestige objective for the defence of which Stalin would be forced to mass his armies, thereby offering the German a chance to destroy them. The second objective was the oilfields of the Caucasus, like Stalingrad 300 miles beyond the German front line, and 350 miles south of it. Hitler was committing his armies to an offensive on divergent lines which was to prove a ghastly miscalculation.

The attack began on 23 August and soon reached the Volga, a thousand miles from the Reich. Supply difficulties were immense and when the southern spearheads reached the foothills of the Caucasus in early autumn they did so only in weak strength and were soon forced to pull back. Meanwhile heavy fighting developed around Stalingrad as units were withdrawn from other fronts and fed into the attack. On 19 November the Russians launched their counter-attack, choosing the point at which weaker Rumanian troops held the line. The fate of Stalingrad was sealed not by Hitler but by Goering when, on 24 November, he gave his guarantee to keep the beleaguered forces supplied by air if all land routes to them were closed. An air supply operation of this type had been successfully carried out during the previous winter to maintain German troops caught in the Demyansk pocket, but there the numbers involved amounted to only 90,000 men, and in any case the operation had taken place when the worst of the winter had passed. Now Goering was offering to supply an army many times that size with an air force weakened by losses and in any case ill-equipped for such an operation. The result was disaster. As the two sides fought over the wreckage of the city — often no more than ten feet apart in the bitter contest for office blocks and factories — food ran short and supplies failed. A fortnight before Christmas the first German soldier died of starvation. By 31 January all further resistance was useless, and von Paulus surrendered the remnants of his Sixth Army to general Mikhail Shumilov, commander of the Soviet Sixty-Fourth Army. Two days later all German resistance ended. Only two German soldiers escaped from the disaster.

For the Russians the experience gained in the battle was probably as valuable as the moral uplift which it gave to all those defending their homeland against the *Wehrmacht*. The Soviet high command learned particularly valuable lessons in mounting a major counter-offensive, and were to apply them with mounting success during the next two and a half years. The Germans learned again the lesson of 1916; that the prestige objective hits both ways. The immediate popular reaction was one of numbness, but gradually the party became the focus of increasing discontent. Within the army and elsewhere Hitler's opponents began, for the first time since 1939, to contemplate active opposition. The regime itself was forced to recognize that greater effort would be necessary if the war was to be won; the German army had entered Russia with 3,300 tanks, but on 23 January 1943 only 495 were left in action.

On 18 February 1943, speaking at the Berlin *Sportpalast*, Goebbels announced the inauguration of an era of 'total war' for Germany. His speech was designed as much to raise morale as to effect drastic changes in the Reich's approach to war: the measures involved in adopting the new posture were mainly regulations aimed at freeing manpower for the armed forces by encouraging women to go into industrial work and redeploying labour. On the morrow of the speech Goebbels himself stressed that the theme to be emphasized was the struggle against bolshevism, a propaganda objective, and ordered that all foreign comment be utilized which demonstrated that hopes of an internal German collapse were illusory. Speer proposed to complement these measures by lengthening the hours of government workers to match those of armament workers, though he warned of the unappetizing social consequences of such moves: 'This means that for the duration of the war, if it goes on for a long time, we shall be — to put it crudely — proletarianized.'[16] The extent to which the catastrophe in the east caused Germany to reorganize her war machine can probably be over-rated: she had already begun a reordering of her economy the previous winter in response to similar, though less extreme, pressures, and the extensive increase in output achieved by Speer over the succeeding eighteen months came more from reorganization and better use of the economies of scale than from any radical structural change. Labour, for example, was always mis-used and ill-treated in deference to the mindless tenets of party ideology.

While considerable pressure had been put upon the Axis by means of air bombardment, propaganda, blockade and the encouragement of indigenous resistance movements, there could be no substitute for a direct military invasion of Europe as the means by which to bring the war to a successful conclusion. Roosevelt's determination to get American troops into action against the Axis powers somewhere in the European theatre during 1942 had played a major part in the decision that the first great direct application of Allied strength would be in the form of the landing in North Africa — Operation TORCH — which duly took place on 8 November 1942. The following January the great Allied conference at Casablanca had laid down the next steps in the process of defeating the Axis: Sicily was to be taken and, if possible, Italy was to be knocked out of the war, whilst a combined bomber offensive paved the way for a landing in north west Europe in 1944. By mid-May 1943 North Africa had been conquered and on 17 August Sicily too fell to the Allies, though this was achieved at the cost of diverting some American troops from the build-up in Britain which was to precede a landing in France — Operation OVERLORD — the following spring.

Fearful of being sucked into a long and costly Mediterranean venture which might be designed less to secure the speedy defeat of Germany than to restore and revive Britain's fortunes as an imperial power, the Americans insisted in May upon a firm commitment to OVERLORD the following spring, no matter what might transpire during operations against Italy. However the prospect of a rapid Italian exit from the war improved dramatically when on 27 July, seventeen days after the landings in Sicily had begun, Mussolini was unseated in a *coup d'état*. With Germany's partner apparently about to succumb there was strong political impetus to land on the mainland itself and despite the very considerable risks an operation was launched at Salerno near Naples on 7 September. Germany, fully aware of the Italian surrender negotiations that had been taking place following the unseating of Mussolini, rapidly moved up a dozen divisions which put up a much stiffer resistance than the Allies had been expecting to encounter from a crumbling Italian army. Naples did not fall until the beginning of October, and thereafter the Germans entrenched on a line bisecting the peninsula between Naples and Rome and began to put up a hard fight to cover the northern part of Italy and their Balkan possessions. Clearly there was to be no 'knocking the props from under Germany' in this war. Despite energetic British attempts to revise Allied agreements and commit further resources to the Italian theatre the Americans held firmly to the promise they had extracted in May and refused to be diverted from a full-scale invasion of Europe the following spring.

The essential preliminary to any invasion attempt which was to stand a fair chance of success was the achievement of command of the air; this was a lesson bitterly learned by the British early in the war, and all their subsequent experience in the western desert and in Italy bore it out. On the strategic plane this command was won by Operation POINTBLANK, a sustained offensive directed against every part of the machine which put the *Luftwaffe* into the air and which lasted from July 1943 until March 1944. The campaign took advantage of weaknesses which were becoming apparent in the German defences: although the production of fighters rose throughout this period — the monthly output of fighters during 1943 averaged 1,369, in June 1944 it was 2,760, and in September 1944, 3,538 — the growing shortage of fuel and the difficulty of training pilots made the *Luftwaffe* increasingly vulnerable. By the spring of 1944 it had almost been eviscerated, but at that point priority in air operations was given to activity connected with the forthcoming invasion and to interdiction bombing — the disruption of road and rail communications and the prevention of the movement of reinforcements up to the battle front. This switch of targets was not altogether a misfortune for Bomber Command; in the five months up to March 1944 it had lost 1,047 bombers in the course of its area bombing programme, the equivalent of its entire front-line strength.

The Allied landing in Normandy on 6 June 1944 was, before all else, an incomparable feat of planning and organization. Seven tons of photographic prints had been used to make the models upon which the details of the operation were first refined, one example of the care, co-ordination and effort which went into every part of the preliminaries to the landing. On D-day itself some 7,000 ships and 11,500 aircraft combined to land 130,000 men from the sea and 22,500 from the air in the successful attempt to break into Hitler's 'Fortress Europe'. Behind them stood a support system designed to land a maximum of 2,500 vehicles and 12,000 tons of stores a day. Skill in combat partnered expertise in operational research as the Allies exerted their strength in the attempt to crush Germany.

With the Allies in Normandy at one hand and the Russians advancing into Poland and Bulgaria at the other, the issue for Germany was no longer whether she could survive against the weight of force posed against her, but simply for how long she could hope to do so. Yet at the moment when success seemed at last to be discernible organizational difficulties impeded the Allies almost as much as did the resistance put up by German forces in the west. On the ground, massive logistical problems presented themselves as the Allied armies at first lagged behind their projected schedule of advance and then suddenly overreached it so that American troops were operating in strength 150 miles beyond the Seine in early September, thirty days before they were scheduled to cross the river at all. By D + 98 days (12 September 1944) the British and American troops had reached positions which it had been forecast would not be occupied until D + 350 days. Whilst advances of this magnitude made dramatic headlines in the newspapers and raised the morale of war-weary populations, they posed severe problems for those charged with supplying and supporting the armies in their advance into Germany and helped to determine that the final assault upon the Reich in the west would take place on a broad front, which could be kept supplied, and not by means of a lightning thrust into the heart of Germany, which could not.

In the air, the strategic bombing forces were freed from their task of supporting the invasion by the middle of August but were still unable to apply their strength to maximum effect. That this was so was due less to the tenacity of the German fighters, whose resistance, though determined, was of little impact, than to the fact that the lords of the air war were quite unable to agree on what the object of their now undivided attentions should be. There was sharp division between those who favoured oil as the most significant target, those who argued that the destruction of Germany's transport system would most quickly bring her to her knees and those who maintained that area bombing and the wreaking of general dislocation was the means best calculated to result in a swift victory. The last act of the air war was in fact to be directed, like the first, at morale. In August 1944 a plan to deliver a crushing blow on Berlin and upon other, previously untouched, German cities — Operation THUNDERCLAP — had been shelved in order to follow the oil plan. However, despite the fact that American ground forces had entered Germany in September, there were signs by the winter that the Germans were not yet about to quit the struggle. The assault of the V-1 and V-2 rockets on England, the appearance of new 'snorkel' U-boats capable of staying underwater and avoiding aerial detection, and the briefly successful German counter-offensive in the Ardennes in December all combined to bring about a reinstatement of THUNDERCLAP.

The unfortunate city upon which the blow fell on 13 and 15 February 1945 was Dresden. The Allies deliberately sought to create what they had accidentally created at Hamburg — a firestorm, which was the consequence of concentrating explosives in a limited area to the point at which temperatures rose high enough for the oxygen in the air to catch fire. Dresden claimed some 30,000 casualties and was, militarily, a success, though with hindsight almost certainly an unnecessary victory. The Russian armies had crossed the Oder on 31 January and were now poised to make their final advance on the capital of the Third Reich. They entered Berlin on 21 April and nine days later, with its Führer dead, the Nazi state abandoned its resistance. For the western allies the war in Europe formally terminated on 8 May, and for the Russians it ended the following day. There remained a war to win in Asia, but this was primarily the concern of the non-European combatants, though it was to be concluded by means of a device designed initially for possible use against Germany — the atomic bomb.

A war which had begun with all sides laying great emphasis on morale as the key to victory had ended with a reassertion of the classic principle of war that defeat of the enemy's forces in being and the physical occupation of his territory were the only sure means by which to guarantee a successful outcome. This might not have held good had the aims for which the Allies fought the war been different; but their fixed intention of dismantling the ruling political regime in Germany and removing every vestige of its influence, together with some questionable ideas about demonstrating not merely the futility but also the illegality of 'aggressive war', determined that the struggle was to be an absolute one. The working populations of each of the combatant countries combined to a more or less complete extent to sustain the war effort of that country, and the whole population became a legitimate target in the search for a means to end resistance and impose what for all participants were war aims of massive scope. These last may have been a mistake; it is certainly clear that the Allied declaration at Casablanca in January 1943 that they would accept only unconditional surrender, although perhaps justified by the politics of the 'strange alliance' between powers as different as Britain, the United States and Russia, certainly contributed to the hardening of the Germans' determination to resist to the end. Against this resolution neither bombing nor blockade were able to achieve all that their proponents claimed for them; the best that can safely be said is that they combined with one another and with the effects of the direct application of strength against the German armed forces to help end the war.

The Second World War perhaps changed non-European

societies more than it changed Europe; movements for national independence were fostered by the Japanese during their reign over south-east Asia, and the old colonial empires of Britain and France did not long survive the ending of the war. To say that it signalled the demise of Europe is to go too far, although it certainly led to a change in her status and attitudes. Within the continent political geography was altered by the division of Germany and by the creation of a Russian sphere of influence encompassing most of the old east European states. Perhaps the most profound social change occurred as a result of the vast movements of population about the continent during and after the war. The immense struggle was seen to have been justified when the bestialities of National Socialism were finally revealed to those who had for so long been fighting against it, thus making the morality of the victors apparently unassailable. But possibly the most significant outcome of the war was the recognition that, when undertaken with all the human and material resources at their disposal, war between advanced industrial states demanded the exertion of such profound efforts and produced at its conclusion problems of such perplexing complexity as to make it a very unattractive arm of diplomacy for nation states. The wars in which the European states would engage after 1945 would be based on different ideologies and resemble more closely the action of resistance movements and partisans than those which had marked the development of war in the age of nationalism which began with Napoleon and ended with Hitler.

Notes

1 Towards revolution

1 W.L. Dorn, *Competition for Empire 1740-1763*, New York, 1940, p. 82.
2 Gerhard Ritter, *The Sword and the Scepter: The Problem of Militarism in Germany*, Miami, 1969, vol. 1, p. 7.
3 S.B. Fay, 'The Beginnings of the Standing Army in Prussia', *American Historical Review*, 1917, p. 772.
4 Michael Mallett, *Mercenaries and their Masters: Warfare in Renaissance Italy*, London, 1974, p. 77.
5 C.G. Cruickshank, *Elizabeth's Army*, Oxford, 1966, p. 26.
6 André Corvisier, *Armées et sociétés en Europe de 1494 à 1789*, Paris, 1976, p. 93.
7 Richard Pares, 'American versus Continental Warfare 1739-1763', *English Historical Review*, 1936, p. 436.
8 L.G. Schwoerer, *No Standing Armies: The Antiarmy Ideology in Seventeenth Century England*, Baltimore and London, 1974, p. 194.
9 Ritter, *op. cit.*, vol. 1, p. 18.
10 A. Goodwin, *The European Nobility in the Eighteenth Century*, London, 1953, p. 29.

2 'Aux armes, citoyens'

1 S.F. Scott, 'The French Revolution and the Professionalization of

the French Officer Corps 1789-1793', in M. Janowitz and J. van Doorn (eds), *On Military Ideology*, Rotterdam, 1971, p. 42.

2 R.W. Phipps, *The Armies of the First French Republic and the Rise of the Marshals of Napoleon I*, Oxford, 1926-39, vol. 1, p. 17.

3 Albert Soboul, *Les Sans-culottes Parisiens en l'an II*, Paris, 1962, p. 110.

4 J.A. Lynn, 'French Opinion and the Military Resurrection of the Pike, 1792-1794', *Military Affairs*, 1977, p. 4.

5 Phipps, *op. cit.*, vol. 3, p. 169.

6 Interpretations of this sort appear in J.F.C. Fuller, *War and Western Civilization, 1832-1932*, London, 1932, and H. Nickerson, *The Armed Horde, 1793-1939*, New York, 1940; see also John Ellis, *Armies in Revolution*, London, 1973, p. 97.

7 J. Colin, *The Transformations of War*, London, 1912, p. 72.

8 Phipps, *op. cit.*, vol. 4, p. 46.

9 B. Schnapper, *Le Remplacement militaire en France: Quelques aspects politiques, économiques et sociaux du recrutement au XIXème siècle*, Paris, 1968, p. 21.

10 Herman Beukma, 'The Social and Political Aspects of Conscription: Europe's Experience', in J.D. Clarkson and T.C. Cochran (eds), *War as a Social Institution*, Columbia, 1941, p. 119.

11 K. Demeter, *The German Officer Corps in Society and State 1650-1945*, London, 1965, p. 72.

12 Gerhard Ritter, *The Sword and the Scepter: The Problem of Militarism in Germany*, Miami, 1969, vol. 1, p. 72.

13 P. Paret, *Yorck and the Era of Prussian Reform*, Princeton, 1966, p. 146.

14 Owen Wheeler, *The War Office Past and Present*, London, 1914, p. 90.

3 The guardians of order

1 R. Holroyd, 'The Bourbon Army, 1815-1830', *Historical Journal*, 1971, p. 529.

2 Alessio Chapperon, *L'organica militare fra le due guerre mondiali 1814-1914*, Turin, 1920, p. 196.

3 Pierre Chalmin, *L'Officier français de 1815 à 1870*, Paris, 1957, p. 24.

4 Michael Howard, *Studies in War and Peace*, London, 1970, p. 70.

5 G.E. Rothenburg, 'The Austrian Army in the Age of Metternich', *Journal of Modern History*, 1968, p. 158.

6 J.S. Curtiss, *The Russian Army under Nicholas I, 1825-1855*,

Durham, NC, 1965, p. 105.

7 G. Harries-Jenkins, *The Army in Victorian Society*, London, 1977, pp. 17, 16.

8 Douglas Porch, *Army and Revolution: France 1815-1848*, London, 1974, p. 41.

9 J. Lassaigne, *Figures parlementaires — L'apport d'un département à la vie politique française*, Paris, 1950, pp. 256-7.

10 Gerhard Ritter, *The Sword and the Scepter: The Problem of Militarism in Germany*, Miami, 1969, vol. 1, p. 109.

11 Gordon Craig, *The Politics of the Prussian Army 1640-1945*, New York, 1964, p. 120.

12 Olive Anderson, *A Liberal State at War*, London, 1967, p. 103.

13 G.P. Evelyn, *A Diary of the Crimea*, London, 1954, p. 72.

14 Anderson, *op. cit.*, p. 111.

4 A decade of violence

1 E.R. Holmes, 'The Road to Sedan: The French Army 1866-70', unpublished PhD thesis, Reading, 1975, pp. 33-4.

2 John Whittam, *The Politics of the Italian Army*, London, 1977, p. 54.

3 Alessio Chapperon, *L'organica militare fra le due guerre mondiali 1814-1914*, Turin, 1920, p. 465.

4 Heinrich Friedjung, *The Struggle for Supremacy in Germany*, London, 1935, p. 196.

5 *The Campaign of 1866 in Germany*, London, 1872, p. 232.

6 H. Bonnal, *Sadowa*, Paris, 1901, pp. 237-8.

7 *Journals of Count Blumenthal*, London, 1903, p. 9.

8 C. di Biase, *Aquila d'Oro: Storia Della Stato Maggiore Italiano*, Milan, 1969, p. 53.

9 F. de Chaurand de St Eustache, *Come L'Italia entrò in guerra*, Milan, 1929, p. 13.

10 Baron Stoffel, *Rapports militaires écrits de Berlin 1866-70*, Paris, 1871, pp. 185-214 (reports of 22 and 29 July 1868).

11 Gordon Wright, 'Public Opinion and Conscription in France 1866-70', *Journal of Modern History*, 1942, p. 28.

12 W.S. Serman, 'Les généraux français de 1870', *Revue de défense nationale*, 1970, p. 1327.

13 G. Harries Jenkins, *The Army in Victorian Society*, London, 1977, p. 137.

14. A Ducrot, *La Défense de Paris*, Paris, 1875, vol. 1, p. 215.

5 Armies and international rivalry

1. D. Ralston, *The Army of the Republic: The Place of the Military in the Political Evolution of France 1871-1914,* Massachusetts, 1967, p. 38.
2. Gambetta to Denfert-Rochereau, 20 September 1871: W. Serman, 'Denfert-Rochereau et la discipline dans l'armée française entre 1845 et 1874', *Revue d'histoire moderne et contemporaine,* 1973, p. 100.
3. Niccola Marselli, *Gli avvenimenti del 1870-71,* Turin, 1873, p. 142.
4. Amadeo Tosti, *Storia dell'esercito italiano 1861-1936,* Milan, 1942, pp. 92-3.
5. T.F. Gallagher, ' "Cardwellian Mysteries": The Fate of the British Army Regulation Bill 1871', *Historial Journal,* 1975, p. 348.
6. A.V. Tucker, 'Army and Society in England: A Reassessment of the Cardwell Reforms', *Journal of British Studies,* 1963, p. 128.
7. *Lettres de la Princesse Radziwill au Général de Robilant (1889-1914),* Bologna, 1933, vol. 1, p. 8 (4 May 1889).
8. Alan Scham, *Lyautey in Morocco: Protectorate Administration 1912-25,* Berkeley, Cal., 1970, p. 7.
9. D. Porch, 'The French Army and the Spirit of the Offensive 1900-1914', in B. Bond and I. Roy (eds), *War and Society,* London, 1975, p. 119.
10. Martin Kitchen, *The German Officer Corps 1890-1914,* Oxford, 1968, p. 35.
11. Hansard, 4th series, vol. CLXIX, 1909, col. 1321; John Gooch, 'Sir George Clarke's career at the Committee of Imperial Defence 1904-1907', *Historical Journal,* 1975, p. 566.
12. Fritz Fischer, *Krieg der Illusionen: Die deutsche Politik von 1911 bis 1914,* Dusseldorf, 1969, p. 246.
13. Henri Contamine, *La Révanche 1871-1914,* Paris, 1957, p. 186.

6 The First World War

1. Pierre Renouvin, *The Forms of War Government in France,* London and New Haven, 1927, pp. 16-17.
2. G. Feldman, *Army, Industry and Labor in Germany 1914-1918,* Princeton, 1966, p. 32.
3. G.E. Silberstein, 'The High Command and Diplomacy in Austria-Hungary 1914-1916', *Journal of Modern History,* 1970, p. 598.
4. L.L. Farrar, *The Short War Illusion: German Policy, Strategy and Domestic Affairs August-December 1914,* Santa Barbara, 1973,

p. 43.

5 John Gooch, *The Plans of War: The General Staff and British Military Strategy c.1900-1916*, London, 1974, p. 312.

6 E. Glaise von Horstenau, *Österreich-Üngarns Letzter Krieg*, Vienna, 1930-8, vol. 7, p. 448.

7 Rudolf Kiszling, 'Der Militärische Zusammenbruch der Österreich-ische-Üngarischen Monarchie 1918', *Österreichische Militärische Zeitschrift*, 1968, p. 406.

8 G. Pedroncini, 'Les rapports du Gouvernement et du Haut Commandement en France en 1917', *Revue d'histoire moderne et contemporaine*, 1968, p. 122.

9 Alistair Horne, *The Price of Glory*, London, 1964, p. 44.

10 Martin Kitchen, *The Silent Dictatorship: The Politics of the German High Command under Hindenburg and Ludendorff, 1916-1918*, London, 1976, p. 113.

11 Pierre Renouvin, 'Les buts de guerre du gouvernement français 1914-1918', *Revue historique*, 1966, p. 21.

12 S.W. Roskill, *Hankey: Man of Secrets*, London, 1970-4, vol. 1, p. 579.

13 H.W. Gatzke, *Germany's Drive to the West: A Study of Germany's Western War Aims during the First World War*, Baltimore, 1966, p. 129.

14 Fritz Fischer, *Germany's Aims in the First World War*, London, 1967, p. 634.

15 Giorgio Rochat, *L'Italia nella prima guerra mondiale*, Rome, 1976, pp. 109, 122; J.M. Winter, 'Britain's "Lost Generation" of the First World War', *Population Studies*, 1977, pp. 449-66; J. Maurin, 'Le combattant lozérien de la classe 1907 lors de la première guerre mondiale', *Revue d'histoire moderne et comtemporaine*, 1973, pp. 124-38.

Expanded horizons

1 Hans von Seeckt, *Gedanken eines Soldaten*, Berlin, 1929, p. 12.

2 John Erickson, *The Soviet High Command*, London, 1962, p. 49.

3 W.D. Jacobs, *Frunze: The Soviet Clausewitz 1885-1925*, The Hague, 1969, p. 96.

4 J.M. Hughes, *To the Maginot Line: The Politics of French Military Preparation in the 1920s*, Cambridge, Mass., 1971, p. 141.

5 D.C. Watt, *Too Serious a Business: European armed forces and the approach to the Second World War*, London, 1975, p. 37.

6 F.L. Carsten, *The Reichswehr and Politics 1918-1933*, Oxford,

1966, p. 28.

7   *Ibid.*, p. 114.

8   Hans von Seeckt, *Deutschland zwischen West und Ost*, Hamburg, 1930, pp. 30-1.

9   J.C. Favez, 'Hitler et le Reichswehr en 1923', *Revue d'histoire moderne et contemporaine*, 1970, p. 49.

10 Gaines Post jr, *The Civil-Military Fabric of Weimar Foreign Policy*, Princeton, 1973, p. 92.

11 P. Pieri and G. Rochat, *Badoglio*, Turin, 1974, p. 557.

12 *Documents diplomatiques françaises*, 2nd series, vol. IX. Col. Palasse to Bonnet, 18 April 1938, no. 192, p. 394.

13 Norman Rich, *Hitler's War Aims: Ideology, the Nazi State, and the Course of Expansion*, London, 1973, p. 18.

14 N.H. Baynes (ed.), *The Speeches of Adolf Hitler April 1922-August 1939*, London, 1942, vol. 1, p. 554.

15 R.J. O'Neill, *The German Army and the Nazi Party*, London, 1968, p. 87.

16 H.C. Deutsch, *Hitler and his Generals*, Minnesota, 1974, p. 276.

17 Alfred Conquet, *Auprès du Maréchal Pétain*, Paris, 1970, p. 33.

18 *Documents diplomatiques françaises*, 2nd series, vol. III. Note du général, Chef du Cabinet du Ministre de la Guerre, au sujet de l'armée de métier, 21 July 1936, no. 9, p. 19.

19 Robert Paul Shay, *British Rearmament in the Thirties: Politics and Profits*, Princeton, 1977, p. 159.

20 R.J. Minney, *The Private Papers of Hore Belisha*, London, 1960, p. 138.

8 The Second World War

1   Alan Milward, *The German Economy at War*, London, 1965, p. 8.

2   Berenice A. Caroll, *Design for Total War: Arms and Economics in the Third Reich*, The Hague, 1968, p. 40.

3   John Strawson, *Hitler as Military Commander*, London, 1971, p. 95.

4   Hans Adolf Jacobsen, *Der Zweite Weltkrieg: Gründzuge der Politik und Strategie in Dokumenten*, Fischer Bucherei, Frankfurt and Hamburg, 1965, p. 67.

5   R.H.S. Stolfi, 'Equipment for Victory in France in 1940', *History*, 1970, pp. 1-20.

6   H.R. Trevor-Roper, ed., *Hitler's War Directives 1939-1945*, London, 1966, p. 60.

7   M. van Creveld, *Supplying War: Logistics from Wallenstein to*

Patton, Cambridge, 1977, p. 198.

8 Brian Bond, ed., *Chief of Staff: The Diaries of Lt. General Sir Henry Pownall*, London, 1972-4, vol. 2, p. 29.

9 A.J.P. Taylor, *The Second World War*, London, 1975, p. 118.

10 Geoffrey Warner, *Pierre Laval and the Eclipse of Modern France*, London, 1968, p. 418.

11 Heinz Hohne, *The Order of the Death's Head*, London, 1972, p. 464.

12 Richard Polenberg, *War and Society: The United States 1941-1945*, New York, 1972, p. 12.

13 Alan Milward, *War, Economy and Society 1939-1945*, London, 1977, p. 92.

14 Marlis G. Steinert, *Hitler's War and the Germans*, Ohio, 1977, p. 153.

15 L.P. Lochner (ed.), *The Goebbels Diaries*, London, 1948, pp. 333-4.

16 Albert Speer, *Inside the Third Reich*, London, 1975, p. 353; W.A. Boelcke (ed.), *The Secret Conferences of Dr. Goebbels 1939-1943*, London, n.d., (1971), p. 334.

Bibliography

What follows is not intended to be an exhaustive guide to
the literature dealing with war and military organization in
Europe since 1750, or even to that portion of it on which the
present work is based; the sheer volume of material involved
in such an exercise would demand not one but several addi-
tional volumes. Rather it is intended to indicate to the reader
who wishes to go more deeply into any of the areas covered
by this book the more obvious starting points. After ten
years of teaching undergraduates I am now somewhat wiser
in the ways of the world as it is, rather than as it ought to be;
accordingly I have thought it better not to make more than
passing reference to books or articles in French and German,
and to make no reference at all to books written in Italian.
Anyone desirous of detailed information on what to read in
French about the French army, or whatever, is best advised
to turn to the bibliographies of the specialist studies in
English as their launching pad into foreign parts.

1 General and introductory works

A number of good general works exist which deal with the
impact of war on Europe in modern times, of which the best
is Michael Howard's *War in European History* (Oxford

University Press: 1976); to it should be added Theodore Ropp, *War in the Modern World* (Durham, NC, Duke University Press: 1959), a pioneering work which has withstood the flood of new materials published since it was written, and J.F.C. Fuller, *The Conduct of War 1789-1961* (London, Eyre Methuen: 1961). General studies of a more fixedly social kind exist in Hoffman Nickerson, *The Armed Horde 1793-1939* (London, Putnam: 1940) and Alfred Vagts, *A History of Militarism* (London, Hollis: 1959; New York, Free Press: 1967), both of which repay reading, although exuding a somewhat dated aroma. For the period before 1789 the best general work is undoubtedly André Corvisier, *Armées et sociétés en Europe de 1494 à 1789* (Paris, Presses Universitaires de France: 1976). Many other works exist, such as Montgomery's *A History of Warfare* (London, Collins: 1968), but in general they draw heavily and less effectively on their predecessors and on the specialized works cited below. Mention should however be made of J.U. Nef, *War and Human Progress* (London, Routledge & Kegan Paul: 1950), an attempt to take the panoramic view which comes as close to pulling it off as any such work could hope to do.

Much useful material is to be found scattered among volumes of essays and collected papers, of which the following are particularly worthy of note: M.R.D. Foot, ed., *War and Society* (London, Elek: 1973), which contains a particularly stimulating essay by V.G. Kiernan on conscription and society; B. Bond and I. Roy, eds, *War and Society Yearbooks* 1 and 2 (London, Croom Helm: 1975, 1976); and Michael Howard, *Studies in War and Peace* (London, Temple Smith: 1970). Geoffrey Blainey, *The Causes of Wars* (London, Macmillan: 1973) deals with a general aspect of war not usually handled outside narrowly specialist studies, and M. van Creveld's *Supplying War: Logistics from Wallenstein to Patton* (Cambridge University Press: 1977) examines one of the fundamental considerations in military activity from a fresh and stimulating viewpoint. A good general introduction to the strategic doctrines of the great European powers in the nineteenth and twentieth centuries is Michael Howard, ed., *The Theory and Practice of War* (London, Cassell: 1965), and to the strategic thinkers themselves, E.M. Earle, ed.,

The Makers of Modern Strategy (Princeton University Press: 1944).

2 The Napoleonic Period

The background to Napoleon's military reforms is examined in B.H. Liddell Hart, *The Ghost of Napoleon* (London, Faber: 1933), and to the regeneration of Prussia in W.O. Shanahan, *Prussian Military Reforms 1786-1813* (Columbia University Press: 1945). Peter Paret's 'Colonial experience and European military reform at the end of the eighteenth century' (*Bulletin of the Institute of Historical Research*, 1964) should also be consulted. The most recent study of the changes wrought on warfare after 1793 by the Revolution and Napoleon is G.E. Rothenberg, *The Art of Warfare in the Age of Napoleon* (London, Batsford: 1977), while J. Colin, *The Transformation of War* (London, Rees: 1912), which treats the same theme, still repays reading.

Although it appeared too late to be consulted during the writing of this book, S.F. Scott's *The Response of the Royal Army to the French Revolution* (Oxford University Press: 1978) is exceptionally valuable. R.W. Phipps, *The Armies of the First French Republic and the Rise of the Marshals of Napoleon I* (Oxford University Press: 1926-39) although now somewhat elderly may still be read with profit. On the Prussian army, P. Paret, *Yorck and the Era of Prussian Reform* (Princeton University Press: 1966) is unsurpassed. Richard Glover, *Peninsular Preparation: The Reform of the British Army 1795-1809* (Cambridge University Press: 1963) examines the changes to British military organization; to it may be added O. Wheeler, *The War Office Past and Present* (London, Methuen: 1914), still the only general study of that institution published to date.

For those interested in the battles of the era, David Chandler, *The Campaigns of Napoleon* (London, Macmillan: 1966) is authoritative. To it may be added Michael Glover, *Wellington's Peninsular Victories* (London, Batsford: 1963), and the same author's *Wellington as Military Commander* (London, Batsford: 1965); A. Brett-James, *Wellington at*

War (London, Macmillan: 1961); and Jac Weller, *Wellington at Waterloo* (London, Longmans: 1967). A fine study of Waterloo is to be found in John Keegan, *The Face of Battle* (Harmondsworth, Penguin: 1978).

3 France

Two good general histories of the French army exist in English, though neither reaches back to 1815: R.D. Challenor, *The French Theory of the Nation in Arms 1866-1939* (New York, Russell & Russell: 1965) is a brilliant work, while P.M. de la Gorce, *The French Army* (London, Weidenfeld & Nicolson: 1963) is attractive and stronger on the more modern period. For those able to read French, Raoul Girardet, *La Société militaire dans la France contemporaine* (Paris, Plon: 1953) is a masterpiece which, shamefully, is both untranslated and out of print.

On the period up to 1870, R.D. Porch, *Army and Revolution: France 1815-1848* (London, Routledge & Kegan Paul: 1974) may be supplemented with Richard Holroyd, 'The Bourbon Army 1815-1830' (*Historical Journal*, 1971) and R.D. Price, 'The French Army and the Revolution of 1830' (*European Studies Review*, 1973). L.M. Case, *French Opinion on War and Diplomacy in the Second Empire* (Pennsylvania University Press: 1954) contains much of interest. The activities of the French army overseas are dealt with in J.A. Dabbs, *The French Army in Mexico 1861-1867* (The Hague, Mouton: 1963). Any aspirant historian of the French army might well consider turning his attentions to the war of 1859, for there exists no modern study in English. The opposite is the case for the war of 1870: Michael Howard's *The Franco-Prussian War* (London, Hart Davies: 1961) is rightly considered the model of its kind.

The military side of the life of the early Third Republic is brilliantly handled in D. Ralston, *The Army of the Republic: The Place of the Military in the Political Evolution of France 1871-1914* (Massachusetts Institute of Technology Press: 1967), to which may be added A. Mitchell, 'Thiers, MacMahon and the Conseil Superieur de la Guerre' (*French Historical*

Studies, 1969). W. Zaniewicki's 'L'impact de 1870 sur la pensée militaire française' (*Revue de Défense Nationale*, 1970) is a good introduction to such matters. The two great civil-military crises of the period may be followed in F.H. Seeger, *The Boulanger Affair: Political Crossroad of France* (Cornell University Press: 1969); Guy Chapman, *The Dreyfus Trials* (London, Paladin: 1974); and Douglas Johnson, *France and the Dreyfus Affair* (London, Blandford: 1966).

For the inter-war period J.M. Hughes, *To the Maginot Line: The Politics of French Military Preparation in the 1920s* (Harvard University Press: 1971), and P.C.F. Bankwitz, *Maxim Weygand and Civil-Military Relations in Modern France* (Harvard University Press: 1967) are essential. R.J. Young's 'Preparations for Defeat: French War Doctrine in the Inter-War Period' (*Journal of European Studies*, 1972) is particularly valuable, as is the same author's 'French Policy and the Munich Crisis of 1938: A Reappraisal', (*Canadian Historical Association Papers*, 1970); both will no doubt be overtaken by Dr Young's full-length study *In Command of France: French Foreign Policy and Military Planning in the Nazi Years, 1933-1940* (Harvard University Press: 1979).

Much has been written about France's best known military figure of the inter-war years, Marshal Pétain; Stephen Ryan, *Pétain the Soldier* (New York, Barnes: 1969) is a mine of information, whilst Richard Griffiths, *Marshal Pétain* (London, Constable: 1970) is the most recent biography and much the best. An interesting corrective to the view of Pétain put out by his detractors since 1940 is Alfred Conquet, *Auprès du maréchal Pétain* (Paris, France-Empire: 1970).

4 Germany

A great deal has been written about the history of Prussia and Germany since 1815 from the military perspective, and much of it is very good indeed. Gordon Craig's *The Politics of the Prussian Army 1640-1945* (Oxford University Press, Galaxy ed.: 1964) is breath-taking. In a more specifically social vein, Karl Demeter, *The German Officer Corps in Society and*

State 1650-1945 (London, Weidenfeld & Nicolson: 1965) is a pioneering study. Herbert Rosinski, *The German Army* (London, Pall Mall: 1966) maintains its value as a general study as, from a somewhat different perspective, does Walter Goerlitz, *History of the German General Staff 1657-1945* (New York, Praeger: 1953). Martin Kitchen's *A Military History of Germany* (London, Weidenfeld & Nicolson: 1975) is a stimulating book from which much can be learned.

For the period up to 1914 non-German readers are fortunate in having available in translation Gerhard Ritter's magnificent *The Sword and the Scepter* (London, Allen Lane: 1970-3), of which volume 1 covers the period 1740-1890 and volume 2 from 1890 to 1914. Otherwise the only significant works on the subject published in the recent past in English are Dennis Showalter, *Railroads and Rifles: Soldiers, Technology, and the Unification of Germany* (Conn., Archon: 1975), and Martin Kitchen's *The German Officer Corps 1890-1914* (Oxford University Press: 1968). For those interested in German military planning before the First World War, Gerhard Ritter, *The Schlieffen Plan* (London, Wolff: 1958) is the essential starting point.

On the inter-war period J.W. Wheeler Bennett, *The Nemesis of Power: The German Army in Politics 1918-1945* (London, Macmillan: 1967) still reads tolerably well, although it is now beginning to show its age. F.L. Carsten, *The Reichswehr and Politics 1918-1933* (Oxford University Press: 1966) is a masterful account of the Weimar period. For those with German, Hans Meier-Welcker, *Seeckt* (Frankfurt, Bernard & Graefe: 1967) is a monumental work. For the period after 1933 R.J. O'Neill, *The German Army and the Nazi Party* (London, Cassell: 1966) is brilliant and indispensable. Alongside it may be placed Harold C. Deutsch, *Hitler and his Generals* (Minnesota University Press: 1974), and the same author's *The Conspiracy against Hitler in the Twilight War* (Oxford University Press: 1968). Much useful information can be found in Berenice A. Carroll, *Design for Total War: Arms and Economics in the Third Reich* (The Hague, Mouton: 1968), and E.M. Robertson, *Hitler's Pre-War Policy and Military Plans* (London, Macmillan: 1963). Matthew Cooper, *The German Army 1933-1945* (London, Macdonald & Janes:

1978) covers ground first traversed by O'Neill and Deutsch and is useful if those works are not readily available, though the author's somewhat wayward views on *Blitzkrieg* should be tempered by Alan Milward's splendid *The German Economy at War* (London, Athlone Press: 1965). For those able to read German, K.-J. Müller, *Das Heer und Hitler, Armee und nationalsocialistisches Regime 1933-1940* (Stuttgart, Deutsche Verlags-Anstalt: 1969) — which an enterprising publisher might do well to translate — is of great value.

5 Great Britain

Here, not unnaturally, there is a wealth of material from which to choose. Corelli Barnett, *Britain and her Army 1509-1970* (Harmondsworth, Penguin: 1974) provides an excellent introduction. On the early Victorian army much can be learned from G. Harries-Jenkins, *The Army in Victorian Society* (London, Routledge & Kegan Paul: 1977), and from Hugh Cunningham, *The Volunteer Force* (London, Croom Helm: 1975) which holds the field until a definitive study is written. A.P.C. Bruce, *The Purchase System in the British Army 1660-1871* (Royal Historical Society) — still awaiting publication at the time of writing — will fill a gap hitherto familiar only to a small but determined band of research students. For the late Victorian army there is a great volume of published work, of which the following are the core: W.S. Hamer, *The British Army: Civil-Military Relations 1885-1905* (Oxford University Press: 1970); Brian Bond, *The Victorian Army and the Staff College* (London, Eyre Methuen: 1972); John Gooch, *The Plans of War: The General Staff and British Military Strategy c. 1900-1916* (Routledge & Kegan Paul: 1974); S.R. Williamson, *The Politics of Grand Strategy: Britain and France prepare for War, 1904-1914* (Harvard University Press: 1969); F.A. Johnson, *Defence by Committee: The British Committee of Imperial Defence 1885-1959* (Oxford University Press: 1960); John Ehrman, *Cabinet Government and War 1890-1940* (Cambridge University Press: 1958); and N. D'Ombrain, *War Machinery and*

BIBLIOGRAPHY

High Policy: Defence Administration in peacetime Britain, 1902-1914 (Oxford University Press: 1973).

A number of valuable articles have been published in the field; worthy of special attention are A.V. Tucker, 'Army and Society in England: A Reassessment of the Cardwell Reforms' (*Journal of British Studies*, 1963), and the same author's 'The Issue of Army Reform in the Unionist Government 1903-1905' (*Historical Journal*, 1966); J.P. Mackintosh, 'The Role of the Committee of Imperial Defence before 1914' (*English Historical Review*, 1962); and John Gooch, 'Sir George Clarke's career at the Committee of Imperial Defence 1904-1907' (*Historical Journal*, 1975). Richard Price, *An Imperial War and the British Working Class* (London, Routledge & Kegan Paul: 1972) is an interesting and informative work written from the social angle.

For the inter-war years Michael Howard, *The Continental Commitment* (London, Temple Smith: 1972) — which also deals with the pre-war years — is an excellent introduction. Detailed studies include: N.H. Gibbs, *Grand Strategy* volume 1 (HMSO: 1976); Robin Higham, *Armed Forces in Peacetime: Britain 1918-1939* (Yeovil, Foulis: 1962); Peter Dennis, *Decision by Default: Peacetime Conscription and British Defence 1919-1939* (Routledge & Kegan Paul: 1972); Brian Bond, *Liddell Hart: A Study of his Military Thought* (London, Cassell: 1977); A.J. Trythall, *'Boney Fuller': The Intellectual General* (London, Cassell: 1977). Particularly useful articles include J.P.D. Dunbabin, 'British Rearmament in the 1930s' (*Historical Journal*, 1975); M.S. Smith, 'The Royal Air Force, Air Power and British Foreign Policy 1932' (*Journal of Contemporary History*, 1977), and the same author's 'British Rearmament and Deterrence in the 1930s' (*Journal of Strategic Studies*, 1978); and R. Quartararo, 'Imperial Defence in the Mediterranean on the Eve of the Ethiopian Crisis' (*Historical Journal*, 1975); while the articles on 'The 10 Year Rule' by Silverman and Booth in the *Journal of the Royal United Services Institute* (1971) form the best guide to that curious regulation.

274

BIBLIOGRAPHY

6 Russia

The standard work on the Russian army before the First World War is J.S. Curtiss, *The Russian Army under Nicholas I, 1825-1855* (Durham, North Carolina, Duke University Press: 1965); the fortunes — or rather misfortunes — of the Russian army in the field may be followed in David Walder, *The Short Victorious War: The Russo-Japanese Conflict 1904-5* (London, Hutchinson: 1973). Otherwise the period before 1917 has attracted little scholarly attention for the English reader to utilize.

The reverse is true of the age of communist Russia, for which a number of good general histories exist. The best is undoubtedly John Erickson, *The Soviet High Command: A Military-Political History, 1918-1941* (London, Macmillan: 1961) which is magisterial; however, the beginner is advised to come to it by way of one or more of the following: B.H. Liddell Hart (ed.), *The Soviet Army* (London, Weidenfeld & Nicolson: 1956); Michael Garder, *A History of the Soviet Army* (London, Pall Mall: 1966); Malcolm Mackintosh, *Juggernaut: A History of the Soviet Armed Forces* (New York, Macmillan: 1967). Both sides of the Russo-Polish war of 1920 are dealt with in Norman Davies, *White Eagle, Red Star: The Polish-Soviet War 1919-20* (London, Macdonald: 1972).

7 Italy

For the non-Italian reader there exists only one work published since 1884: John Whittam, *The Politics of the Italian Army* (London: Croom Helm: 1977).

8 The First World War

A number of useful general histories exist, of which the most stimulating is Marc Ferro, *The Great War* (London, Routledge & Kegan Paul: 1973); C.R.M. Cruttwell, *A History of the Great War* (Oxford University Press: 1964) still provides the best narrative outline of military events, and E.L. Woodward, *Great Britain and the War of 1914-1918* (London, Methuen: 1967) is a useful synthesis. A.J.P. Taylor, *The First World War: An Illustrated History* (London, Hamish Hamilton: 1963) contains some of the best picture captions ever, and much else besides. Arthur Marwick, *Britain in the Century of Total War* (London, Bodley Head: 1968) is of some value, while J.C. King, ed., *The First World War* (London, Macmillan: 1973) is one of the few really useful collections of documents in an overrated genre.

If all the battle studies of the First World War were laid end to end it would still not deter aspiring authors from writing more of them; some are good, many are adequate, but only a few can be singled out for special mention: Leon Wolff, *In Flanders Fields* (London, Longmans: 1959); Barrie Pitt, *1918: The Last Act* (London, Cassell: 1962); A.H. Farrar Hockley, *The Somme* (London, Batsford: 1964); Alistair Horne, *The Price of Glory* (Harmondsworth, Penguin: 1964); R.R. James, *Gallipoli* (London, Batsford: 1965); Martin Middlebrook, *The First Day on the Somme* (London, Allen Lane: 1971); and Norman Stone, *The Eastern Front 1914-1917* (London, Hodder: 1975). There are many, many others.

The best introduction to the question of what the powers were fighting for and how they hoped to get it is Barry Hunt, ed., *War Aims and Strategic Policy in the Great War* (London, Croom Helm: 1977). German war aims may be studied in Fritz Fischer, *Germany's Aims in the First World War* (London, Chatto & Windus: 1967); Hans Gatzke, *Germany's Drive to the West: A Study of Germany's Western War Aims during the First World War* (Baltimore, Johns Hopkins University Press: 1966); L.L. Farrar, *The Short War Illusion: German Strategy, Policy and Domestic Affairs August-December 1914* (Santa Barbara, Cal., A.B.C.-Clio: 1973); and the same author's *Divide and Conquer: German Efforts to conclude a Separate Peace 1914-1918* (Columbia University Press: 1978). British war aims are analysed in V.H. Rothwell, *British War Aims and Peace Diplomacy 1914-1918* (Oxford University Press: 1971), which may be supplemented with W.B. Fest, 'British War Aims and German Peace Feelers during the First World War' (*Historical Journal*, 1971). French war aims await a sustained treatment; meanwhile the best introduction is Pierre Renouvin, 'Les buts de guerre du gouvernement français' (*Revue historique*, 1966), alongside which may be put C. Andrew and A.M. Kanya-Forstner, 'The French Colonial Party and French Colonial War Aims 1914-1918' (*Historical Journal*, 1974).

On the home fronts F.P. Chambers, *The War behind the War* (London, Harcourt Brace: 1939) is still useful, and John Williams, *The Home Fronts: Britain, France and Germany 1914-1918* (London, Constable: 1972) contains a number of good anecdotes. Germany is brilliantly treated — but from quite opposite poles — in Gerald Feldman, *Army, Industry and Labor in Germany 1914-1918* (Princeton University Press: 1966) and Martin Kitchen, *The Silent Dictatorship: The Politics of the German High Command under Hindenburg and Ludendorff 1916-1918* (London, Croom Helm: 1978), as well as by volumes 3 and 4 of Gerhard Ritter's *The Sword and the Sceptre* (see above, section 4). Also useful are G. Feldman, 'Fondements sociaux de la mobilisation économique en Allemagne 1914-1916 (*Annales*, 1969); R.H. Lutz, ed., *The Causes of the German Collapse in 1918* (Conn., Archon: 1969); and D.J. Goodspeed, *Ludendorff* (London, Hart Davies: 1966). On France Pierre Renouvin, *The Forms of War Government in France* (Yale University Press: 1927) is still useful and may be supplemented with J.C. King, *Generals and Politicians: Conflict between France's High Command, Parliament and Government 1914-1918* (Conn., Greenwood: 1971); G.H. Cassar, *The French and the Dardanelles* (London, Allen & Unwin: 1971); and David Dutton, 'The Fall of General Joffre' (*Journal of Strategic Studies*: 1978). Useful works on Britain are P. Guinn, *British Strategy and Politics, 1914 to 1918* (Oxford University Press: 1965); Arthur Marwick, *The Deluge: British Society and the First World War* (London, Bodley Head: 1965): and Cameron Hazlehurst, *Politicians at War, July 1914 to May 1915* (London, Cape: 1971). On Russia the best guide is Norman Stone, *The Eastern Front* (see above).

9 The Second World War

Two very useful recent works dealing with the onset of war from the military viewpoint are D.C. Watt, *Too Serious a Business: European Armed Forces and the Approach of the Second World War* (London, Temple Smith: 1975), and A. Preston, ed., *General Staffs and Diplomacy before the Second World War* (London, Croom Helm: 1978).

Though there can never be too many good books, the choice of general works on the Second World War is almost embarrassingly large. Gordon Wright, *The Ordeal of Total War 1939-1945* (London, Harper & Row: 1968) is perhaps the best general textbook on modern history written this century, while Henri Michel, *The Second World War* (London, Deutsch: 1975), which is of somewhat larger dimensions, is a reliable source for any aspect of the war. Alan Milward, *War, Economy and Society 1939-1945* (London, Allen Lane: 1977) is immensely stimulating; P. Calvocoressi and G. Wint, *Total War* (Harmondsworth, Penguin: 1974) is useful, as is A.J.P. Taylor, *The Second World War: An Illustrated History* (London, Hamish Hamilton: 1975); and B.H. Liddell Hart, *The Second World War* (London, Cassell: 1970), though flawed by its author's preoccupation with the Western Desert, is none the less serviceable.

The plethora of battle and campaign studies threatens to exceed that for the First World War, if it has not already done so; the best approach is perhaps made by way of the excellent series 'The Politics and Strategy of the Second World War', published by Davies Poynter of which the following volumes have appeared to date: A.F. Upton, *Finland 1939-40* (1974): Brian Bond, *France and Belgium 1939-40* (1975); Charles Cruickshank, *Greece 1940-41* (1976); Geoffrey Warner, *Iraq and Syria 1941* (1974); Robert Cecil, *Hitler's Decision to Invade Russia 1941* (1975); Louis Allen, *Singapore 1941-42* (1977); Keith Sainsbury, *The North African Landings 1942* (1976); Raymond Callahan, *Burma 1942-45* (1978); and W.G.F. Jackson, *'Overlord': Normandy 1944* (1978).

No major studies of the war aims of the major participants comparable to those for the First World War have yet been published in English.

Domestic aspects of Germany's war are best covered by Marlis G. Steinert, *Hitler's War and the Germans* (Ohio University Press: 1977), which may be supplemented with Alan Milward, *The German Economy at War* (see above, section 4); and Gordon Craig's essay in his *War, Politics and Diplomacy: Selected Essays* (London, Weidenfeld & Nicolson: 1966). On Britain see Angus Calder, *The Peoples' War: Britain 1939-1945* (London, Cape: 1969); Henry Pelling, *Britain and the Second World War* (London, Fontana: 1970); and Paul Addison, *The Road to 1945: British Politics and the Second World War* (London, Cape: 1975). Much of the domestic history of France in the wartime years, not unnaturally, deals with the Resistance, with which this study has not been concerned. However, those who desire more information may profitably consult Henri Michel, *The Shadow War* (London, Deutsch: 1972); H. Noguères, *Histoire de la Résistance en France de 1940 à 1945* (Paris, Laffont: 1967, 1969); and H.R. Kedward, *Resistance in Vichy France* (Oxford University Press: 1978). For the other side of the coin, see S. Hoffman, 'Collaboration in France in World War II' (*Journal of Modern History*, 1968). The best general survey of resistance is M.R.D. Foot, *Resistance: An Analysis of European resistance to Nazism 1940-1945* (London, Methuen: 1976). On Russia, A. Werth, *Russia at War 1941-1945* (London, Barrie: 1964) can be used alongside John Erickson, *The Road to Stalingrad* (London, Weidenfeld & Nicolson: 1975).

Finally three impressive recent works should be mentioned which together indicate the direction which historical scholarship would seem to be taking on the Second World War, now that the basic narrative (with the exception of the impact of ULTRA) has been fairly clearly established: Gabriel Kolko, *The Politics of War* (London, Weidenfeld & Nicolson: 1969); W.R. Louis, *Imperialism at Bay: The United States and the Decolonization of the British Empire, 1941-1945* (Oxford University Press: 1977); and Christopher Thorne, *Allies of a Kind: The United States, Britain and the War against Japan 1941-1945* (London, Hamish Hamilton: 1978).

Index

280

INDEX

INDEX